Ever since the first publication of Freud's ideas, the scientific status, therapeutic efficacy and morality of psychoanalysis have come under attack from an often sceptical public and from certain sections of the academic community. Yet psychoanalysis has grown in public stature over the last century. It is held in high regard by many important thinkers for its valuable exploration and interpretation of human development in all its aspects. In academic disciplines ranging from literary criticism and feminist studies to psychotherapy, psychoanalysis provides a key building block in understanding human subjectivity.

In *For and Against Psychoanalysis*, Stephen Frosh explores questions of meaning and interpretation in psychoanalysis, the aims and effectiveness of psychoanalytic therapy, and the application of psychoanalytic theory to social concerns. He shows how the elements of politics, therapy, subjectivity and science – which exist concurrently within psychoanalysis – provide us with an enormous number of things to say about its value and limitations. In presenting arguments both for and against, the author enables us to appreciate more clearly what psychoanalysis has to offer, and what it does not.

Essential reading for psychoanalysts, counsellors and psychotherapists, *For and Against Psychoanalysis* provides a first-class introduction to the ideas behind psychoanalysis and the place it occupies in the modern world.

Stephen Frosh is Reader in Psychoanalytical Psychology at Birkbeck College, University of London, and Consultant Clinical Psychologist and Vice Dean of the Child and Family Department, Tavistock Clinic, London.

For and Against Psychoanalysis

Stephen Frosh

London and New York

First published 1997
by Routledge
11 New Fetter Lane, London EC4P 4EE

Simultaneously published in the USA and Canada
by Routledge
29 West 35th Street, New York, NY 10001

Typeset in Times by Routledge
Printed and bound in Great Britain by
Mackays of Chatham PLC, Chatham, Kent

British Library Cataloguing in Publication Data
A catalogue record for this book is available from the British Library

Library of Congress Cataloguing in Publication Data
Frosh, Stephen.
    For and against psychoanalysis / Stephen Frosh.
    Includes bibliographical references and index.
    1. Psychoanalysis. I. Title.
    BF173.F897   1997
    150.19′5–dc21   97–9748
    CIP

ISBN 0–415–13138–3 (hbk)
ISBN 0–415–13139–1 (pbk)

In memory of my mother, Ruth Frosh

Contents

Preface

For more than ten years, I have been exploring different aspects of psychoanalysis, trying to understand its hold over me. Throughout that time, I have taught psychoanalysis in a university department of academic psychology, and for the past six years I have also worked as a psychologist in an institution (the Tavistock Clinic) best known for its psychoanalytic work. Yet I have not applied to train as a psychoanalyst, a decision prompted partly by practical reasons (I want to have a life), partly no doubt by unconscious hostility (a typical psychoanalytic explanation) and partly by my discomfort with too close an attachment to this ambivalent object. Psychoanalysis, at least for me, is aggravating and infuriating, yet also exciting and enlightening – all at the same time. I prefer the (perhaps) dilettantish stance of maintaining a position as a sympathetic critic on the margins looking in, not dependent on psychoanalysis for a living yet engaged enough for it to be part of my professional identity.

In the past ten years the margins on which I stand have become less uncomfortable than they were. Academic psychology is now much more respectful of some concerns shared by psychoanalysis, for example of how to collect and interpret meaningful data, employ the subjectivity of an investigator in the service of research, and address the limits of people's capacity to tell a story about themselves and their experience. Psychoanalysis has become more self critical with regard to its evidential basis, more aware of social and cultural issues and more sophisticated in its exploration of its own therapeutic processes. Both disciplines seem less defensive and less dogmatic. Under these conditions, I am beginning to feel that it is possible to move the debate about psychoanalysis forward, rather than constantly retrenching and reviewing old arguments.

This book has elements of retrenchment in it; I want to take stock of the standing of psychoanalysis. However, it is also an attempt to respond constructively to what I think of as a real cultural need – the need for psychoanalysis to be accountable, responsive to criticism, and respectful of evidence and argument, while still being provocative and challenging. It seems to me that psychoanalysis should always disrupt common sense and perhaps even upset people by overturning cherished beliefs. But this cannot be a random procedure; some integrity is required, some basis for scrutiny and argument, some capacity to reflect honestly on the strengths and limitations of psychoanalysis.

I hope this book is enjoyable and challenging. A small part of Chapter 7 draws on material first published as 'Postmodernism and the adoption of identity', in A. Elliott and C. Spezzano (eds) (1997) *Psychoanalysis at its Limits: Navigating the Postmodern Turn*, Northvale, NJ: Jason Aronson. The section entitled 'New sexual agendas' in Chapter 8 is based on material first published as 'Psychoanalytic challenges: a contribution to the new sexual agenda', in *Human Relations*, 50: 3 (1997). As ever, I am grateful to various friends, students and colleagues for comments that have sent me off in all sorts of directions.

BEGINNING

A story, apparently true, is told about the funeral of a famous psychoanalyst. Being a secular funeral, the coffin was brought into a hall prior to the body's cremation. The hall was full of the friends and colleagues of the dead person; it probably contained a fair sprinkling of enemies too, for such is the lamentable state of psychoanalytic affairs. As is usual in such circumstances, the body was lying down. The wish of the deceased had been that there should be no religious ritual at the funeral, so the respectful crowd stood for a few minutes in the presence of the corpse, and then sat down. No one spoke. After several minutes of silence, a few people crossed their legs. Still no one spoke. About a quarter of an hour passed, with little more than a few coughs and grunts, and the rather over-regular breathing of a number of elderly analysts who had fallen asleep. Then, clearly thinking that the silence had gone on for long enough, the most senior training analyst present said, apparently to the body: 'Seemingly, you are finding it hard to know where to begin'.

Introduction

Chapter 1

The psychoanalytic heritage

Once Freud had 'made it', once psychoanalysis was a recognised science, something happened both to him and to his discovery. They both aged. They lost something essential. Freud and psychoanalysis slowly became respectable and that may have squeezed the life out of both.[1]

Do not assume as analyst, because you are in a position of seeming authority, that the patient, the one who suffers, is not reading *you*.[2]

For most people, psychoanalysis begins and ends with Freud. Here and there are pockets of knowledge about Jung and Adler – early schismatics from the psychoanalytic movement – and in Britain at least there is also some awareness of the contribution of Donald Winnicott, Melanie Klein and Freud's daughter, Anna. But more than fifty years after his death, and a hundred years since the first genuinely psychoanalytic study was published,[3] it is Freud with whom people are still obsessed and who represents those psychoanalytic ideas which have infiltrated the popular culture of the twentieth century. The fascination with Freud shows no signs of abating, whereas interest in his successors is limited to those who are aficionados of the psychoanalytic movement.

Why is this? One possible answer is that it is Freud's moral stature, rather than his scientific credibility, which draws an audience to him. Freud developed an account of persons that purported to see through the surface of action and conscious intention to the unspoken and sometimes unspeakable wishes and anxieties beneath. Whether or not he was correct in his specific formulations of the nature of these unconscious elements, he painted a picture of what has come to be called 'psychological man' to which many people could respond.[4] Freud put a name to the widely shared feeling that sometimes we act in ways which we experience as outside our control, as mysterious yet revealing of ourselves. In addition, Freud spoke the language of morality; he presented himself as faced with unpleasant truths which he nevertheless had a duty to speak about. He would rather not have seen what he saw, but having seen it he had no choice but to speak of it.

Perhaps Freud stands in for an entire pantheon of lost father figures. In other times or places these might have been prophets; male seers who can comprehend the inner truth, who can see more deeply and accurately than is normal, and who are compelled to speak the truth they see. Most of the biblical prophets seem to have been drawn unwillingly to their task, with Jonah only the most glaring example of a line of doubters, shirkers and hedgers. Freud's beloved Moses was one of them. He did not think he would be believed and did not regard himself as up to the task of delivering the Israelites from Egypt. Freud had more self-confidence, but as he acknowledged late in life, he was no less reluctant to be the instrument of truth. At the end of *Civilisation and its Discontents* he writes:

> I have not the courage to rise up before my fellow men as a prophet, and I bow to their reproach that I can offer them no consolation: for at bottom that is what they are all demanding – the wildest revolutionaries no less passionately than the most virtuous believers.[5]

Yet it is as a prophet that Freud has been received, as a figure who might know what people are really like, who might see through the surface appearance to the messy reality underneath. Perhaps it is because reality is messy, uncomfortable, embarrassing and often shameful that Freud is experienced as a critical, judgemental father figure (in psychoanalytic terms, as a super ego, someone to fear, respect and rebel against).

It may be that Freud has a confessional function for us all, in the contemporary, secular West at least. For him, the accomplishments of civilisation and culture were tenuous, built upon the energy generated by impulses which might be socially unacceptable and sometimes downright destructive. It does not require a detailed history of the twentieth century to see that the unleashing of irrational destructiveness is an issue with which many people have had to grapple. Freud's warning, his 'no consolation', resonates strikingly with one dominant experience in post-Freudian life: that the potential for violence and destructiveness in humanity is more-or-less inexhaustible. Psychoanalysis does not excuse this, but it does at least give it meaning. Freud, lamenting and despairing of anything good in people, acid in his commentary on human nature even when he was gentle and sombre in his judgements on individual human beings, can come to represent the 'one who knows', the one who has seen and said it all before.

So Freud the father stares down at us, implicitly judging us in terms of our inner nature, seeing through the veneer of civilised conduct to the beast below. Whatever the content of his theories – and to most people these are only hazily known – Freud has the stature and problems of a judgemental father who understands what we are up to and does not like what he sees. Freud himself seems to have had a transference onto Moses, and given the structure of the history of the western world, it is perhaps not surprising that so many of us have a transference onto Freud. It is therefore equally unsurprising that Freud and his psychoanalysis should have given rise to such intense feeling and such energised debate that the controversies it spawned nearly a hundred years ago still roll on, sometimes in new guises but often remarkably unchanged. Discussion still rages around the existence and functions of the unconscious, the place of trauma in psychological suffering, the possibilities of 'cure' for psychological disturbance and the efficacy or otherwise of psychoanalysis in bringing about such cures, the relationship between fantasy and reality, the importance and the dimensions of human sexuality, the extent to which psychoanalysis can throw light on the workings of society, and whether psychoanalysis is abusive or empowering. Most of these issues would have been recognised by Freud himself as part of the debate surrounding psychoanalysis in his lifetime; the language in which they are discussed has been modernised but the issues themselves are not all that different in form. At one level, this is simply because they are good questions about psychoanalysis, with answers that are by no means clear cut. However, the reason they continue to excite interest may have more to do with the way psychoanalysis, with the figure of Freud behind it, seems to name the issues which lurk unresolved at the edges of individual and social life, issues concerning the anxieties, wishes and fantasies around which so much human activity circulates.

What I am suggesting here is that a large part of the fascination with Freud is generated not so much by the content of his work as by his symbolic function as one of the last patriarchs – a man who laid down the law, judged us rigorously and with rancour but also with some sympathy; a man who could be turned to with confessions, secrets and doubts. Here was someone who might be trusted to judge fairly, to penalise us when we deserve it but also to care enough about us to pay us attention. Squirming under the father's gaze it is good at least to know that a father is there, when it is so hard to find one anywhere else in the world. Freud seems to have had considerable awareness of his transferential function, at least to the extent that it affected the politics of the early psychoanalytic societies. He went to some lengths to consider questions of preference and succession, to establish his own special relationship with some of his followers and to nurture ties which he believed would be in his own interest and in the interests of the 'family business' – the psychoanalytic empire which he was intent on building. That he made some serious mistakes in this regard, the most glaring being in the case of Jung, does not detract at all from the analogy. Patriarchs tend to do such things, to be blinded by their emotions and their wishes and not necessarily to see through the flatterers and schemers who are closest at hand.

As might be expected given this analogy, psychoanalysis is built heavily around the structures of authority. Power does not come via the expression of an individual talent – though this can help (or hinder) progress – it comes via the gradual accrual of status in an insular and labyrinthine social network. The stages of achievement here consist very largely in the passing of time under critical scrutiny by authority figures. For example, training as a psychoanalyst in the British Psycho-Analytical Society involves several years of five-times-a-week personal analysis, plus the management of two five-times-a-week cases under weekly supervision involving discussion of very detailed 'process' records in which the supervisee writes down everything she or he can recall of the sessions. Added to this are theory seminars and often an 'infant observation' in which a young child is watched on a weekly basis, the trainee again taking detailed notes about her or his own responses as well as the child's behaviour. Given the enormous investment of time and money in the training – particularly the personal analysis – plus the exposure of one's own secret longings, impulses and failures to the scrutiny of someone who, until the very last minute, is in a position to refuse the trainee entry to the professional society, it would not be surprising if what was produced were dogmatic, conformist and scared neophytes unable to challenge any of the received wisdom to which they have been exposed. Moreover, assuming the reality of the phenomenon which analysts call transference, it would also not be surprising if the thinking of newly hatched analysts was heavily influenced by their emotional dependence upon, or perhaps opposition to, the figures with whom they have been in such intimate contact and who have had such a powerful hold upon their lives and potential livelihood. This might also explain the fact that when an analyst becomes critical of the movement, it is experienced as a betrayal, polarising both camps – the case of Jeffrey Masson being the most obvious recent one here. Even psychoanalysts who have not fallen out with the movement can have trouble remaining sane within it. Lamenting the tendency of psychoanalytic institutions to 'silence creative but dissenting voices', Ricardo Steiner comments:

> Of particular concern to me is that peculiar criterion of validation we tendentially use in our discussions, in our promotions of candidates, members, training analysts etc, based on what I would call the 'diagnostic fallacy'. I refer here to a buried assumption in some of these processes that if you do not think like me you must be mad or in need of more analysis (of the type valued by my group or sub-group).[6]

Induction into the analytic movement, it seems, is not a matter of learning certain skills, but of absorbing certain values.

More than that, it is a matter of bowing the head to authority. Understandably, most critical attention has been paid to the personal analysis component of the training, particularly the question of whether this amounts to a form of indoctrination. It is hard to imagine that a trainee who resisted the appraisals of her or his analyst and supervisors by more than a modicum would prove acceptable to the British Psycho-Analytical Society. In practice, what happens is that trainees sometimes spend many years seeking out a training analyst with whom they feel comfortable, whose insights and approach they trust and who represents the school of psychoanalysis with which they would like to be associated. They then have a period of analysis before they are accepted by the society for training, and then another period before they are allowed to take on cases under supervision themselves – effectively prolonging the period of trial until both the training organisation and the trainee feel sure that they are right for the task. It is not clear how many potential students fall by the wayside before becoming fully engaged in the training, but once they have got so far as to take on training patients it seems that most stick out the journey to the end. In all likelihood, this is because the initial screening procedure is so prolonged, unpredictable, arbitrary and arduous that it is only survived by those potential trainees who feel themselves in important ways to be analysts already. People who regard the system as irrational and unfair are not likely to keep on; those who accept it are likely to incorporate its values before the training proper begins.

It should be noted that this is not a completely irrational procedure and it is not part of my argument here to see it as such. Psychoanalysis as a clinical practice is based on intimate understanding of the patient in relationship with the analyst. It is therefore reasonable to stress the importance in training of the experience of exploring oneself in relation to one's own analyst. It seems a fair argument that people whose relationship with their own analyst is deeply problematic are likely to find the intense reiteration of that relationship with patients difficult to tolerate. Moreover, the technique of analysis is based on microscopic interpersonal interchanges, so the detailed recall and scrutiny of sessions is a powerful and appropriate training procedure. Michael Rustin, offering a defence of psychoanalytic practice from the perspective of a sympathetic outsider, makes the following claim concerning its self-regulatory mechanisms and its training procedure:

> Psychoanalysis undoubtedly has a real object for scientific study and has organised itself in such a way as to produce rational and consensual means of generating knowledge. The evidence of scrupulous attention to reliable method in analytic training, and for the advance of analytic knowledge in the face of perceived anomalies and therapeutic failures, seems to me to exist for inspection. . . . Observation of the routine work of analytic therapy in Britain suggests . . . a strenuous commitment to understand individuals as they are and to tolerate extreme uncertainty in the process of finding out what ideas might best explain psychic phenomena.[7]

Rustin is emphasising here the way that the careful work of experienced practitioners percolates down to trainees so as to encourage them to take note of the detailed aspects of their encounters with their patients. In this way they learn to postpone judgement, to be cautious in their explanatory accounts and to tolerate uncertainty. They also enter a consensual community which is not different in kind from any other scientific community which takes for granted the premises of its occupation and philosophy of study. Rustin is claiming that this is not an idealised version of psychoanalytic training and practice, but a description of what actually happens – at least in Britain, where observational studies and rigorously grounded interpretative work is favoured.

The effect of this goes further than these rational considerations might suggest. The skills and insights obtained during psychoanalytic study are probably very substantial, even if they operate within a narrow area and still seem to be contentious among analysts. However, the state of mind inculcated in the trainee is a still more substantial force. Perhaps it is true that some or all trainees absorb a tolerance of uncertainty and a respect for competing data and the complexities of causal attributions on the basis of equivocal evidence. They almost certainly learn or have reinforced a capacity to tolerate isolation, boredom and criticism. But on top of this they accept the yoke of the psychoanalytic community; they become incorporated into it if not as full believers, then at least as quiet assentors. They do not rock the boat; they accept the authority of the psychoanalytic view of the universe and of its priests here on Earth, and they practice according to its precepts.

Freud's attractiveness in the contemporary world remains centred around the issue of authority, and the psychoanalytic movement as a whole has shown a profound understanding of this point in the way in which it has organised itself. This authority is not necessarily irrational or persecutory, though it does at times have that aspect, perhaps because of the very personal nature of the interchanges between patients and analysts, trainees and supervisors, and the consequent apprehension about what people might know and think about oneself. This secrecy, however, gives rise to a sense of an authority which is unaccountable and yet all-pervading. Moreover, because psychoanalysis trades in unconscious factors, it is never possible for someone encountering it to be sure that one's motives, whether critical or accepting, are what they seem to be. If one's analyst seems persecutory and thoughtless, it may be because one is in the grip of a negative transference towards her or him; if the analyst seems perfect, this is still more suspicious. If the psychoanalytic movement turns out to be a secret society run by elitists on patriarchal lines, it is because one is full of envy for those who are already in the inner sanctum, the parental bedroom to which everyone aspires. In fact, if there is any truth in the claims made by psychoanalysis, all these things are always so: no action, emotion or perception is fully what it seems. However accurate this claim might be, it does make criticism difficult.

Up to this point, I have been suggesting that the continuing fascination with Freud is produced in part by his fantasy value as a rather stern but prescient father, one of the last in a long line now pined for within a culture where such figures are absent – some might say, mercifully so. I have also been arguing that the psychoanalytic movement is itself bound up closely with questions of authority, and that that can be seen in the way it organises its training programmes. Given their centrality to this argument, it is perhaps worth considering the notions of authority and transference more fully before moving on to look at what has come 'after Freud'.

AUTHORITY AND IDENTIFICATION

The psychoanalytic method of treatment is built around recognition of the phenomena associated with transference. In Freud's thought and in that of the 'classical Freudians', transference is understood to be based on the psychological mechanism of displacement: a set of intense feelings is diverted from the person to whom they belong and instead is directed towards some other person, in this instance the psychoanalyst. Freud's first formulation of transference, in the 'Dora' case study, stresses the way such transferences represent, but are not in fact the same as, the unconscious complexes from which they arise. Transferences are

> new editions or facsimiles of the impulses and phantasies which are aroused during the progress of the analysis; but they have this peculiarity, which is characteristic of their species, that they replace some earlier person by the person of the physician. To put it another way: a whole series of psychological experiences are revived, not as belonging to the past, but as applying to the person of the physician at the present moment.[8]

One of the striking elements in this definition is the idea of a 'new edition'. Some basic 'ur-text', usually a set of feelings towards a parent, is the original and true source of the peculiar interactions found in the analytic situation. Importantly, this means that the psychoanalytic encounter can only be understood in the light of this ur-text; there is not enough in the surface exchanges between analyst and patient to justify the intensity of the patient's feelings unless it is understood that the analytic situation functions as a kind of trigger for the emergence of some passion which was already there. This is experienced as a new feeling, but in reality it is a recapitulation, a facsimile. It is 'a *specific illusion* which develops in regard to the other person, one which, unbeknown to the subject, represents, in some of its features, a repetition of a relationship towards an important figure in the person's past'.[9]

One of the key notions in this definition is contained in the phrase 'unbeknown to the subject'. The strong argument here, maintained through all the developments in the notion of transference which have occurred during the last fifty years, is that one might be aware of very intense emotions when in a relationship with another person, without recognising the source or, hence, the original and continuing meaning of those emotions. Interestingly, even a strong critic of psychoanalysis such as Ernest Gellner shows considerable respect for this idea. Whereas much of psychoanalysis is woolly in its epistemology and outrageous in its claims, transference, he says, is a 'crisp fact':

> [Here] there is a striking generalisation which could *not* have easily been anticipated, whose truth seems genuinely evident (rather than being poised, as the others are, between equally heavy weights of positive and negative examples), and whose meaning seems reasonably precise. There is an almost comic contrast between the overwhelming and genuine evidence for this one phenomenon and the sketchy, dubious evidence for most other psychoanalytic ideas, notably the claim of therapeutic effectiveness.[10]

Gellner is one of several critics who appreciate that transference can operate organisationally as well as interpersonally, and that this might be one source of the enormous passion (both positive and negative) which many people show towards the institutions of which they are part – including the institutions of psychoanalysis. Indeed, Gellner suggests that the psychoanalytic movement is held together by transference: 'psychoanalysis is powerfully addictive, and "transference" is the name, though not in any serious sense the explanation, of this phenomenon'.[11]

What is the significance of this for understanding the nature of the psychoanalytic enterprise? The problems are immediately obvious and form a subset of the problems created by the notion of the unconscious upon which psychoanalysis is founded. If we can never be sure of the sources of our emotional attachments to others, to our analyst or to the organisational structures of psycho-analysis, then those attachments can always be interpreted in terms of something other than the way they appear to be. So if an analysand attacks her or his analyst, it is likely that at least some of the energy of this attack derives from unconscious feelings towards people other than the analyst – usually parents. Similarly, if the institutions of psychoanalysis (or the whole enterprise itself) are adored or hated, this is not just because of their actual value but because of the reminiscences they produce, the resurrection of some original state of affairs or trauma which has nothing intrinsically to do with psychoanalysis at all.

The power of this account is very great in numerous ways. As Gellner notes, it does seem to make sense in relation to the intensity of people's feelings about those with whom they have relationships, including the peculiar relationship known as psychoanalysis. It also offers, at least in outline, the beginning of a theory of organisations and social forms – an account of what binds each of us to others and to organisational structures which may be experienced as aversive or oppressive in many respects. On the other hand, it makes it very difficult to know when to stop; that is, it makes reality so completely imbued with fantasy that one can never be confident about calibrating anything – any excess or persecution, any act of love or generosity. Motives become obscured, not clarified; interpretation can be a weapon.

Finding a fixed point in this slippery realm leads back to the question of authority. The controversial French analyst Jacques Lacan refers to the psychoanalyst in the transference as 'the subject supposed to know',[12] implying by this that there is a common way of relating to the analyst as if she or he possesses a particular knowledge or truth, and that part of the process of analysis is discovering that this is a fantasy – that no one owns the kinds of truths we all look for. This is a notion which offers considerable leverage when challenging simplistic ideas of the purpose of therapy or aspirations towards 'cure'. But it leaves open another question: if the individual can never know the source of her or his desire – if the origins of transference are 'unbeknown to the subject' – then who *can* pronounce upon it? Who can give a judgement of whether the analyst is persecutory or the analysand simply feels persecuted, whether the institutes of psychoanalysis are conservative or their attackers envious, whether psychoanalysis itself is fraudulent or its critics simply scared of its emotional truths? Only those who do know, which can either mean each one of us to the limits of our flawed and unconsciously riven understandings, or someone elected – for unconsciously determined and transferentially induced reasons – to a position of authority.

What might it be like to 'know' the unconscious in this way, and how might we recognise the kind of person in whom authority might be appropriately invested? Although there are many psychoanalytic accounts of leadership, these are couched in a rather disappointingly social psychological framework and do not really help when it comes down to the question of who might be a legitimate authority to whom one can bend the knee. They tend to rely on notions of external sanction plus the capacity to come to terms with inner sources of one's authority – internal 'objects' from whom a sense of authoritativeness might derive. Thus Anton Obholzer, working from within the 'group relations' model of organisational consultation, writes: 'Good-enough authority, at its best, is a state of mind arising from a continuous mix of authorization from the sponsoring organization or structure, sanctioning from within the organization, and connection with inner world authority figures.'[13]

This may be an adequate description of the characteristics of individuals in whom authority can be invested – that they have the power to be authoritative and that they feel confident about their right to use that power – but it does not help with the question of what makes for *legitimate* authority, psychoanalytically or in any other way. Specifically in the context of the standing of psychoanalysis, one needs to ask who can own the kind of knowledge that allows them to pronounce on the nature of another's subjectivity – on the truth of their unconscious life?

One straightforward yet problematic answer to this question is that nobody has this knowledge, that 'the subject supposed to know' can never actually know. In different ways, several psychoanalytic thinkers have come to this point of view. It is implicit in the Lacanian phrase itself, and was certainly acted out in ironic, perhaps mischievous ways, by Lacan himself. For example, Lacan was often known as the 'Master',[14] yet his theory – particularly the theory of the phallus – seems to imply that no one can 'master' the unconscious, that all investments of full knowledge and authority in someone else are spurious. If one takes the notion of the phallus as connoting power – which is at least one strand in its complex use in

Lacan's work – then Lacan's idea that the phallus 'can only play its role as veiled' and that it can never be known directly suggests that it is not the kind of thing which can be possessed by any being, human or otherwise.[15] Authority therefore becomes a matter of style, of the projection of an authoritative stance; it has no absolute substance of its own. Indeed, one might suggest from here that the analytic cure consists mainly in discovering that there is no cure, that no one can solve the enigma of anyone else's life.

While this might seem a cynical view of authority, it is not so far removed from other psychoanalytic formulations. For example, the British post-Kleinian analyst Wilfred Bion famously enjoined analysts to enter into their work without 'memory or desire', leaving their knowledge, preconceptions and expertise outside of the consulting room. 'It is important,' writes Bion, 'that the analyst should avoid mental activity, memory and desire, which is as harmful to his mental fitness as some forms of physical activity are to physical fitness.'[16] Moreover, 'the capacity to forget, the ability to eschew desire and understanding, must be regarded as essential discipline for the psycho-analyst. Failure to practice this discipline will lead to a steady deterioration in the powers of observation whose maintenance is essential.'[17] In this view, it is not a particular kind of knowledge that designates the analyst as 'the subject who knows', but a particular attitude of mind, an observational stance towards the patient which communicates itself as an openness to being surprised and a willingness to accept what comes. In Bion's work, this is named as 'reverie' and identified first of all with the way a mother appreciates and accepts her infant – the kind of authority which in some ways may really be 'inside knowledge',

> Reverie is that state of mind which is open to the reception of any 'objects' from the loved object and is therefore capable of the reception of the infant's projective identifications whether they are felt by the infant to be good or bad.[18]

The one who knows something of the unconscious here becomes not a person invested with a specific knowledge, but one capable of communicating a transforming stance, an experience of the kind of balanced 'not knowing' that both respects the workings of the unconscious and makes something of it – that makes one's body dance with the rhythm rather than fight against it. One knows who is in authority because of the effect that person has.

This is not necessarily the way in which the psychoanalytic

movement presents itself to the rest of the world. Not all psycho-analytic learning is aimed at freeing the analyst from preconceptions; on the contrary, psychoanalysis makes many truth claims concerned, for example, with the mechanisms of the mind, the course of human development, the causes of psychological distress and the vicissitudes of sexuality.[19] The possible evidential status of these claims is one of the issues discussed in the next chapter. However, psychoanalysis itself – with its stress on uncon-scious phenomena as motivating devices in human belief and behaviour – would suggest that conscious and balanced evaluation of evidence is unlikely to be the main source of individuals' commitment for or against the system. As has been noted above, the institutions and training mechanisms of the psychoanalytic movement are not organised so as to encourage rational, critical debate, but rather so as to provide firm guidelines and transferen-tial objects – people and practices with whom to identify – in which trainees and members invest.

It is partly in recognition of this attribute of psychoanalysis that many of its critics argue that it is more like a religious or mystical movement than a science. For example, Ernest Gellner again:

> Psychoanalysis is, in a very strict sense of the term, a mystical experience. Mystical experience can best be defined as follows: an intense emotional experience, which at the same time purports to be and is felt as being the acquisition of knowledge which is important, privileged, and out of the ordinary.[20]

Leaving aside for the moment the question of whether much 'ordi-nary' science might also be characterised as mystical in this way, the suggestion here is that it is the personally transformative quality of psychoanalytic encounters that attracts adherents, rather than any socially consensual demonstration of knowledge, expertise or even effectiveness. Coming into contact with 'the subject supposed to know' and feeling affected by this contact is what leads to belief – an 'intense emotional experience' which makes one feel that some important insight has been gained, some new knowledge acquired. Psychoanalysis seems set up to work in this way. The analyst offers a 'container' of sorts for the patient so that she or he can experience all of her or his passion and yet not be destroyed by it, or else the analyst frustrates and provokes the patient until an awareness of her or his own pre-existing inner knowledge comes to the fore. Institutionally, psychoanalysis avoids spontaneity and freedom of expression; it is a kind of decentred total institution in which everything feeds back into itself.

Under these conditions, commitment to psychoanalysis can rarely be a matter of rational decision making. Instead, the primary means through which commitment occurs is something closely related to transference: identification with significant individuals or with the culture of psychoanalysis itself. By experiencing the power of the analyst or the system of which she or he is part (a power to offer thinking space, surprises and insights which at least feel like they have meaning), the individual aspires to this person or system – works to take it in as an aspect of her or his own personality. This is, perhaps, the primary way in which people form themselves in childhood. In relation to the ego, for instance, Freud suggested that its character might be 'a precipitate of abandoned object cathexes' containing 'the history of these object choices',[21] meaning that it might be built up on the basis of internalisation in fantasy of objects lost or renounced in reality.

From many differing perspectives, and to some degree (particularly for the Lacanians) with different evaluations of the process, psychoanalysts now argue that psychological development is in large part a process of taking in external 'objects'. This means that fantasies of people or parts of people (the maternal breast is the primary instance here) become part of the mind (they are 'introjected'), available as sources of nurture or all-too-present as causes of persecutory disturbance, but generally accessible not just as entities with which to have relationships, but as *causes* of belief, desire and mental structure. This is a model, too, of the analytic experience, for instance in Bionian thought the task of the therapist is to retain the stance of reverie so that the patient can feel fully known and tolerated, able to make use of her or his psychological resources, capable of facing her or his own thoughts and dreams.[22] The patient's 'task' is to incorporate this stance of the analyst, to be able to introject it as a way of relating to her or himself and thus to employ it as a prompt to further integration of the personality and to creative psychic work. This goes a lot further than the original Freudian idea that analytic progress derives from revelation of the underlying cause of neurosis and is measured by the capacity of the ego to function without too much interference. Instead, most contemporary psychoanalysts have a more fluid vision of the analytic process, in which what matters are the patterns of identification and internalisation seized on by the patient, so that she or he can derive sustenance for the integration of personality attributes which might otherwise be left fragmentary or denied.[23]

The authoritative psychoanalyst, the one who knows the unconscious, is the one who can become an object of identification. None more so than Freud himself, for reasons touched on at the beginning of this chapter: he functions as moralist, patriarch, prophet – the one who seems to know, who speaks of a certain way of being in the world which is both intimidating and reassuring. Freud represents the individual who is willing to take upon himself the weight of all our troubles. Perhaps it is this that is characteristic of the appeal of many individual psychoanalysts and of the whole psychoanalytic edifice – that psychoanalysis appears to offer a model of personal searching and transformation which is not only sought after, but needed throughout the contemporary Western world. Gellner is only one of several cultural critics who have taken this view:

> Psychoanalysis does not need to make any explicit promises (though, in fact, it quite often does so). A truly tremendous promise is immediately, visibly and dramatically implicit in its entire presentation of the human condition, and that vision in turn has enormous plausibility.[24]

Among the many problems inherent in this irrationalist stance, however, is the difficulty encountered by psychoanalysis and by individual analysts in living up to this idealised, transference-imbued picture of what can be achieved, a difficulty which always threatens to provoke denigration. Switching between the poles of this fantasy (psychoanalysis is everything, psychoanalysis is nothing) can lead and has led to neglect of the relatively ordinary achievements and limitations of the psychoanalytic movement, forcing a choice between 'for' *or* 'against'.

THE PSYCHOANALYTIC HERITAGE

The psychoanalytic inheritance, derived first and repeatedly from Freud, thus consists of a promise of effectiveness, of light thrown on individual impulses and desires, hopes and frustrations – light leading to transformation as well as illumination. In addition, it promises something equivalent concerning human development, social relations and culture; in fact, it has taken as its domain almost every aspect of human experience, commenting sometimes cautiously, often imperiously, from the point of view of the one who might really know. Most of these commentaries derive directly from Freud: on sexuality, on psychopathology, on child development; but also on religion, politics, history and culture. They have been used in almost equal measure by psychoanalysts and by cultural and literary critics making use of psychoanalytic formulations to flesh out their hypotheses about human causes. They continue to be contentious, unreliable, exciting and provocative. To a considerable extent, they have defined the culture of modernism.

But what, in fact, *is* psychoanalysis now? Even in these first few pages, I have referred not just to Freud but to a few of the many developments of Freudian ideas, including the work of Lacan and Bion – two provocateurs of psychoanalytic dissent. As has been described in numerous writings, including some of my own,[25] there are considerable variations to be found in the assumptions, emphases and formulations of differing approaches, all of which would call themselves psychoanalytic. Some of these differences have led to vituperative debates, particularly around the Kleinian and the Lacanian positions, and there are certainly differences of theory and practice among some adherents of different schools of thought which might make one wonder if they truly belong to the same movement at all. Not that this is unexpected, given the account of the nature and mode of transmission of psychoanalytic knowledge outlined above. So much depends on the accident of choice of one's own analyst, of the school of thought in which one becomes immersed through training or reading, of the particular zeitgeist making one or other analytic position fashionable. So little depends on the kind of evidence which might make it possible to make rational choices. Would the division between Freudians and Kleinians in Britain have been as marked and agitated as it has turned out to be if the main players had not been two women fighting over Freud's heritage, both intent on developing child psychoanalysis – especially as one of these was Freud's own daughter?

In the past, the main fault lines discriminating between differing psychoanalytic approaches have been relatively easy to identify. For example, the earliest schismatics split from Freud over differences in the relative emphasis to be placed on sexuality versus other drives such as aggression. The debate between Anna Freud and Melanie Klein revealed substantial differences in models of infant develop-ment, beliefs about the structure of the mind, emphasis placed on unconscious versus egoic structures, and the place given to object relationships and to fantasy life. Object relations theorists themselves, such as Winnicott and Fairbairn in Britain or their close cousins in self theory in the United States, disputed the causal significance of biological drives and argued that quality of interpersonal relationships was the primary determinant, not just of mental health but of the whole developmental structure of consciousness and the unconscious. Thus Guntrip, using the traditional translation of Freud's 'trieb' as 'instinct', claims:

> Instincts can only operate satisfactorily when they belong to a stable ego, and therefore cannot be the source of the ego's energy for object-relating. It seems more conceivable that the energy of the ego for object-relating is the primary energy; as Fairbairn put it, 'libido is object-seeking'.[26]

Transformed into crude non-technical language, this means that sexual energy does not lead to relationships; rather, the urge to form relationships leads to sex. Psychoanalysis this may be, because of its continued use of the concept of the dynamic unconscious, but Freud it is not.

The clarity of differentiation between the various schools of psychoanalysis seems to have become less apparent in recent years. To a considerable degree, all the mainstream psychoanalytic schools have turned their attention to what is best termed 'intersubjectivity' – the ways in which mental representations of relationships are formed and the effects these have on the development and actual social relationships of individuals. Although substantial variations in terminology and emphasis still apply, there is far more overlap among the mainstream proponents of psychoanalysis than at any time in the post-Freudian period. For instance, contemporary Freudians and Kleinians differ considerably on the centrality they accord to early fantasy life, to unconscious emotions and to cognitions, with Freudians being willing to credit the ego with more capacity for imagination and control than do Kleinians, who in turn remain more wedded to a vision of the infant mind as one already full of complex emotions and fantasy states. Yet, proponents of both approaches can be found who are concerned with the ways infants form mental representations of their own functioning and of other people, and of how this can be understood in terms of creative interplays between autochthonous elements of the mind, early experiences and unconscious impulses.[27] Indeed, it is fairly hard to find any contemporary psychoanalyst who does not accord central significance to object relationships, even if they differ on many other aspects of theory (such as the place of drives or the order of developmental accomplishments) or practice (such as the way interpretations should be phrased, or the use of the negative transference).

As in many other things, Lacanians are an exception to this trend. Although this is not the place to develop the Lacanian position in any detail, it is worth holding in mind their rigorous critique of object relational ideas. This is not because they deny the importance of social relationships, but because they are antagonistic to the idea that mature relationships are possible in any straightforward sense – or that knowledge of another, that is, intersubjectivity, is an achievable state of human affairs. For Lacanians, all interpersonal relationships, and indeed the structure of the individual human subject as well, are penetrated by cultural and social forces with distorting and obscuring effects. It is therefore not possible to achieve unmediated knowledge of the other of a kind that could give rise to the types of resolved, reciprocal relationships postulated by object relations theorists and often taken as a loose yardstick of mental health. Moreover, Lacanians suggest that even in the intimate and intense encounter of the psychoanalyst with the patient, something interferes with the capacity of either partner to understand or recognise the other. Intersubjectivity even here is blocked by some other feature – the limits of language, the structure of authority, the impossibility of being fully at one with any other person.

What is preserved in the Lacanian critique of the object relational tendency of most contemporary psychoanalysis is one of the more radical elements of psychoanalytic thought: a pessimism concerning the possibility of positive knowledge as against negative knowledge or critique. Michael Rustin expresses this comparison in a particularly clear way, taking as his context the differing relationships with political thought held by British and Lacanian psychoanalysis,

> On the one hand, there is an emphasis in the Lacanian tradition on the necessarily 'negative' and 'antagonistic' aspects of psychoanalytic and other 'critical' modes of social thought. The idea of the 'negative' focuses attention on the inherent limits of human self-understanding, and its inherent distortions and falsifications

involved in representation. . . . By contrast, the object relations and Kleinian traditions postulate a 'positive' core of ideas about human nature and its more benign forms of development. . . . The first tradition is above all adapted to the unending investigation of the inauthentic, idealised and self-regarding aspects of human consciousness. The second tradition regards psychoanalytic investigation not only as a method of recognition of illusions and self-deceptions, but also as a source of grounded understanding of 'authentic' states of feeling and object relations, conceived as the foundation of creative forms of life.[28]

Rustin's own sympathies lie more with the British tradition. He argues that Kleinians, for example, are not 'positive' in the sentimental sense, but are well versed in the negativity of experience and indeed have been its principal theorists, with their notions of envy and projective identification and their emphasis on aggression and destructiveness. Their positive stance comes from a perspective on development which embraces the possibility of dealing with destructiveness in more or less creative ways – with the prospect of what Kleinians term 'reparation'. Rustin notes:

> The idea that the disruptive phenomena of the unconscious can be contained in more and less destructive ways, that relatively benign relationships between the inner world and external reality can be conceived in theory and to some degree sustained in reality, has led to some commitment within the object relations tradition to projects of social improvement.[29]

Differentiating between 'negative' and 'positive' traditions in psychoanalysis is, of course, only one possible take on the variety of ways in which the psychoanalytic field can be divided. Nevertheless, it is a powerful one, reflecting the complexity of the critical positions taken up by psychoanalysis and the alternative possibilities of different attitudes towards therapeutic, political or cultural change. In Rustin's reading, 'positive' and 'negative' refer to particular perspectives on the possibility for social progress and for authentic communication, not on the capacity of a theory to recognise destructiveness. In general, negative theories such as those to be found in the Lacanian tradition are concerned with critique, with pulling away the veils to reveal what is underneath (usually a horror, as one might expect); positive theories are more 'therapeutic' in tone, holding out the prospect of transformation. Thirty years ago, Philip Rieff named a similar division as that between the 'analytic' and 'ecstatic' attitudes.[30] He clearly preferred the analytic, with its tendency to detachment, irony and pessimism and its commitment to rigorous understanding over therapeutic consolation (Freudianism was the exemplar of the analytic attitude). Rieff's book was called *The Triumph of the Therapeutic*, and was one in a line of works from differing perspectives which documented the decline in the radical vision of psychoanalysis.[31] On the other hand, as Rustin argues, being aware of negativity does not preclude the development of socially progressive projects. In fact, one might argue that it is only out of such awareness that truly constructive activity can arise. Viewing everything as already all right removes the motivation for change; envisioning progress as inevitable means it is likely to fall at the gates of greed, envy and human destructiveness.

Where this leads us, then, is to a view of the psychoanalytic heritage not so much as a collection of core theories, but as a stance or group of stances on human development and possibility. There are, of course, specific theories to consider, for example concerning the place of 'real' experience on sexuality, child development, the mechanisms of therapeutic change and so on. Discussion of some of these points will form a substantial part of this book as it unfolds. But over it all stands a different kind of question about what psychoanalysis contributes; a question of impact, of what difference it makes to have a theory of this sort. It is a critical, heterogeneous theory and its one universal claim is that there is more to human activity than meets the eye, that there is – in Gellner's words – a 'Beast' at work,[32] something which lies within us and which systematically disrupts everything we think and do. How this Beast should be construed, what its origins and tendencies are, to what extent it can be appeased or transformed – on all these points, there are a variety of psychoanalytic answers. The heritage of psychoanalysis resides here. It resides, too, in the sets of practices and institutional frameworks which characterise psychoanalysis in action around the world. It can also be found in the identifications and emotional investments of analysts, analysands and critics, perhaps even in the orientation of 'ordinary people' towards therapy or causal explanations of human motives.

So what are we left considering, when evaluating the viability of psychoanalysis – its 'for and against'? It is a set of theories, a pattern of work, a perspective and a critical stance. It contains intimations of alternative social orders and transformations of individuals through therapy. It is infused with truth claims and denials, with attachments, passions, identifications and enmities. It makes people question, it gives them answers, it doubts the answers and the very possibility of fully answering anything. It claims to be a science, it claims all science is flawed. Perhaps it is the most encompassing social theory ever invented; perhaps it is all a fraud. I shall try to develop a genuine 'for and against' argument in the following chapters as I explore questions of meaning and interpretation in psychoanalysis, the aims and effectiveness of psychoanalytic therapy and the application of psychoanalytic theory to social concerns. It will already be clear, however, that the ambition to develop a 'for and against' argument begs numerous questions, including those of affiliation and personal motivation mentioned in the Preface, but also more abstract considerations of 'objectivity' and 'subjectivity'. Quite clearly, if psychoanalysis reveals anything at all, it shows that it is not possible to sustain a clear differentiation between what is objective and what subjective – the two orders of experience merge into one another in a slippery and contaminating way. This is a position congruent with recent developments in the philosophy of science as well as in psychology generally, which have recognised the part played by subjective elements in the research process. However, psychoanalysis suggests something more reciprocal than that. Subjective investments will influence perceptions of external 'reality', but this same subjectivity will itself be infiltrated by that reality. In a famous phrase, Lacan claimed that 'Man speaks, then, but it is because the symbol has made him man'.[33] The individual does not control her or his subjectivity, does not even own it – the unconscious is saturated with the structures of the social and cultural order, above all with language. Jane Gallop's gloss on this is as follows:

> Castration for Lacan is not only sexual; more important, it is also linguistic: we are inevitably bereft of any masterful understanding of language, and can only signify ourselves in a symbolic system that we do not command, that, rather, commands us.[34]

In the context of evaluating psychoanalysis, this highlights the difficulty of distinguishing between subjective investment, social construction and anything resembling an objective assessment of the standing of psychoanalysis.

Given all this confusion, what criteria can one employ when attempting to establish the value of the psychoanalytic enterprise? In this book, I am not going to claim that it is possible to set up objective standards with which everyone would agree; indeed, part of the argument developed in the next chapter is that the tradition of 'scientific' evaluations of psychoanalysis, which has tried to do this, is wrong headed in some important ways. To adopt the terminology of postmodernism, there is no 'meta-narrative' against which the standing of psychoanalysis can be unequivocally measured. On the other hand, I am also not about to support a relativistic free for all in which psychoanalysis is reduced to being an interesting story about human psychology, valuable for its literary merits alone. Psychoanalysis claims to say important and truthful things about human functioning; it would not rest content with being a beautiful (or ugly) fairy story.

My approach here is not to be too grand, but instead to get involved in the specifics of the arguments surrounding psychoanalysis at some key points: its standing as a causal or hermeneutic theory; its efficacy as a mode of therapy; and its potency as a contributor to debates around identity construction, gender, sexual orientation and racism. At each of these points, something can be said about what psychoanalysis does, about whether it deepens our understanding of human functioning, whether it is consistent with its own perceptions and theories or seems subservient to social pressures and norms, whether it is coherent or muddled, evocative or sterile. In each case the criteria for assessment will be different, but the argument I am developing is fairly precise. Psychoanalysis, to be taken seriously, needs to have a project which is specifiable, a set of theories which are coherent and which relate to that project, and a practice which is consistent with the theory and which has comprehensible effects. Moreover, for psychoanalysis to be desirable, it should maintain a critical vision of its own, functioning in tension with social norms and capable of throwing light on psychological phenomena which might otherwise seem obscure, bizarre or frightening.

It will be seen that there is no one answer to all the questions which could be asked about the standing of psychoanalysis, that the conjunction 'and' in 'for and against psychoanalysis' is more appropriate than the alternative 'or'. The concurrent presence of all these confusing elements of subjectivity, science, politics and therapy, all operating on different planes yet all bearing on the standing of psychoanalysis, leaves us with an enormous number of different things which might be said about psychoanalysis, its value and its limitations. My hope is that by the end of this book, some of these things will have been said in a way that makes it possible to appreciate more clearly what psychoanalysis has to offer, and what it does not.

Part I

Knowledge

Chapter 2

Science, mysticism and subjectivity

Throughout the history of psychoanalysis there have been acrimonious debates about its standing in relation to truth. How does one evaluate the claims made by a body of theory which is heterogeneous, often vague, enormous in its scope (dealing with issues ranging from slips of the tongue to the history of civilisation), and which requires of its practitioners immersion into structures and institutions of intense belief? What criteria can be employed to assess an approach which suggests that all theories and claims to knowledge – that all rational activities – are under the sway of unconscious forces which cannot be known in any direct way, yet which can be employed as explanations for almost any eventuality? Psychoanalysis, it might be argued, possesses some of the most versatile explanatory concepts in intellectual history, so versatile that they are immune to appraisal by rational means because they do not stay still for long enough.

Much of the debate about the standing of psychoanalysis as theory has revolved around the question of whether it can be considered to be, in any meaningful sense, a scientific pursuit. Freud's view on this, expressed most firmly in his new introductory 'lecture' on *The Question of a Weltanschauung*, was unequivocal: 'Psychoanalysis, in my opinion, is incapable of creating a *Weltanschauung* of its own. It does not need one; it is a part of science and can adhere to the scientific *Weltanschauung*'.[1]

Psychoanalysis is 'a specialist science, a branch of psychology',[2] unfit to create its own attitude towards or view of the world. The fact that it deals with subjective issues – what Freud calls the 'mental field' – makes no difference, 'since the intellect and the mind are objects for scientific research in exactly the same way as any non-human things'.[3] In fact, if

> the investigation of the intellectual and emotional functions of men (and of animals) is included in science, then it will be seen that nothing is altered in the attitude of science as a whole, that no new sources of knowledge or methods of research have come into being.[4]

What psychoanalysis contributes is an application of the scientific method and point of view to wishes and other unconscious mental events, although this does not mean that it can proceed in a wish-fulfilling way itself. Psychoanalysis can neither adopt the ways of art nor of religion, though it can be used to analyse these; it cannot even allow that these might be alternative ways of expressing human truths. Science, and with it psychoanalysis, must contest the ground of explanation and triumph:

> It is simply a fact that the truth cannot be tolerant, that it admits of no compromises or limitations, that research regards every sphere of human activity as belonging to it and that it must be relentlessly critical if any other power tries to take over any part of it.[5]

Freud's espousal of the values and perceptions of science could hardly be more categorical, and his claim that it is in the scientific sphere that psychoanalysis is properly placed is strongly stated and tenaciously defended. Others, of course, have not always been so sure. Hans Eysenck, an irrepressible prophet of the demise of psychoanalysis, pronounces of Freud:

> He was, without doubt, a genius, not of science, but of propaganda, not of rigorous proof, but of persuasion, not of the design of experiments, but of literary art. His place is not, as he claimed, with Copernicus and Darwin, but with Hans Christian Anderson and the Brothers Grimm, tellers of fairy tales.[6]

Psychoanalysis is a series of tall tales, for some reason taken seriously – perhaps because of their excitement and literary merit. As will be seen, some defenders of psychoanalysis adopt a position rather similar to this one of Eysenck's, but without his acerbic attitude towards the truth claims of psychoanalysis. They simply argue, *pace* Freud, that the genre of novels and fairy tales – of narratives – has something considerable to offer in the pursuit of human understanding.

From a more sophisticated critical perspective, Ernest Gellner has something similar to say. Psychoanalysis is a 'mystical experience'; where it differs from other forms of mysticism is not in its scientific standing, but in its use of mystical means to attain knowledge of the natural rather than the spiritual world,

> Psychoanalysis does indeed consist of the penetration of a Special Realm, discontinuous from the ordinary world though dominating it, and accessible only to forms of exploration distinct from those prevalent in the ordinary world: success is heralded by intense emotion, and a deep transformation of the knower himself. All this it shares with older forms of mysticism. But: this Other Realm *is part of Nature*. This is mysticism with a naturalistic face.[7]

Gellner is pointing here to an aspect of psychoanalytic knowledge which was dwelt upon in the previous chapter: its *transformative* capacity. One unusual feature of psychoanalysis is that knowledge is given the status both of 'scientific' advancement – pursuing understanding of the general functioning of human subjects, of the unconscious, of psychopathology and so on – and also as the route to personal change. It is through a particular kind of psychoanalytic knowledge – 'insight' – that the therapeutic action of psychoanalysis has its effect. In principle, it might be argued that this latter facet of psychoanalytic knowledge need not contaminate its scientific aspect; therapy might be seen as the application of general discoveries to the individual case. In this way, it could be equivalent to other attempts to derive scientific 'laws' through one mode of investigation and then to apply them in a set of more specific spheres. However, what complicates the position of psychoanalysis is that the transformative capacity of psychoanalytic knowledge is held to be integral to the theory itself. Studying a mental phenomenon 'from the outside' will not produce the kind of knowledge which counts as genuinely psychoanalytic, just as reading *about* psychoanalysis in books is held never to produce a true understanding of it.

A brief example to clarify this point can be given from the field of observational studies of children.[8] Among developmental psychologists working within an empirical tradition, the task of an observer is to systematically record children's behaviour, reducing as far as possible distortions caused by the various biases which might enter into the observational process. Among these biases, or sources of 'error', are included particular attributes of the observer, and one way to check on this is to use additional observers whose observations can be compared with one another. As Jerry Wiggins points out in his classic text on the subject, this 'problem' of inter-observer reliability is best understood as an empirical question concerning the extent to which the findings made by one observer can be generalised to those which would have been made by another.[9] Nevertheless, the central point is that psychology strives to make sources of variation in observational studies explicit so as to approach as near as possible to an account of the child's behaviour which is not mediated by subjective aspects of the observer's own functioning.

Several psychoanalytically oriented developmental psychologists have used a similar observational framework with the goal of elaborating children's emergent subjectivities, thereby producing data congruent with psychoanalytic understanding. They are thus working within the 'scientific' frame of empirical psychology, but applying it to psychoanalytically relevant phenomena. Among the most influential of these researchers is Daniel Stern, whose painstaking work on the fine detail of interactions between mothers and infants has been received with considerable interest both by developmental psychologists and by psychotherapists.[10] Interestingly, however, the relationship between *psychoanalytic* knowledge and the kind of knowledge produced by observational studies of this kind, even when the latter has a psychodynamic gloss, remains controversial. Writing about Stern's work, Roszika Parker notes:

> Many writers have commented that this is a world of interpersonal rather than intrapsychic events. Stern's baby does not develop images of the mother mediated by its unconscious phantasy, or archetypal imagery. It seems that Stern's view is that as unconscious conflicts cannot be observed in babies, they cannot be taken into account.[11]

The problem here, from a psychoanalytic point of view, is almost exactly the opposite of that which would concern empirical psychology. *Because* Stern relies on observation of behaviour without mediating it through the observer's own subjectivity, he *cannot* produce an account of the infant's emerging selfhood from the point of view of its psychodynamic – that is, at root, its unconscious – determinants. This is because, as Gellner suggests in the quotations given above, psychoanalysis suggests that the *only* reliable route into the unconscious of another is through the unconscious of the self, through what Parker calls 'unconscious to unconscious communication'.[12] This is why the main British tradition of infant observation – nowadays an important component in all psychoanalytic psychotherapy training courses – requires the observer to record not just the child's behaviour, but the feelings evoked in the observer as well. This is not, as might be the case from an empirical position, in order to take into account the 'distorting' impact of these feelings on the observer's objectivity; rather, it is because the observer's emotional responses are taken to be the most useful – the most 'valid' – indices of what is going on for the child her or himself. Margot Waddell describes this approach to infant observation as follows:

> It is a method with no claims to impartiality or objectivity. Rather the reverse, it is one rooted in subjectivity of a particular kind – with the capacity to look inward and outward simultaneously; . . . one that struggles to prevent observation being clouded and distorted through preconception. It is a method which requires the observer to be as minutely cognisant of his or her internal processes as of those of the subject of observation.[13]

Although there is an element here of the observer becoming aware of her or his internal processes in order to reduce their impact (the method is 'one that struggles to prevent observation being clouded and distorted through preconception'), the capacity to understand the child is seen as dependent on the ability to register the unavoidable, in fact the *essential*, subjective responses of the observer in the child's presence. Comprehending a (here, preverbal) child's state of mind – the focus of psychoanalytic work – can only be achieved through comprehension of one's own unconscious response.

From Gellner's point of view, this indeed looks like a variety of mysticism: full psychoanalytic understanding, whether of oneself or of others, can only be achieved when something extracognitive takes place, some unconscious responsiveness. If one does not believe in the possibility of 'unconscious to unconscious communication', it is not only impossible to carry out psychoanalytic therapy, but also impossible to do psychoanalytic science. Knowledge of this kind is personally transformative, hence full of personal investments, subjective resonance, wishes, conflicts and ambivalence. In most canons, this would rule it out of science.

But is this necessarily so? All the claims and considerations outlined here warrant considerable discussion, for they bear not just on the very specific but well-worn question of whether psychoanalysis can reasonably claim to be a science, but also on the wider issue of what kind of knowledge of subjectivity is possible and legitimate. However, it might be worth making a preliminary point here, concerning the narrowness of the view of science which dominates in discussions surrounding psychoanalysis. It seems fair to say the scientific standing of psychoanalysis has generally been explored using a 'positivist' image of science, containing a number of assumptions which have themselves been brought into question in the social sciences in recent years. Principal among these assumptions is the notion of *realism*, that is, the position that there exists a domain of objective 'truth', of actual reality, which with the right methods can be identified and explored directly – even if this is a very difficult task. So, to follow up the example of child observation procedures given above, there is an actual 'truth' of the child's behaviour which can be described accurately, given robust enough measures and the taking of forceful enough steps to reduce error due to sampling and observer bias. Following from this assumption, positivism assumes a dualist or objectivist epistemology, in which findings are taken as having objective existence of their own, independently of the researcher. Reliance is therefore upon methodologies (usually quantitative ones) emphasising the neutrality of the researcher and the manipulation of experimental conditions to separate out true from factitious events.[14]

Intriguingly, in the social sciences in general, this view of correct science has increasingly been disputed. To a considerable degree, the form this debate has taken has been around the competing virtues of qualitative and quantitative methods of research. In an article in the conservative *British Journal of Psychology*, Karen Henwood and Nick Pidgeon advance the case for qualitative research methods as follows:

Qualitative methods are privileged within the naturalistic approach because they are thought to meet a number of reservations about the uncritical use of quantification in social science practice: in particular, the problem of inappropriately fixing meanings where these are variable and re-negotiable in relation to their context of use; the neglect of the uniqueness and particularity of human experience; . . . and because of concern with the overwriting of internally structured subjectivities by externally imposed 'objective' systems of meaning.[15]

What Henwood and Pidgeon are suggesting is that the attractiveness of qualitative procedures resides in their responsiveness to the complexity and variability of human meanings – and that this complexity and variability is lost in approaches which try to fix upon a universal 'true' meaning of human behaviour and experience. In essence, an argument is being made for the classic division between *Naturwissenschaften* (natural sciences) and *Geistesswissenschaften* (moral/human sciences) – the latter requiring an approach based on uncovering meaning or understanding, usually viewed as a human process of interpretation. The problem with positivist science is that it fails to appreciate the extent to which psychological data derived from humans requires interpretation before it can be understood, with the particular form of interpretation being based on interactive and discursive processes – the kind of interpretive activity which people engage in all the time in everyday life. This kind of social science approach, codified recently in text-based modes of research work such as 'narrative analysis' and 'discourse analysis'[16] makes claims about the relative poverty of positivist research and the need for more broadly rhetorical and interpretive methods of human understanding. It is perhaps only experimental psychologists who might be surprised by this; psychoanalysts should not be, because they need only look to related situations of human judgement to find parallel cases. For example:

Historians and biographers as well as legal judges infer motives and beliefs of other human beings on the basis of indirect evidence. They do not only rely on explicit verbal utterances in acknowledging the mental states in question. . . . If only scientific evidence were sufficient for the ascription of mental states for which we do not have direct evidence, our legal systems would be paralysed.[17]

Much of this discussion, particularly concerning the status of interpretive activity in knowledge production, is reflected in the continuing debates on 'hermeneutic' approaches to psychoanalysis, debates which will be discussed in the next chapter. Here, I want to draw attention to the position of the researcher in this 'new paradigm' (as it has come to be called) – social science research.

Qualitative research grows out of a critique of positivist and neo-(or post-positivist) positions with their focus on the observability of the 'real' perceived by a neutral or potentially neutral researcher. It is linked with what are termed constructivist rather than realist epistemologies, indicating that it embraces a view of knowledge as something produced through human activity. The end point of research might be various constructed versions of experience, rather than full knowledge of an objective and fixed external reality. Not only does this allow for heterogeneous, multiple 'readings' of psychological and social phenomena, it also acknowledges that the process of knowing something changes it, creating of it something new. For example, interviewing a research 'subject' comes to be seen as a process of 'co-constructing' a narrative of the subject's experience, as opposed to tapping into some pre-existing fixed account of things. In practical terms, this means recognising that the interviewee might be thinking about an issue for the first time in the course of the research interview, testing and evolving various new ideas in conversation with the researcher. The task of the interviewer, therefore, shifts from one of eliciting the interviewee's 'real' views to creating the conditions under which a thoughtful conversation can take place. Clearly, in doing constructivist work of this kind, the person of the researcher is deeply implicated. Here is a further comment from Henwood and Pidgeon, this time in the context of *feminist* research methods,

> One implication here is that the knower and known cannot be unambiguously separated, as is assumed by the norm of objectivity. . . . Accordingly, the role of the researcher must be seen as central to the research process; . . . revealing the personal in research then becomes a part of explicating the bases for knowledge. The conventional approach to conducting and reporting science, where researchers' attitudes are not revealed, recognised or analysed (in the attempt to be 'objective' and 'value-free') contrasts with the feminist view that researchers' commitments should be fully described and discussed and their values 'acknowledged, revealed and labelled'.[18]

Note that this argument is not presented as having anything to do with psychoanalysis. Nevertheless, it resonates with the set of issues surrounding psychoanalytic subjectivity described above. Just as psychoanalytic knowledge depends on the subjectivity of the knower being fully incorporated and theorised (for example through exploring countertransference feelings), so critics of positivism are saying that claims to objectivity and value neutrality are specious, leading to impoverished or misleading versions of psychological understanding. Instead, 'revealing the personal in research . . . becomes a part of explicating the bases for knowledge'. 'Truth' as the object of scientific pursuit recedes into the distance. Instead what we are left with are constructed accounts, mediated by the person of the researcher, never able to take more than provisional form, always unstable versions of possible reality. If this is science, then perhaps psychoanalysis can join the club.

There are, however, numerous difficulties with this simple equation of psychoanalytic and new paradigm research. One concern is what is meant by comments such as that 'researchers' commitments should be fully described and discussed and their values acknowledged, revealed and labelled'. Here, psychoanalysis is considerably more sophisticated, but also more problematic than social psychology or even ethnography. Henwood and Pidgeon seem to imply that describing researchers' investments in their work might be a relatively simple, technical matter – perhaps an issue of confession or self-revelation. But what is to be revealed? The researcher's gender, class and race position may well be relevant and it may be important to declare them as a way to increase the transparency and richness of the data produced. This is, indeed, the strategy employed by some of the best practitioners of the new social science.

Psychoanalysis, however, suggests that this declaration of relatively explicit, structural aspects of the researcher's persona will never be complete enough to understand what her or his contribution to the research might be – let alone to comprehend the nuances of the interpretive strategy employed in data analysis. There are likely to be complex unconscious processes interacting with the research work, encouraging some ways of going about things, inhibiting others. For example, Catherine Riessman's work on divorced women, described in her book *Narrative Analysis*,[19] seems to have derived some of its motivation from her own experience. Certainly Margaret Wetherell acknowledges that her work on racism in New Zealand is influenced by her own history as a white New Zealander.[20] How is the impact of this to be reckoned with? Even Wendy Hollway's exceptionally full description of her personal and professional development at the start of her exemplary book *Subjectivity and Method in Psychology*, raises as many questions as it answers – including further questions on topics which she spends time discussing, such as those concerning her personal investment in understanding heterosexual relations, and the impact of her commitment to feminism on her reading of her data. In the particular case of Hollway's work, some of these issues become available to scrutiny through the way her text moves between polemic and description, and especially through the use of transcript material which includes her own active voice. For instance, the following (characteristic) interchange offers as much opportunity for interpretation of the researcher's position as it does for that of the 'subject'. In fact, it makes everyone involved in the research open to interpretive scrutiny. Hollway is here questioning a woman she knows about her relationship with her partner, Will:

WENDY (THE RESEARCHER)   Why didn't you tell Will that you actually enjoyed two nights on your own?
BEVERLEY   'Cos I didn't want to hurt him. *(All three laugh.)*
WENDY   There you are you see. You both end up doing something that won't suit either of you, for the sake of some notion about what you should do for *love*.[21]

There is certainly not much evidence of the neutral researcher here. Indeed, Hollway has gone to considerable lengths to establish her own involvement in the work. But psychoanalysis might suggest that even more is required, that the only way to fully explore a researcher's investment in a particular piece of research would be through a dialogic encounter involving the potential for interpretation of the researcher's activity and checking out the impact of this interpretation on her or his understanding and future conduct (why is 'Wendy' apparently so disparaging of the notion of 'love' and what is the impact of her position on the evolution of the interview? What exactly is the relationship context in which this takes place? What do Beverley and Will make of Wendy?). This seems rather a tall order, although perhaps not an impossible one. At the very least, psychoanalysis enjoins suspicion of any final reading of an interpersonal encounter, whether it be for purposes of therapy or research – human motivations are too slippery and volatile ever to be completely understood.

ON METHODS AND UNCONSCIOUS CUNNING

If the perception of the complexity of the researcher's motivational commitments is more subtle in psychoanalysis than is shown even in most new paradigm social research, the same cannot be said for some of the other components of its scientific activity. One of the outstanding attributes of the 'narrative turn' in psychological research is the extent to which it has relied on scrupulous documentation of evidence and – as far as possible – transparency of analytic procedures. With the apparent demise of positivism and the marginalising of Popper's notion of 'falsifiability' as the primary criterion for establishing whether an approach is scientific or not,[22] this respect for evidence and for rigorous standards of data presentation and critique is perhaps as close as one can get to a characterisation of the scientific method. It is perhaps along these lines that the following piece of polemic from the psychoanalyst Donald Spence should be read:

> What does it mean to call a field of inquiry a science? First of all, it suggests that there is a widespread respect for data and that these data, furthermore, are in the public domain and available to all interested parties. Second, it suggests that theory is data-determined, that it changes in response to new observations, and that these observations are given priority over unfounded assumptions. Third, it suggests that progress is cumulative and that earlier models provide the building blocks for later theory. Fourth, it suggests that argument is grounded on evidence and not on authority and that the basis for a given conclusion is accessible to any party and does not depend on who is speaking. Science, by this account, is fanatically democratic. Fifth, it suggests that all theory is tentative and subject to revision, but that revision should be based on evidence rather than fashion.
> Psychoanalysis fails on every count.[23]

This is a critique that requires sustained attention, for it calls into question not just the status of psychoanalysis as a science, but its claims to be taken seriously at all.

Debate over the scientific standing of psychoanalysis has often taken place from within the positivist tradition, centring on the question of whether the 'conjectures' made by psychoanalysis are in principle refutable or not – that is, on whether psychoanalysis obeys the criterion of falsifiability put forward by Popper as decisive in assessing a theory's scientificity. As suggested above, this no longer seems to be a crucial issue. It may rather be that the hallmarks of scientific activity in the social and human sciences are better regarded as a systematic collection of evidence using transparent means (that is, methods available to scrutiny) and tolerating the possibility of alternative explanations to those promoted by any particular theory. Some of the methodological assumptions of positivism, notably the idea that the researcher's personal contribution to the work is a form of controllable 'error', may even be counter indicated in this sphere of work. In addition, the idealised view of science perpetrated by the positivist tradition could itself be regarded as 'unscientifically' imbued with ideology, having an axe to grind, particularly in promoting certain forms of Western rationality to the top of the tree of 'good' knowledge. In this connection, Michael Rustin suggests that the criteria established in the empiricist tradition of the philosophy of science might have been devised 'with the specific intent of excluding psychoanalysis and Marxism from the domain of legitimate human sciences'.[24]

Given the prestige with which science is held in the West, setting up solely positivist rules for entitling something to be termed 'scientific' acts to marginalise other approaches to knowledge. Probably not coincidentally, these other approaches include some with potentially critical political agendas. Whether the claim that the empirical tradition is politically motivated can be sustained at a general level or not (though it does seem to hold true of some aspects of Popper's work), it suggests that certain issues – particularly connected with forces which could disrupt rationalist assumptions – might have been ruled out of science by fiat. The philosopher David Will is even more robust in refuting the positivist principle, in line with arguments which have already been rehearsed above,

> An empiricist theory of science is so utterly embedded in the closed system of experiments that it can only account for scientific activity in such systems. However, it fails to do this adequately since it cannot sustain the notion of the reality of the phenomena described by science, nor can it account for the intelligibility of the very experimental activity it purports to explain. But, even more seriously for the human sciences, empirical realism is quite unable to give any account whatsoever of the possibility of scientific activity in open systems in which a constant conjunction of a non-trivial kind are rarely produced.[25]

The argument here is that the kind of approach to scientific testing advocated in the positivist, empiricist tradition is inappropriate to the human sciences. This is, first, because it cannot account for 'intelligibility', that is, for the meanings embedded in human actions, including the activity of constructing experiments – a debate which has been well worked out in the context of critiques of artificial intelligence.[26] Second, the empiricist approach is geared to highly controlled ('closed system') situations which are not representative of the actualities of human circumstances. In reality, so many factors impinge on people as they go about their lives, it is impossible to 'control' for the extraneous ones. Will's argument here merges into the rationale for interpretive, hermeneutic approaches to be discussed in the next chapter.

On the face of it, this work suggests that the positivist account of science has little to offer when evaluating the status of psychoanalysis. However, this does not mean that psychoanalysis can consequently be declared 'scientific'. More importantly, it does not resolve the arguments which are really at issue here. There are, of course, gains to be had when something is denoted a science: the label implies authority, objectivity, truthfulness, accountability and the like, and political and economic consequences for the practitioners of the science may well follow. This is undoubtedly one set of reasons why psychoanalysts have aspired to the label, even when they have also argued that what matters to them is their craft and their patients' wellbeing, rather than whether or not they are practising a 'science'. But behind the status conferred by the label, there is a set of issues around the credibility of the psychoanalytic process. It will be recalled that in Spence's description of science, given earlier, emphasis is placed upon the rigour of procedures, in particular the way evidence for claims is produced in an accountable way. Spence makes the bald statement that psychoanalysis fails in this respect. His view is that the standards of data presentation by psychoanalysts are shoddy in the extreme: 'Respect for data is rarely observed in coming to public conclusions; published statements are, more often than not, *ex cathedra* rather than closely reasoned; and published argument is founded more on authority than on appeal to evidence.'[27]

Spence despairs of the consequences of this failure to obey basic rules of evidence, of the way psychoanalysts have been willing to adduce small pieces of clinical material, often taken out of context to illustrate (but not test) theory. In place of a bank of well-founded knowledge offering cumulative guidance on the strengths and weaknesses of various aspects of analytic theory and practice, psychoanalysis possesses something which might better be called a mythology: 'Instead of an archive, we have a literature of anecdotes, a dumping ground of observations which have little more evidential value than a 30-year-old collection of flying saucer reports.'[28]

Spence writes as an insider to psychoanalysis, despairing of his profession's inability to establish appropriate standards of reporting, debate and judgement. Interestingly, the relative outsider (though sympathetic commentator), Michael Rustin is more optimistic about the standards used by his psychoanalytic colleagues. As noted in Chapter 1, he argues that, in practice, psychoanalysts and psychoanalytic psychotherapists behave with great respect for evidence, scrutinising their work closely, making it available for peer review, debating its implications for theory. As such, they operate as an authentic scientific community. To repeat part of the quotation given earlier, Rustin states that 'Observation of the routine work of analytic therapy in Britain suggests . . . a strenuous commitment to understand individuals as they are and to tolerate extreme uncertainty in the process of finding out what ideas might best explain psychic phenomena.'[29] This claim, so different from Spence's, is based on Rustin's close knowledge of the writings and training structures of British psychoanalytic psychotherapy, particularly child psychotherapy at the Tavistock Clinic in London, which is built around intensive supervision, shared 'workshops' in which cases are presented and discussed, detailed observational studies and associated seminars, and 'real-world' work in the public health service. Rustin's view here is clearly that what psychoanalytic psychotherapists *do* is rather better than what they *write* – the latter being the source of Spence's strictures.

In considering how contemporary psychoanalysis treats evidence, Spence describes laxity, Rustin portrays scrupulous integrity. It is, of course, possible that both things are true of different parts of the analytic community, or of the community as a whole at different times or in different aspects. What the work of both these writers suggests, however, is that setting up what Rustin refers to as 'idealised' notions of scientific activity and then finding psychoanalysis wanting is to miss the point about the conditions of worthwhile work. Whether or not psychoanalysis fits a particular mould as a science is of much less interest than whether or not it does what it does in an honest way.

Unfortunately, the debate over science cannot be escaped so easily, because the question remains of what kind of truth claims are being made by psychoanalysis, and on what grounds. In this context, Ernest Gellner's more sustained assault on psychoanalysis in his book *The Psychoanalytic Movement*, presents a lively and troubling picture. Gellner argues that psychoanalysis offers a great deal to people seeking answers to big questions, and also that some of its major claims – particularly the existence of a dynamic unconscious and the reality of the phenomenon of transference – are well supported in everyday experience. However, even when noting these positive attributes of psychoanalysis, Gellner does not resist the temptation to impugn the integrity of its other claims – the 'almost comic contrast' between the 'overwhelming and genuine' evidence for transference and the 'sketchy, dubious evidence for most other psychoanalytic ideas' being a case in point.[30] But it is not the actual lack of evidence for psychoanalysis which is so damning from Gellner's perspective. Indeed, he seems to find this rather endearing, as it points to the other factors which compel people to believe in systems for which there is no evidence – along the lines of his description of psychoanalysis as 'mysticism', described above. Instead, he focuses on the principled disavowal by psychoanalysis of the possibility of uncontaminated evidence. There are many elements in this critique, including a powerful indictment of psychoanalysis' claims to special knowledge of the unconscious, which he rejects on the grounds that there can be no self – and other – knowledge of this kind which is direct and theory independent. Thus, psychoanalysis is not exempt from its own general rule that there is no privileged access to the unconscious, that, being hidden, the unconscious can only be reasoned or theorised about from observation of its activities. Hence, psychoanalysis faces problems which are no different in kind from other ways of understanding psychological phenomena. Conversely, even if psychoanalysis is an efficient means of exploring the unconscious, there are likely to be other available means as well.

This introduces Gellner's view that the crucial obstacle to empirical scrutiny of psychoanalysis derives from the nature of the unconscious itself. For Gellner, the portrayal of the unconscious in psychoanalysis is as a cunning adversary, something which is always disruptive and always interfering with evidence. 'The Unconscious,' he writes, 'is a kind of systematic interference, which hampers full and proper contact between the mind and its object, and thereby prevents effective knowledge.'[31] As a consequence, there are no data which can be held to be representative of the unconscious, because the unconscious ruins the possibility of actual knowledge – it calls everything into question. Thus, when psychoanalysts present incomplete information, when they argue *ad hominem* among themselves and against adversaries, when they take 'no' to mean 'yes', they are not guilty of poor standards, as Spence might suggest. They are, instead, acting in the spirit of their discipline:

> The central idea – a cunning Unconscious – is totally polymorphous in its manifestations in daily behaviour. Its cunning is displayed in controlling those manifestations, *and* our interpretations of them. It is this which makes the idea untestable through ordinary behaviour. . . . It also means that *ad hoc* evasions of evidence are not really *ad hoc* within the system at all, but follow directly from its central insight, and thus have a kind of natural feel.[32]

Psychoanalysis does not just describe the unconscious; it enacts it in its structures and beliefs:

> The attribution of cunning to the Unconscious, and a habit of tampering with evidence, is not something added to the theory more or less surreptitiously when it flounders and is in difficulties. In all good faith, *it was always there*. The evasion was not brought in to save the theory: it *is* the theory.[33]

Gellner's point here is that, given the portrayal of the unconscious in psychoanalysis, it is not possible to have evidence which is transparent to consciousness – in fact, Freud overvalued consciousness when he ascribed to it powers of rationality superior to the cunning of the unconscious. As the unconscious disrupts everything, it disrupts evidence as well; it is never going to be possible to see clearly what is going on. Gellner's portrayal of the psychoanalytic movement as imbued with the cunning of its own creation – the Freudian unconscious – is surprisingly close to some evocations of their work by psychoanalysts themselves. Lacan in particular springs to mind here, with his endless ironies, puns and paradoxes, all given in the name of the unconscious. Whatever one thinks of the creative and imaginative possibilities to be found in this mode of activity, it would spell death to any attempt to root psychoanalysis in evidence derived from practice and theoretical work. If everything slips away, disrupted by an unconscious constantly on the lookout for pranks to play, then not only can one not trust the evidence of one's senses – a useful point to remember – but even with all the caution in the world one could not build up an evidential basis for the development of academic, theoretical and research activity. It would not matter how careful one's observations were, because something would always slip in regardless – an extra '0', a slip of the recording pen, an oversight. This could indeed be read as one of the enduring messages of the psychoanalytic movement, and it makes good poetry and cultural criticism.

But does this imply that there can be no progress in the psycho-analytic enterprise? Is there no way of establishing what is known and what can be (even to a limited extent) understood? In the next chapter, which engages primarily with issues of clinical evidence and accountability, it will be suggested that the process of argument which goes on around psychoanalysis is a genuine knowledge endeavour however slippery and unlike traditional images of science it may appear to be. Moreover, despite all the operations of the cunning unconscious as it trips up everyone and everything, and also despite the acknowledged impossibility of ever formulating a once-and-for-all account of the real world, some theories, clinical practices or evaluative and critical studies might be better grounded than others.

Chapter 3

Knowledge and interpretation

KNOWLEDGE IN THE SETTING OF ANALYSIS

The question of the weight which can be given to the kind of data produced in the psychoanalytic setting has in recent years been most interestingly debated in the context of *clinical* evidence. Here, the influential neopositivist critique of psychoanalysis by Adolf Grünbaum repays attention.[1] It should be noted that since it was first published in 1984, Grünbaum's book, *The Foundations of Psychoanalysis: A Philosophical Critique*, has been much discussed in the literature on psychoanalysis and science and has been criticised on a number of grounds. The most important of these is to the effect that Grünbaum adopts an idealised and basically Popperian view of science which he employs to evaluate an abstract and dated variant of psychoanalysis – classical Freudian theory as promulgated by Freud himself. Implying that these historical foundations of psychoanalysis remain the epistemological foundations of current analytic practice, Grünbaum mixes a rigorous reading of Freud with a reductionist approach to psychoanalysis as a whole. Post-Freudian developments, which have changed psychoanalysis out of all recognition, are ignored, and the complex network of psychoanalytic claims and debates are reduced to a relatively simple question of how psychoanalysis fares on one specific point, which Grünbaum terms the 'Tally Argument'. This is an important criticism of Grünbaum's work and it will be argued below that it does indeed vitiate the strength of his claims. Nevertheless, he raises in an exemplary way a set of issues surrounding the kind of evidence which bears on the standing of psychoanalysis.

Grünbaum starts from the well-documented position that Freud always insisted that psychoanalysis has the status of a science, meaning by this a causal, explanatory system built on the model of the natural sciences rather than on the interpretive approach characteristic of hermeneutics. Interestingly, in arguing against a hermeneutic rendering of Freud, Grünbaum is at one with many of his critics, who wish to defend psychoanalysis both from Grünbaum's attacks and from the apparent watering down of an explanatory theory into a literary, descriptive or evocative one.[2] Where Grünbaum is particularly interesting is in his assertion that the key area of scientific enterprise is not to be found in Freud's theory making – the so-called 'metapsychology' – but in his *clinical* activity. Metapsychology was, for Freud, 'speculation';[3] what appeared in the consulting room were clinical facts. Thus, Grünbaum claims, Freud 'saw himself entitled to proclaim the *scientificity* of his clinical theory *entirely on the strength of a secure and direct epistemic warrant from the observations he made of his patients and of himself*' (emphasis in the original).[4] Freud's criterion of scientificity was therefore methodological, depending on the scrupulousness of his clinical activity (particularly 'observations') rather than on claims about the nature of the theory as a whole. In this regard, if Grünbaum is correct, Freud's view was much in line with the position adopted in the previous chapter, that true science depends not so much on a single test of falsifiability as on the rigour with which evidence is collected and examined.

The problematic notion of what constitutes evidence of this kind – 'clinical facts' – has returned in recent years to haunt Freud's successors, labouring in a philosophical climate in which constructivism has taken hold and in a psychoanalytic world in which the 'real' events of the consulting room have become occluded by the power of fantasy (transference). Indeed, it will be argued that contemporary psychoanalysts show more appreciation than Grünbaum of the complex nature of any judgement of what should count as clinical data. Nevertheless, Grünbaum's tendentious argument that the scientific credentials of psychoanalysis rest on clinical rather than metapsychological concerns does enable him to move on to some far-reaching further ideas.

The first of these is that Popper's dismissal of psychoanalysis' standing as science on the grounds of the logical impossibility of finding empirical data to falsify its claims, is itself false. Grünbaum contends that when the focus of investigation is placed on the clinical rather than the metapsychological theory, psychoanalysis does in fact throw up a number of testable assertions or hypotheses. As an example of such an instance in which a psychoanalytic theory is shown to be available to refutation by evidence, Grünbaum quotes Freud's 1915 paper, 'A case of paranoia running counter to the psychoanalytic theory of the disease'. In this, Freud allows that his theory that paranoia is caused by repressed homosexuality could be disproved by the discovery that a young woman patient was paranoid but showed no evidence of homosexuality. Grünbaum comments that this paper demonstrates that 'the psychoanalytic aetiology of paranoia is empirically refutable *and* that Freud explicitly recognised it'.[5] It has to be noted, however, that by the end of this paper Freud finds the evidence he expects both for delusions *and* for homosexuality, so the theory does not get refuted after all and one therefore wonders what this particular example really shows. Freud may have allowed for the possibility of refutation (so the theory was logically falsifiable), but one would not get high odds on him actually disproving his own theory. Rather, Freud consistently demonstrates a remarkable capacity to identify phenomena which appear to contradict his ideas, only to triumphantly demonstrate subsequently that the contradiction is no contradiction at all but further support for what he had claimed all along. In this way, the idea of refutation is invoked as a rhetorical device, but the chances that Freud's conjuring act will produce real refutation always look slim.

Despite this, Grünbaum claims, in the context of a discussion of Popper, that 'the inability of certain philosophers of science to have discerned *any* testable consequences of Freud's theory betokens their insufficient command or scrutiny of its logical content rather than a scientific liability of psychoanalysis'.[6] What he sets about demonstrating is that claims to the scientific status of Freud's clinical method are in fact fatally flawed not by some very general principle of non-falsifiability, but for a much more specific reason: that in every case it is impossible to trust the evidence of the consulting room, because of what Grünbaum terms 'suggestion' and what has been more generally termed here the constructivist impact of the presence of the analyst or researcher. It is important to understand the force of this claim. As Grünbaum notes, a common way of defending psychoanalysis is to argue that the clinical interactions of analyst and analysand represent a mode of repeated experiment which supplies data superior to that offered by traditional empirical psychology. This is because the context of the 'experiment' is one where a rich and deep interpersonal encounter can take place, making its findings more valid in terms of the reality of the individual's life. One-off experiments under controlled conditions can only be a poor reflection of this reality. The argument, however, requires that the data collected during the 'repeated experiment' can be relied upon. Grünbaum claims that no such reliance is possible, that all psychoanalytic data are contaminated by the presence of the psychoanalyst and hence that psychoanalysis cannot offer any valid information at all.

There are several strands to Grünbaum's argument here which repay attention. At the centre stands a two-fold claim attributed to Freud: first, that accurate analytic interpretations are distinct from suggestions, but instead map out something which is 'true' of the patient; and second, that psychotherapeutic successes are produced by such accurate analytic interpretations. Taking the second point first, Grünbaum outlines what he calls Freud's 'necessary condition thesis' (NCT) relating to the causal properties of analytic treatment. This NCT has two components:

> (1) only the psychoanalytic method of interpretation and treatment can yield or mediate to the patient correct insight into the unconscious pathogens of his psychoneurosis, and (2) the analysand's correct insight into the aetiology of his affliction and into the unconscious dynamics of his character is, in turn, *causally necessary* for the therapeutic conquest of his neurosis.[7]

As Grünbaum notes, the NCT is rather a brave assertion, depending on evidence that psychoanalytic psychotherapy works and that other forms of therapy do not work or work less well. In principle, this is a falsifiable claim, making psychoanalysis potentially 'scientific' – although this is vitiated by the tendency of some analysts to argue in a *post hoc* fashion that patients who appear cured have received genuine psychoanalysis, while those who continue to have difficulties (including troublesome psychoanalytic colleagues) have been incompletely or inadequately analysed. Leaving that aside, a more severe problem for the NCT is the continued uncertainty over the measurement and documentation of psychotherapeutic change, particularly of the rather subtle psychodynamic variety postulated by psychoanalysis. This point will be returned to in a later chapter, but for the moment it is hard to challenge Grünbaum's conclusion that evidence for the clinical effectiveness of psychoanalysis is scarce, and hence that the NCT has little warrant. In Grünbaum's view, this is a devastating blow to psychoanalysis, for he has Freud making the whole edifice depend on evidence of therapeutic effectiveness. Freud's epistemological claim is held to be that,

> actual *durable* therapeutic success guarantees *not only* that the pertinent analytic interpretations *ring* true or credible to the analysand *but also* that they *are* indeed veridical, or at least quite close to the mark. Freud then relies on this bold intermediate contention to conclude nothing less than the following: collectively, the successful outcomes of analyses do constitute *cogent* evidence for all that general psychoanalytic theory tells us about the influences of the unconscious dynamics of the mind on our lives. In short, psychoanalytic treatment successes as a whole vouch for the truth of the Freudian theory of personality.[8]

The sophistication of this argument should be dwelt on a little. Grünbaum is suggesting that Freud has put forward a potentially falsifiable – hence scientific – proposition, and that this has indeed been falsified. Therapeutic successes would provide evidence not just for the effectiveness of psychoanalytic *therapy*, but for the 'Freudian theory of personality' – the body of work as a whole. Conversely, without such successes there is no warrant for belief in the theory and hence, as the clinical evidence for the superiority of psychoanalytic therapy over other forms of therapy is weak, psychoanalysis as a whole loses credibility.

Setting aside for later discussion the vast problems involved in evaluating any form of psychotherapy, including psychoanalysis, the suggestion that the whole of psychoanalysis stands or falls on the question of therapeutic success is extremely disingenuous. Psychoanalysis makes a vast array of claims across a wide variety of different disciplinary areas and has had a significant impact on art, culture and politics (through, for instance, the feminist movement) as well as on psychology. The links between many of these claims and therapeutic outcome – which will always be susceptible to impact from numerous sources of influence – is weak in the extreme. Consequently, to bracket out all these other ideas while restricting the debate over the scientificity of psychoanalysis to clinical claims is to distort not just current activity in the psychoanalytic world (as Grünbaum is wont to do through neglecting everything but Freud), but to disavow much of Freud's own work, including some of his most influential legacies. The broadening of psychoanalysis away from a merely clinical procedure has escalated in post-Freudian work, making verification by any one criterion even more problematic,

> Psychoanalysis . . . changed from a set of aetiological hypotheses into a theory of human nature in general. Its core is a theory of development and of mental functioning under conditions of conflict, which forms the frame for the understanding of psychopathological phenomena. Psychoanalysis has become the most complex theory of twentieth-century psychology, covering an enormous scope. At present it is impossible to isolate simple aetiological hypotheses from this body of thought without distorting its nature.[9]

Evaluating the standing of psychoanalysis, as science or as a more general intellectual discipline, requires a wider survey of evidential sources than just the therapeutic effect.

In some ways, the other claim concerning the scientific credentials of the clinical theory – that accurate analytic interpretations are distinct from suggestions – relates to an area of evidence separate from the issue of outcome. Here, Grünbaum has some things to say which come close to the heart of the debate in this chapter, particularly in relation to the impact of the scientist's subjectivity on her or his readings of evidence. Grünbaum refers to Freud's claim that psychoanalytic interpretation is more than suggestion as the 'Tally Argument', deriving this from the following important statement of the claim by Freud:

> After all, [the patient's] conflicts will only be successfully solved and his resistances overcome if the anticipatory ideas he is given tally with what is real in him. Whatever in the doctor's conjectures is inaccurate drops out in the course of the analysis; it has to be withdrawn and replaced by something more correct.[10]

The claim here is that only interpretations which accurately express 'what is real' in the patient will survive and have an impact. Everything else – including the pet ideas of the analyst which do not correspond to the truth of the patient – will fall away during the course of treatment. Again, this is a claim of considerable specificity but also great potential circularity. Reading forwards, it suggests that there is such a thing as an accurate or truthful interpretation, reflecting what is 'real' in the patient rather than what is invented by the analyst, and that only such interpretations will survive the test of time ('the course of the analysis'). Read backwards, however, it is an invitation to *post hoc* declarations that the interpretations which take hold – on which, for example, patient and analyst agree – are truthful and (the crucial point) *independent of the influence of the analyst*, whereas all others are mere suggestion. One obvious, if epistemologically minor, point is that analysts do not necessarily regard the failure of an interpretation to take hold as the essential test of its veracity. The interpretation might have been premature (that is, the patient resisted it, perhaps precisely because it contained an unpalatable truth) or badly phrased or not presented with enough compelling evidence. Even at the end of treatment, a patient might still be resisting an insight which the analyst believes to be correct.

However, the point taken up by Grünbaum bears more closely on the question of who can know what in the context of psychoanalysis. The issue here is that which Freud calls suggestion and Grünbaum, with his eye on the scientific status of evidence, calls 'contamination'. Given the setting of psychoanalysis, in which an intense, personal and unchaperoned encounter occurs between a person looking for help, self knowledge and insight, and an authoritative expert who is, in Lacan's eloquent phrase, 'supposed to know', how is it ever possible to be sure that the interventions of the analyst only have an effect if they 'tally with what is real'? When can a patient's 'yea' to an interpretation be regarded as a genuine 'yea', and when is her or his 'nay' a genuine 'nay'? This is particularly problematic when, in a strategy legitimated by Freud's work on negation, an energetic refusal of an interpretation by a patient might be taken as evidence of its significance.[11] As Grünbaum hints, the crucial issue here is the set of fantasies cohering around the transference relationship, which itself is a testimony to the impossibility of seeing things 'as they are' in psychoanalysis, independently of any interpersonal mediation. What occurs between analyst and patient is a constructive process in which 'reality' is revealed to be penetrated by fantasy processes which are constantly productive. That is, no reading of 'what is real' in the patient can ever be a stable one because every reading is a new construction of reality, with reality itself being an interpersonal product; something arising out of the encounter between self and other.

Grünbaum takes this difficulty as fatal for Freud's claim that it is possible ever to know when one has spoken the truth about a patient. Grünbaum acknowledges the sophistication of Freud's position here, for example in showing that Freud believed an analyst could only legitimately override a patient's stated objection to an interpretation if there was compelling additional evidence supporting the analyst's view. However, Grünbaum argues that all the information available to the psychoanalyst is in principle contaminated, in the same way as is the patient's response. So, what he terms Freud's appeal to 'consilience' (converging lines of independent evidence) must be spurious because no data separate from what goes on between analyst and patient is allowed into the analytic setting. If the patient reports an occurrence which occurred outside the consulting room and which seems to support a line of analytic enquiry, she or he is still *reporting it* in the context of her or his relationship with the analyst, under the analyst's influence, as it were – perhaps to please or appease the analyst. If analyst and patient are involved in a relationship powerful enough to imbue everything with fantasy elements, no statement or behaviour of the patient can be genuinely independent. Hence, Grünbaum argues,

the purported consilience of clinical inductions has the presumption of being *spurious*, and this strong presumption derives from the fact that the *independence* of the inferentially concurring pieces of evidence is grievously jeopardised by a *shared* contaminant: the analyst's influence.[12]

What remains after everything else has dropped out is still something created between analyst and patient. Whether or not this should be called suggestion, it certainly dispossesses Freud of the argument that it is possible to distinguish between what is 'in' the patient and what is produced by the analytic process. The evidence which can be used by an analyst to support any particular contention concerning a patient simply does not lie about in a pure, 'uncontaminated' form. It always already shows signs of disturbance and reconstruction.

EVIDENCE AND INTERPRETATION

At its simplest, Grünbaum's argument concerning the nature of psychoanalytic evidence boils down to a statement that it is untrustworthy. Psychoanalysis proposes the existence of various unconscious psychological factors within each individual and claims that the method of analysis makes these available to scrutiny and influence within the psychoanalytic encounter. Grünbaum points out that the nature of this encounter – its intensity, the fantasies it produces, the workings of transference – make it impossible to separate out what 'actually' lies within the individual and what is put there by the analyst. Psychoanalysis might therefore be more a procedure for creating facts than discovering them.

Grünbaum's focus on Freud alone is a principled one, in the sense that he regards himself as examining not just the historical foundations of psychoanalysis but also its epistemological ones. There is some warrant for this in the practices and writings of contemporary psychoanalysis, where appeals to Freud's authority continue to proliferate. However, Grünbaum's strategy runs up against the enormous changes which have occurred in psychoanalysis since Freud, in clinical theory and practice as well as in the wider articulations of the theory with social and artistic issues. It also results in a failure to appreciate the increasing sophistication of psychoanalysts' own discussions of clinical evidence, in particular their understanding of its constructed nature. The question which needs resolving here, is whether these developments modify Grünbaum's conclusion that Freudian ideas fail to withstand scientific testing.

At first glance, nothing much changes. Here, for example, is a full and impressive statement of the kind of material required to establish a psychoanalytic finding, by the influential American psychoanalyst Otto Kernberg:

> The validation of an interpretation . . . requires the emergence of new information in the patient's free associations, thus broadening and deepening the understanding of a certain conflict; the emergence of deeper understanding of a dominant, defensive object relation and its underlying, dynamically-opposite object relation, with a corresponding shift in affective expression; a change in the patient's transference relationship or in his/her internal relationship to an extra-analytic object; and a rapprochement between the patient's experience and the analyst's understanding of it. The new information available to the patient and to the analyst should somehow affect the patient's symptoms, character and fantasies, and broaden the patient's capacity for psychic experience, as contrasted with his expressing unconscious conflicts by somatisation or acting out.[13]

Taking this slowly, the first requirement for validation of an interpretation is that new information should be produced, visible in the patient's free associations – the basic material of psychoanalysis. This information should bear on an unconscious conflict, hence being relevant to the concerns of the psychoanalytic situation. Understanding of the object-relational basis of the conflict should increase and be registered by alterations in the patient's emotional state and in the transference relationship. The patient and the analyst should concur, or, rather, there should be a *rapprochement* between the patient's experience and the analyst's understanding of it. Finally, in various ways the patient's symptoms should improve and her or his capacity for engagement with life should increase.

Nothing in Kernberg's detailed formulation can be exempted from Grünbaum's strictures. Free association, changes in understanding, alterations in transference and, particularly, the idea that the patient's experience and the analyst's understanding should be in agreement – all these things take place within the circuit of the encounter between analyst and patient and are irremediably influenced by it. Even the requirement of improvement in the patient's symptomatology does not guarantee the evidential base of the interpretation, for such an improvement might easily be a placebo effect, a kind of gift to the analyst for trying. That is, there might be a psychological cause for the patient's improvement without there being a specifically psychoanalytic one, and certainly without it being linked causally to the content of an interpretation. Alternatively, within the context of a transference relationship, an interpretation might have an impact without being accurate. So, for example, a Kleinian-style interpretation of a patient's doubts about the analyst's capacity for understanding might be given in terms of the patient's envy of the analyst's creativity and intelligence. This might produce a rich flow of associations concerning envy in other areas of the patient's life and could indeed be helpful to that person in blocking envious responses when with others, hence leading to an improvement in her or his emotional state. But this does not mean that the initial interpretation was actually accurate as a statement of the patient's unconscious feelings towards the analyst. Perhaps the analyst had simply been crass, bored or stupid up to that point, and the patient's doubts were well placed, yet stimulated the analyst to say something worthwhile. That the patient was able to make use of what was said is in no way a direct test of its veracity; it might simply attest to the power of the analytic situation.

We are, here, on crucial terrain not just for discussions of the validation of psychoanalysis, but also for debates over the criteria for science. Grünbaum, accurately paraphrasing Freud, emphasises the truth claims of psychoanalysis, particularly that there might be something tangible in an unconscious conflict which becomes visible and nameable during the course of a psychoanalysis. This is a position which still influences psychoanalysts either explicitly or implicitly. Thus Kernberg can write of the 'validation of an interpretation' in terms of the kind of evidence required to show its accuracy. On the other hand, what is increasingly common as a position within psychoanalysis is the argument that analytic interpretations do not name simple truths, but instead have effects – they produce readings of the unconscious which are helpful in that they open out new spaces for growth and self discovery. A slightly different rendering of Kernberg's criteria for validation might be used to reference this position as well. This would take his list of requirements not as proof of the accuracy of the interpretation in naming something which was 'really' going on inside the patient, but rather as the necessary criteria for evaluating the impact of the interpretation. What is a good, 'valid' interpretation? One that improves the flow of free associations, leads to deepening effect and a better relationship with the analyst, is connected with symptomatic and relationship change and so on. In this reading, interpretations are 'performative'; their value is in their effects, not necessarily in their truthfulness.

This argument is once again close to that of the hermeneuticists, raising familiar questions about the connection between this kind of literary account of psychoanalysis (it tells good, meaningful stories with which people can connect) and science. But before getting to this it is worth considering in slightly more detail what psychoanalysts themselves now have to say about the status of their data – about what might be called a 'clinical fact'.

There are indications that the analytic community views the question of the evidential status of what are regarded as its basic data – what occurs in the analytic setting – as an important one. There have been many publications and also conferences on this issue, including a particularly revealing special seventy-fifth anniversary issue of the prestigious *International Journal of Psycho-Analysis* devoted to the topic of 'What is a clinical fact?'.[14] Two themes dominate this publication. Several writers, including David Tuckett in his editorial comment, lament the existing standards of reporting in the analytic literature, along the lines of the strictures from Spence quoted in the previous chapter. Tuckett writes, 'by and large our standards of observation, of clarifying the distinction between observation and conceptualisation, and our standards of discussing and debating our observations are extraordinarily low'.[15]

Alongside this recognition of a lack in the psychoanalytic approach to observation and recording comes an injunction to improve standards, in essence by making an effort to describe the events in the consulting room more fully and carefully, distinguishing between what happens and the interpretations which might be placed upon these happenings. Thus, in his substantive article in the special issue, Tuckett contends that,

> if there is a reasonably detailed clinical account intended to describe what has actually gone on in the session, then that account is usefully considered as providing the *clinical facts*. The account will include information about what the analyst has noticed and also, through hints that other analysts will quite probably notice, can even provide significant information about what was noticed unconsciously but not immediately apprehended, or even what was completely ignored.[16]

The recommendation here is to offer descriptions of sufficient detail and complexity for others to be able to make judgements, including in principle to be able to reject the assertions of the writer or at least to be able to scrutinise what she or he has been doing unconsciously. In essence, this is an appeal to what Spence calls 'thick description' – description relatively free from theory, but detailed enough to enable formulation of alternative views.[17] In most psychoanalytic writings, clinical accounts are presented in order to illustrate rather than test theoretical points; what Tuckett and Spence are advocating is a reversal of that procedure, more in line with accepted scientific practice.

The problem with this idea is the one debated above, that such a differentiation between facts and theories may not be possible, given the nature of the psychoanalytic enquiry. This does not mean that the relatively 'thick descriptions' of activity in sessions would not improve matters, making it more possible to assess the various influences which might have had a hand in producing certain kinds of effects – much as contemporary social psychology is attempting to do. However, the impossibility of ever making an absolute differentiation between what is to be found and what is to be made is well recognised by the analysts writing in the *International Journal of Psycho-Analysis* – and is treated as simply a characteristic of psychoanalysis rather than as something to be hidden or denied. In every case of this kind, what is being suggested is that the special relationship between analyst and patient is not distorting the facts, as Grünbaum might argue, but rather supplies the necessary conditions under which significant facts can be known. The claim is that it is only because of the intense relationship between analyst and patient that important truths come to light; and that these are interpersonal, intersubjective truths – the merging of unconscious fantasies out of which something meaningful might become known. Thus, Edna O'Shaughnessy, having acknowledged that the 'facts' she offers are always seen from her point of view, states:

> My clinical observations were not made by observing 'basic data' and then making inferences or invoking an hypothesis or a theory, but by experiencing phenomena in a certain way. It is an individual way of seeing, hindered by my limitations, using what capacities I have, infused with theory, or with knowledge of my patient, or with memories of our psychoanalytic endeavours, sometimes devoid of theory or even contrary to theory.[18]

On the face of it, this looks like an admission of the tendency of psychoanalysts to appeal to whim, authority, or personal idiosyncrasy in making their evidential claims. Yet, O'Shaughnessy goes on to assert that the similar assumptions, training and working conditions of psychoanalysts make for a shared 'paradigm' in which it becomes possible to read and understand the clinical material presented in each case. Ornstein and Ornstein also accept the constructed nature of clinical facts ('our psychoanalytic clinical facts are thoroughly intertwined with and dependent on the interpretive process, and on the theory we hold')[19] but go on to argue that the regularity and detail of the psychoanalytic encounter confer substance on these constructions, making them communicable and, in traditional psychometric terms, valid. Interestingly, there is here a very strong emphasis on what the analyst brings to the encounter, yet this is seen as adding to, rather than detracting from, the meaningfulness of the resulting data:

> The clinical facts are shaped not only by what becomes activated in patients in the analytic situation, but also – importantly – by all of the analyst's responses, especially those directed at the patient's transference expectations and demands. These facts, as they emerge in a context in which their meaning is continually

negotiated, can be observed with reasonable certainty and their meaning can be inferred with growing certainty over time. It is this ongoing negotiation between patient and analyst (with all that its turbulence entails), that shapes the clinical facts and captures their meaning(s).[20]

Finally, Joseph and Anne-Marie Sandler (having warned against the irrationality of various psychoanalytic beliefs, preserved often because of the theorist's own transference to her or his analyst or other influential figure), comment in a similar vein as follows:

> The analytic facts we derive from our clinical work are constructs. As the analysis proceeds we automatically and unconsciously register what we perceive, inevitably in a selective manner. As observers, we organise our perceptions, and in this process the unconscious theories and models we have built over the course of years play a central part. Much of this unconscious theory is 'good' theory, i.e. it is theory which is effective and geared to reality.[21]

What is most striking about this material is the way these illustrious psychoanalysts accept the constructive process by which clinical facts are created and remembered, acknowledge its subjectivity, lay stress on the contribution of the analyst to it, and yet claim that this does not in itself make analytic evidence invalid. Quite the contrary, it seems: the deep relationship of analyst to patient makes a certain kind of understanding possible – knowledge of the patient's 'interiority'.[22] Moreover, the 'unconscious' theory used by the analyst is likely to be a 'good' theory. Although it is not articulated, it is nevertheless geared to reality, it is potentially one (perhaps the only) route to comprehension of the patient's unconscious state of mind. Is this a reasonable account of an exceptional method, built around the detailed exploration of one unconscious by another and hence exempt from the usual requirements for scientific activity? Is it an approach which might apply to *all* human and social science? Or is it special pleading aimed at covering over scandalous transgressions of acceptable research methodology?

REACTIVITY, HERMENEUTICS AND THE LIMITS OF PSYCHOANALYTIC SCIENCE

Increasingly, the idea that psychoanalysis seeks to express the 'truth' about an individual is falling into disuse – even among those who use the word 'truth' quite freely. 'When I make a truth claim, I do not claim to know *the* truth, or *all* the truth, but only *a* truth. Other true formulations are always possible.'[23]

What is being played with here is a different notion of truth from the causal, mechanical one espoused by Freud and defended with such vigour by Grünbaum and others. For many writers in this area, the distinction is grounded in a critique of the viability of ever uncovering 'historical truth', seen as the limiting aim of classical psychoanalysis. Spence makes the link as follows: 'To search for historical truth is to live out the metaphor of analyst as archaeologist and to believe, along with Freud, that pieces of the past lie buried somewhere in the person's unconscious.'[24]

Spence regards the attempt to bolster the historical truth view of psychoanalysis as part of a misguided search for scientific respectability, doing violence to the actuality of the human contact which lies at the heart of the psychoanalytic endeavour. Crucial in this is recognition of the way psychoanalytic formulations are worked out in the context of particular individuals struggling to relate to one another. This also means that as this context shifts, as the relationship changes, so psychoanalytic understanding of what is happening might also have to shift dramatically. 'No interpretation is sacred. If context is boundless and ever-expanding, the grounds for reaching a conclusion about this or that meaning are forever shifting. An archive can be constructed, but its contents will always be open to interpretation and elaboration.'[25]

What Spence is calling into question here is perhaps not so much a specific notion of *historical* truth – that at the source of a neurosis there is a causal event – but rather the more general claim that there can be any one 'truth', any final understanding of a person, any clear single or indeed multiple cause for their activity. Psychoanalytic understanding, he suggests, depends on the subjective exploration of one person by another; by implication, this means that something different will always be produced whenever different analysts work, or when different theoretical perspectives dominate, or when social contexts shift. Spence argues that the task of the analyst includes identification with the internal state of mind

of the patient – the attainment of what he terms an 'inside' stance
from which the motives of the patient may be perceived:

> It is this inside stance which allows us to make a judgement as to
> what are the 'facts' of the case, where one ends and another
> begins; this state of affairs comes about because not all 'facts' are
> visible, because many do not emerge until we put ourselves in the
> shoes of the figure in question, and because the final meaning is
> always coloured by both theory and context.[26]

Hence, any psychoanalytic finding can only be provisional,
constrained by the conditions under which it has been produced:

> If our hermeneutic position is correct, then it must follow that
> the meaning of the material is highly dependent on who is
> listening to it, and that what was true for the treating analyst, at
> a particular time and place in the treatment, will never be true
> again.[27]

The relativity of the notion of truth being worked with here
certainly frees psychoanalysis from the invidious position of
making claims to absolute knowledge which cannot be sustained,
but it does present its own difficulties. The most obvious of these is
the question of what criteria are available for enabling distinction
between all the possible 'provisional truths' which might arise –
including all the provisional or perhaps absolute falsehoods. Can
any tale told by a psychoanalyst be believed? At least Freud tried to
suggest the kind of things which might be regarded as evidence.
Can the critics of his causal, explanatory approach articulate ways
of regulating the freedom to imagine all sorts of impossible things –
a freedom which sometimes seems very attractive to psychoanalysts,
as well as to their patients?

The answer coming from advocates of what has come to be
known as the hermeneutic position within psychoanalysis is that
causal, explanatory truths about people may not be available, but
meaning-imbued 'narrative truths' are, and that some of these
might have causal functions of a sort. The model for this in the first
instance is the reading of literary texts: the richer the text, the more
alternative and even contradictory meanings might be pulled out of
it. In fact, the availability of rich networks of associations may be
one element in the aesthetic appeal of a work of art.[28] Narrative
truths convince because of their capacity to evoke and structure
experiences, to offer coherence where there is fragmentation, to

articulate half-understood meanings and throw light on obscurity. This is not an arbitrary process; it is quite possible to make interpretations of a text which have no coherence at all and which fail to communicate anything. These would be failed, 'false' interpretations. But while the search for narrative truth is not arbitrary, it is difficult. Not only is there a strong element of relativity brought into the situation by the variety of different narratives which might be available at any one time, but also as the context for interpretation shifts – as culture changes, for example – so do the narratives which take hold and which hold conviction. To mention one of the founding texts of psychoanalysis as an example, Freud presents interpretations of his patient Dora's dreams as evidence of her masturbatory tendencies and various aspects of her Oedipal conflicts. Later on he revises his view of her to include homosexuality as a central motivating tendency. Later still the interpretations are read by feminists and others as evidence of *Freud's* state of mind and his immersion in patriarchal culture.[29] Each of these accounts offers narrative intelligibility, each has a certain degree of coherence but also embodies inconsistencies. Each reading is intriguing and none of them as far as one can tell is bought into by the protagonist – by Dora or, in the last reading, by Freud. The question here is, under such conditions of rich variability, how stable is any psychoanalytic finding? What roots a particular narrative account in evidence as opposed to speculation? Returning to Eysenck's view, what, if anything, makes this more than a fairy story?

The usual criteria for narrative truth put forward by the hermeneuticists include theoretical coherence, inner consistency and narrative intelligibility.[30] The first of these suggests that the interpretation needs to make sense in terms of existing theory, and in some formulations this relates not just to psychoanalytic theory but to its more general context. 'The theory should be *consistent with accepted background knowledge embodied in other disciplines, and cohere with it.*'[31] The second criterion, of inner consistency, implies some rational order to the narrative, while the third is really an appeal to the believability of the narrative, that it should somehow 'make sense'. Strenger places the whole process in its sociological context:

> The ultimate criterion for the validity of an interpretation must consist in the consensus of the interpretive community that a text

has indeed become intelligible. This in turn means that it has become integrated into the frame of meaning within which the interpretive community lives – a frame which for reasons of principle cannot be formalised. This is quite different from what happens in the natural sciences.[32]

It is not at all apparent from any of these claims that the story has been moved forward. Psychoanalytic interpretations would probably rarely fulfil the charge that they should meet with the acceptance of 'the interpretive community' if that community is defined in anything other than the narrowest of terms. Does this mean that their narrative holds little potency? Indeed, in the early days of the psychoanalytic movement it was claimed by Freud that the *resistance* of the academic community to his 'news of the plague' was in some ways evidence of its truth value. While one might not want to hold too strongly to this position one might nevertheless want to preserve the possibility that an unpopular theory might nevertheless be in some way 'true'. This point also poses problems for the notion of external coherence, the idea that the theory has to be compatible with what is known elsewhere. On the one hand, it is conceivable that psychoanalysis might be in advance of knowledge elsewhere; certainly, it would not want to be particularly congruent with some other branches of psychology. On the other hand, when one looks at the remarkable penetration of selected psychoanalytic ideas into disciplines such as literature, cultural studies and geography, it begins to seem possible that this apparent congruence is a form of mass delusion. In many ways, the 'consistency, coherence, intelligibility' triad adds up to little more than an elaboration of the truism that a story – a theory or interpretation – should be persuasive. The words keep circulating, defined in terms of one another: interpretation, meaningfulness, intelligibility. An interpretation is meaningful if it makes a person's experience intelligible; intelligibility is derived from being able to make sense of experience in a consistent and coherent way; coherence depends on congruence with theoretical and cultural values; congruence of this kind means that a relevant community should agree that the interpretation is intelligible. Perhaps we all know what is meant here, but reliance on common sense might not be the best way forward for a dissenting, troublesome discipline such as psychoanalysis.

In his famous articulation of the hermeneutic position,

Habermas takes this further by suggesting that the final arbiter of analytic correctness, at least in the clinical setting, should be the patient. Analytic insights, he argues,

> possess validity for the analyst only after they have been accepted as knowledge by the analysand himself. For the empirical accuracy of general interpretations depends not on controlled observation and the subsequent communication among investigators but rather on the accomplishment of self-reflection and subsequent communication between the investigator and his 'object'.[33]

Note that this is not merely a claim about the value of specific interpretations. Habermas explicitly mentions 'general interpretations' and seems to imply that the translation of general psychoanalytic propositions into specific interventions which are then accepted by the patient is a crucial test of the validity of the general propositions themselves. A kind of feedback system is in operation here, in which the psychoanalyst, versed in the theory and practice of her or his discipline, puts forward a proposal to the patient in the form of an interpretation. This intervention has an effect of some kind, and in the light of this the analyst modifies his interpretation – his narrative of the patient's experience – until the patient can relate to it more completely. Eventually, an emancipatory process occurs in which the patient is led to a form of linguistically mediated self-knowledge which places her or him in more control over the experience; this process is confirmation of the power of the analytic narrative. None of this is presented as simple; there may be very awkward, subtle navigation of the space between analyst and patient before anything like a confirming response to the psychoanalytic story can be brought about.

At first glance, Habermas's idea that the patient's response should decide the value of the analytic story has some compelling positive and negative features. It offers a way of rooting theory in what actually takes place in the clinical situation and – assuming the good faith of both analyst and patient – suggests that psychoanalysis is a collaborative enterprise aiming at constructing meanings which have affective as well as cognitive force. In this regard it is close to many working psychoanalysts' accounts of the way they test the value of an interpretation: as in the quotation from Kernberg given earlier, they tend to suggest that a good interpretation will bring on richer associational material, a change in the patient's emotional state and alterations in the relationship with the analyst. All these could be seen as variants of Habermas's ideas. On the other hand, most psychoanalysts would also argue that there may be perfectly good 'narrative truths' which pass patients by or are actively refuted by them, because their truth lies in the complex of negative personal attributes and feeling states to which they draw attention. In fact, as Grünbaum points out, unless and until a patient's resistances have been overcome, psychoanalysts would *expect* denial of any interpretation which is remotely meaningful.[34] Moreover, there seems here to be an ironic inconsistency in the hermeneutic stance. If a patient is convinced of the truth of an interpretation, then she or he is failing to appreciate the hermeneutic discovery that there are no truths, that there are only varieties of story. A patient's statement, 'That's an interesting story' might not be as gratifying for the patient or for the psychoanalyst as 'Yes, that's right!', but in this context it is all that can be asked for.

The hermeneutic point of view moves the argument about scientificity on considerably, but also leaves it in a mire. The tendency has been to set up the natural sciences as one form of knowledge and the human sciences as another, then to argue that psychoanalysis is a mode of story telling, a narrative enterprise close to literature and textual analysis, but full of human meanings and deriving its healing properties from those. Questions of scientificity are then set aside as psychoanalysis is evaluated in terms of its persuasiveness – to the intellectual community or to the patient. However, this does not seem to solve any problems in a final way, for the criteria by which one might evaluate a particular psychoanalytic narrative, and indeed the grand narratives of psychoanalysis itself, remain poorly articulated and slippery. 'Psychoanalysis is persuasive when it persuades' does not seem like a very promising mast to pin one's colours to, particularly given the contentiousness of most major positions in psychoanalysis even within its own institutions, let alone in the wider world. In addition, there is the question of whether, in treating the discourse of patients like 'texts', something important is being lost from the psychoanalytic project. Ricardo Steiner, balancing an appreciation of what hermeneutics offers with a concern for the preservation of the knowledge claims and moral standpoint of psychoanalysis, expresses this well. Certain kinds of application of hermeneutics, he writes,

do deprive psychoanalysis of some of its fruitful potential: the insistence on psychoanalysis as a pure interpersonal dialogue, as a clinical encounter, which, following the suggestions of the hermeneutic interpretive tradition, aims at understanding meanings and not at explaining causes, for example, leads to a reduction of the whole of psychoanalysis to a simple province of the exegetical disciplines applied to texts.[35]

In a similar way, a contributor to the *International Journal of Psycho-Analysis* issue on hermeneutics to which Steiner's paper is the introduction, argues that 'The framework for thinking about psychoanalysis should not be causality *versus* interpretations of meaning in psychic reality, but causality *via* interpretation of meaning in psychic reality. Causality versus interpretation is a false dichotomy'.[36] From this point of view, the hunt for meanings is purposeful, not simply conversational; some meanings have more meaning than others and psychoanalysis neglects this fact at its peril. Indeed, put at its strongest, this might be the specific contribution of psychoanalysis to the 'narrative turn' in psychology and the discursive position in general, that it provides some insights into the places from out of which particular narrative stances emerge. To use an analogy from Freud himself, there is a comment in *The Interpretation of Dreams* that dream thoughts have no definite endings, 'they are bound to branch out in every direction into the intricate network of our world of thought'. Nevertheless, he writes in a footnote to the 'Dream of Irma's injection' that 'There is at least one spot in every dream at which it is unplumbable – a navel, as it were, that is its point of contact with the unknown'.[37] It is as if all this untrammelled speech which is available to hermeneutic analysis is enriching and, when elaborated, creates a network of meanings – but behind it lies another voice, 'the unknown' from which it arises. Perhaps it is recovering this voice that is the ultimate aim of psychoanalysis.

However, it is possible that some first principles are being forgotten here. In the final section of this chapter I want to return to the issues of constructionism and subjectivity with which the last chapter began, considering again the notion of truth (but this time with more of a postmodernist gloss) and the possible ways in which psychoanalysis might be evaluated. As a starting point, a reminder of what happens when transference enters into the picture might help.

SUBVERTING THE TRUTH

In the following passage, Jane Flax presents an account of the interpretive process which is close to Habermas but which makes more explicit the context in which psychoanalysis actually takes place:

> Both transference and rational insight are necessary for the patient's emancipation, but this rational insight is of a very special sort. It is necessarily intersubjective and is more like a mutually-agreed-upon reading of a text than a solution to a problem of quantum mechanics. The patient has the particular experience that she/he is trying to remember and work through with the help of the analyst who has a general schema which is useful to both of them in explicating the meaning of the patient's experience past and present (especially transference phenomena). Their goal is not 'truth' in the empiricist sense of what 'really' happened to the patient, but rather *understanding* which includes a powerful affective and experiential component. The past is lived through the transference; it is not merely grasped intellectually.[38]

Rationality is here emancipated from the demands of supposed cognitive 'objectivity'; instead, the notion of what is rational is expanded to incorporate the intersubjective dimension which is so crucial to psychoanalysis. In addition, even though Flax retains a view of psychoanalysis as dealing with *past* events ('the patient has the particular experience which she/he is trying to remember'), she nevertheless makes it clear that a live process of emotional engagement and change is part of what is meant by analytic 'understanding', and she is thus in line with those contemporary psychoanalysts who see their work as directed at patients' *current* representations of themselves; most significantly, this happens within the transference, that is unconscious fantasies infiltrating the relationship between analyst and patient are part of the data for exploration (the conventional psychoanalytic view) – and are also the medium through which understanding comes. Psychoanalytic rationality is not just an intellectual act, but an activity full of emotion.

As with the hermeneutic renderings of psychoanalysis described above, Flax presents an account in which questions of discovery ('what is the real event at the source of the patient's neurosis?') are transformed into questions of reading and textual interpretation. This lays stress on the relativity of analytic findings – alternative readings are always possible – and on their intersubjective character: the reader has an active role in constructing the reading. Moreover, because psychoanalysis is usually dyadic, what occurs within it is a negotiation, or sometimes a conflict, between different ways of reading the 'text' produced by the encounter between patient and analyst. Perhaps Flax is right in suggesting that analytic progress depends on the production of a reading which is 'mutually agreed', an idea which might relate to that of Habermas when he refers to 'communication between the investigator and his "object"'. However, I want to take up what might be a more novel claim implicit in Flax's argument, concerning the nature of psychoanalytic rationality itself. As noted above, she seems to suggest that this cannot or should not be reduced to the usual notion of 'reason', but rather extended to include emotional, intersubjective and unconscious (for instance, transferential) components. Although the idea that psychoanalytic 'insight' covers all these areas is a familiar one, the claim that it is a form of rationality is a bold one, rooted in analytic tradition (Freud's identification of rationality with the ego and the task of analysis as widening the ego can be seen as moving along the same lines), but nevertheless presenting a challenge to conventional ideas concerning what might count as rational understanding. At its strongest, one might suggest that what is at stake here is not just the kind of evidence appropriate to the evaluation of psychoanalytic claims, but also what it is that constitutes 'rationality' itself.

Rather than taking on the whole of this enormous issue here, I want to explore two linked aspects: the place of emotional insight and the extension of the notion of rationality to include subjective understanding. Psychoanalysis explicitly privileges something it terms 'insight' over purely cognitive understanding. What is meant by this is a mode of self knowledge built on an intellectual grasp of the unconscious dynamics of a motivational state – the reasons 'why' the person acts in this or that way – accompanied by a transformative experience of having been through something. In the quotation from Flax given above, this is referred to in the phrase: 'The past is lived through the transference; it is not merely grasped intellectually'.

In Moore and Fine's dictionary on psychoanalytic concepts, the entry on 'insight' includes the following:

As resistances are interpreted, repressed ideational content returns and is now accepted by the ego, so that psychic reorganisation is facilitated. The resulting insight has two significant components, affect as well as cognition, for cognitive awareness alone does not lead to therapeutic insight. Often the cognitive awareness of insight is repressed again in the process of psychic reorganisation, but the new emotional freedom is maintained.[39]

Insight is here named as something involving both cognitive and affective dimensions but implicit in the definition seems to be a notion of insight as something which is not necessarily conscious – the 'cognitive awareness of insight' might be lost, while the 'emotional freedom' brought by insight is maintained. This suggests a view of insight as a transformative process only loosely coupled with cognition, a problematic notion for any conventional view of understanding as dependent upon knowledge which can be articulated in consciousness.

At its most general, what is being described here is the psychoanalytic emphasis on 'learning from experience'. The kind of knowledge which is of interest is transformative knowledge – knowledge which makes a difference to the knower, leaving her or him not only with *more* information than before, but in a different state of mind. This kind of knowledge can be deeply resisted because it is troubling or challenging, as indicated by Moore and Fine's comment that the cognitive awareness of insight might become repressed. Nevertheless, it is the only form of knowledge worth having. In the psychoanalytic view, it is unlikely to arise from a solely cognitive process. Rather, it is when the emotions are mobilised, when irrational, unconscious structures are exposed and experienced in the context of the therapeutic or pedagogic transference (for this is not just something confined to therapeutic situations), that insight might be acquired – that learning from experience might occur. Learning of this kind comes about through investment of the self in the learning situation, through a willingness to experience all that the situation might contain and to let it act on oneself, even in excess of one's initial capacity to keep track of it or comprehend it. Cognitive understanding – coding the transformational experience in words, for example – is important, but it might come later and might never be completely achieved.

Freud's vision was of the triumph of consciousness: 'where id was, there ego shall be'.[40] In making the unconscious available to inspection, he was colonising the sphere of the irrational for rationality. No longer need dreams elude us, for we can interpret them; we know what they mean and whence they come. Scientific practice in this sense is concerned with constructing a coherent intellectual system around events and experiences, including those which at first sight seem irresponsibly out of order. But, as Flax comments in a later work, 'Much as Freud desired it otherwise, psychoanalysis simply does not and cannot fit within the empiricist or rationalist models of science or knowledge'.[41]

What has happened over time is that something present in nascent form in Freud's early formulations has come to be much more important: an awareness that this intellectual colonisation of the irrational is never comprehensive, for rationality has its own erratic, excessive underside. Unconscious factors influence all aspects of human behaviour, including apparently rational behaviour; knowledge itself, as Melanie Klein and her followers have been particularly keen to reveal, is achieved in response to unconscious impulses.[42] Victoria Hamilton points out that for Freud, 'knowing is regarded as a secondary development to more primary needs and wishes; their frustration or gratification precipitates the search for knowledge'.[43]

Whatever one thinks of the specific claim here (Hamilton is critical of what she terms psychoanalysis' 'tragic vision' of knowledge as something driven by the need to overcome loss, to fill in gaps), it is clear that there can be no simple separation between the achievement of rational thought or reason, and the operations of emotion and of the unconscious. Flax notes that this view of human functioning is radically different from traditional philosophical positions, calling into question claims of the possibility of intellectual knowledge of anything resembling an 'objective' variety. In particular, the Enlightenment tradition of rationality – to which empiricist science belongs – is challenged. According to Freud, Flax writes,

> humans are originally and primarily desiring beings. Our being is not defined by the capacity to reason, as Plato and Kant believe; by the ability to speak, reason and engage in political deliberation, as Aristotle argues; or by the power to produce objects of value and need, as Marx claims. 'The core of our being,' according to Freud, consists of 'unconscious wishful impulses' that cannot be destroyed.[44]

Knowledge of oneself or others which is built upon the denial of desire – of emotion and feeling states – cannot therefore be complete knowledge. As personal and interpersonal knowledge is the focal area of psychoanalysis, then the process of finding something out – of knowing anything – must involve emotion. Hence, the post-Freudian conceptualisation of analysis as a setting in which knowledge comes about through personal interconnection is promoted to become a critique of Enlightenment forms of rationality. Real knowledge involves emotion at its core,

> Psychoanalysis also calls into question the assumption that rational thought and the accumulation of reliable knowledge require suppression or control of 'subjective' feeling and that 'reason' is the only or best source of knowledge. . . . The feeling states of both patient and analyst provide important information about and insight into the patient's inner world as well as the relationship between the two members of the therapeutic alliance.[45]

How does the analyst know what interpretation to place on the patient's words? Through their impact on her or his feeling state, that is through the analyst's capacity to register and reflect upon the emotions generated in her or him by the patient at that particular moment in the context of that specific individual analysis. So not only does the end state of the patient's self knowledge (insight) require emotional transformation if it is to be regarded as legitimate, but the moment-by-moment process of coming to know about self and other requires the employment of emotion rather than (as would be the case with alternative accounts of scientific rationality) its suppression.

What is strongly implicit in this is an account of rationality as something which cannot be restricted to 'pure reason' if it is to supply meaningful knowledge about human subjectivity. As noted above, this has two facets. First, it is not possible to divorce reason from emotion in the way postulated by positivistic science: there is no 'unbiased' part of the mind which could be called upon to act as neutral observer of events. Consciousness has unconscious forces pushing it all the time, and the ego is itself subject to the whims and fancies of desire. Therefore, second, human understanding must incorporate subjectivity, must be recognisable as something emerging out of an intermixing of subject and object, of the process of being and becoming part of another. What psychoanalysis suggests is that rational understanding *depends upon* the capacity to allow expression to subjectivity. Psychoanalysis suggests that scrupulous examination of the 'reading process' occurring within the researcher or clinician is necessary not so as to reduce sources of 'bias', but so as to be able to understand human data at all.

Finally, this leads us back to the questions of the scientific standing of psychoanalysis and the kinds of evidence which can be drawn upon in evaluating its worth. It should be apparent that psychoanalysis offers a critique of those notions of science which decry subjectivity and insist upon an absolute division between the subjects and objects of knowledge. At least in the sphere of human understanding, subjective and interpersonal processes are necessary elements for comprehension of 'data' and for inclusion in formulations of theory – whether hermeneutic or explanatory. In this sense, rationality is considerably extended, not only in that apparently irrational aspects of human psychology become amenable to rational explanation, but because the process whereby this occurs is itself imbued with recognisably subjective phenomena. Thus, 'subjective bias' comes to be seen as a necessary component in the formulation of rational understanding. Without it, the analyst could not construct the kind of contact with the patient that enables an interpretation to be made, for it is from the moment-by-moment monitoring of the analyst's emotional responses that hypotheses about the patient's inner world arise. More formally, psychoanalysis proposes that there is no mental agency which is not imbued with unconscious, hence 'irrational' processes, and this provides the necessary context from which psychological study emerges.

None of this means that it is impossible to give an account of people which might be communicable to others and might make rational 'sense'. Indeed, the opposite is the claim: theories of personhood that acknowledge the existence of subjectivity and human (especially interpersonal) meanings, must be built out of the kind of resources employed by psychoanalysis, particularly the personal meanings and subjective states of the researcher. The fact that social psychologists working in 'new paradigms' are grappling with these issues, even though they are not necessarily employing specifically psychoanalytic ideas, attests to the power of this claim. If science aims to offer the fullest possible explanation for phenomena, the notion of science as applied in the human sphere needs to be extended further than simple empiricism – or even than the more subtle, but still positivistic, conceptualisation embraced by

Grünbaum and others. However, there remains the very substantial difficulty attested to in much of the discussion in this chapter and the last: if so much that is subjective goes into the process of formulating psychoanalytic theory, what criteria for validation can be employed? To this, the answer must be: broader criteria than those which are simply empirical. Criteria, for example, which make an appeal to meanings, which require the articulation of subjective and intersubjective processes, including acknowledgement of the location and feeling states of the 'researcher'. Such criteria can be rigorously pursued – their adoption does not mean that permission is given for mysticism or for total nihilism in the articulation of theories. But their pursuit requires skills which are traditionally located outside science as narrowly conceived. It requires interpretive and literary skills, as hermeneuticists and postmodernists might both suggest, and also self-reflective skills by which the investigator, whether clinician or researcher, demonstrates that her or his own feeling states have been engaged with and understood.

Part II

Psychotherapy

Chapter 4

Psychoanalytic psychotherapy
Does talking make things worse?

The structure of psychotherapy is such that no matter how kindly a person is, when that person becomes a psychotherapist, he or she is engaged in acts that are bound to diminish the dignity, autonomy, and freedom of the person who comes for help.[1]

In doing psychoanalysis I aim at:
Keeping alive
Keeping well
Keeping awake.[2]

Psychoanalysis as a profession is concerned principally with the practice of psychotherapy. Whether this is an appropriate focus has always been a source of debate. Freud himself was ambivalent on the matter, declaring in a famous letter that, 'We do analysis for two reasons: to understand the unconscious and to make a living.'[3] Subsequent critics of psychoanalysis, particularly those writing from a philosophical or radical political perspective, have often distinguished between the strengths of psychoanalysis as a theory and its weaknesses as a mode of therapy. Russell Jacoby, a long-time critic of conformist tendencies in psychoanalysis, is a good example. 'Psychoanalysis is a theory of an unfree society that necessitates psychoanalysis as a therapy. To reduce the former to the latter is to gain the instrument at the expense of truth: psychoanalysis becomes merely medicine.'[4]

For Jeffrey Masson, quoted at the start of this chapter, the situation is equally severe: *all* forms of psychotherapy, but particularly psychoanalysis, are assaults on the freedom of the individual, ways of coercing people to behave according to the dictates of other people and to believe things about themselves and their experience which are not true. Psychotherapy is a form of social control:

The therapist claims that she or he is always attempting to

determine what will benefit the patient. All behaviour on the part of the therapist and all prohibitions with respect to the patient are being done for the patient's 'own good'. Yet this is what everybody says who wants to change another person's behaviour.[5]

From this perspective, when psychoanalysis reduces itself to therapy, it connives with an oppressive society to disempower its clients; moreover, it does so in such a way that the recipient believes that the opposite process is occurring. A measure of psychoanalytic psychotherapy's underhand mode of operation is that those who are most completely 'cured' are the people who are most taken in by psychoanalysis. They know not what has been done to them.

Interestingly and ironically, although this strand of antagonism towards psychoanalytic psychotherapy has been present and much discussed in the critical literature, an equally strong argument against psychoanalysis as therapy has come from a completely opposed perspective. This argument says, more or less simply, that psychoanalytic psychotherapy does not work. The data bearing on this claim will be discussed in a later chapter, but it can be stated here that there is at best little evidence that psychoanalytic psychotherapy does 'work' in any straightforward sense. Putting the two critiques together we have: psychoanalytic psychotherapy is retrograde because it acts as a mode of social control, converting people's accurate appreciation of the oppressive features of society into the belief that their troubles are caused by personal pathology, and then influencing the individuals concerned to act in a more controlled, less subversive way. Furthermore, it does not even work.

One might think that it would be necessary first to establish whether psychoanalysis as a therapy really does have effects on people before debating whether these effects are good or bad. However, this has not happened in the literature, except in a small overlap area in which critics of psychoanalysis have argued that it is pernicious because it claims to be helpful when in fact it is not.[6] Psychoanalysis is pilloried by these critics for misleading the public, making false claims, charlatanry and so on – in general, theirs is a consumer-protection portfolio. Overall, however, the field seems to be divided between those who think that psychoanalytic psychotherapy works and is a good thing (but has little empirical evidence to support it), those who think it works and is a bad thing (usually social theorists), those who think it does not work but that there might be alternative approaches which do (traditionally, behaviourists) and those who think no psychotherapies work but other forms of treatment might (such as drug treatment). There are also those who believe that psychoanalytic psychotherapy would work if it were done properly, and those who are genuinely agnostic but carry on practising psychoanalysis as a way of making a living. As noted above, this latter was at times Freud's own position and is perhaps the only rational one to take.

In all this the question of what it might mean to suggest that psychoanalytic psychotherapy 'works' is a major one. What is it trying to do and is what it is trying to do worth doing? It is the complexity of this question which makes it impossible to address the issue of the standing of psychoanalytic psychotherapy by turning first to the empirical studies. How these are to be read depends in large part on what one understands psychotherapy to be and on what one thinks of as its aims and intentions. For example, debates about the effectiveness of psychoanalytic therapy - often become polarised around the relative importance of improvements in patients' '*symptoms*' as opposed to alterations in 'underlying causes' or personality attributes. Studies which evaluate outcome usually pay most attention to changes in observable behaviours or in self-reported mood states (for example scores on depression inventories or other questionnaires), although sometimes ratings by clinicians (either the treating therapist or an independent one) are used. Psychoanalysts have traditionally ignored this research on the grounds that it does not measure changes in the deeper, characterological areas in which they are interested. As most psychoanalysts also tend to regard these features of a person as not easily measurable – or not measurable at all – this neatly sidesteps the problem of taking on board the negative findings of research. Nevertheless, there is a real issue here, not just to do with the level of outcome measurement (symptom, personality attribute, etc.) but also in terms of understanding the purpose and principles of psychoanalytic psychotherapy sufficiently well to set up meaningful criteria for evaluating effectiveness. Put bluntly, if psychoanalysis neither claims nor tries to 'treat symptoms' it cannot be called to task for failing to deal with them. On the other hand, if it does, then its reputed failure in this area is a cause for considerable concern. Moreover, if psychoanalysis does not aim to reduce troubling symptoms, one has to ask what it is doing in the field of therapeutics at all.

ADVOCACY VERSUS INTERPRETATION

Jeffrey Masson's repeated assaults on the truthfulness of psychoanalysis has had the virtue of clarifying the arena of psychoanalytic claims. What does psychoanalysis stand for? In terms of therapeutic activity, is it a procedure built around the dismissal and abuse of the patient, a charge Masson indefatigably presses, or is it something which can be employed in an empowering way, having at its heart an appreciation of the needs of patients as they struggle with their heritage and current conditions of existence? Considering psychoanalysis as a mode of therapy, Masson is unequivocal: it is a method of writing off the patient's actual experience so as to shift the source of responsibility for distress from the social world in which it belongs (reality, in Masson's terms) to the individual. The method whereby this is achieved, he argues, is through adjudging real events (trauma) to be products of the patient's fantasy – the quintessential version of this being his claim that psychoanalysis is built on Freud's suppression of the 'seduction theory' in favour of the fabrications of unconscious wishes derived from infantile sexuality.[7] In the context of therapy, this becomes part of the power game played by the analyst at the patient's expense – a kind of political re-education goes on, so that real aspects of an oppressive and abusive world are converted into elements of the patient's imagination. The analyst holds all the cards, makes all the judgements, is the sole arbiter of what truly happened and what is only made up. Generalising broadly, Masson writes that a person's account in therapy of a traumatic event 'is not to be taken literally, as referring to something real that happened in the real world', but is rather interpreted as a symbol of unconscious impulses – a symbol which can only be decoded by the analyst. Analytic doctrine dictates that the patient's memory can never be trusted because it is infiltrated by fantasy; only the therapist can work out what is real and what is not:

> To find out what happened, in this view, requires an external, objective source, a person trained in a demasking procedure: the therapist. . . . The idea that only the analyst can judge whether something is real or merely a fantasy became standard doctrine, and the very foundation of psychoanalytically oriented psychotherapy.[8]

Given this description of the analytic encounter, it is not

surprising that psychoanalysis should be a bruising experience. At its core is the insertion of one person's values into another; knowledge and healing play little part in this. At worst (although this might be Masson's view of the usual arrangement), the analyst uses the therapeutic situation to bolster her or his own sense of potency. It is nothing more than an exercise of power,

> Too often interpretations are used as disguised insults, or ways of forcing another person to accept the analyst's opinions. 'Insight' comes no easier to the so-called analyst than it does to the so-called patient. . . . One has only to think of the great case histories to realise how often Freud was wrong.[9]

In this version of things, psychoanalytic psychotherapy is a mode of abuse, distorting reality to obscure the actual origins of people's distress, and doing so by means of a set of procedures which reduce to rhetoric – to the manipulation of conditions of persuasion and power so that the patient will believe what she or he is told.

Authority, power, persuasion; these are indeed problematic and catalytic elements in the therapeutic process. As discussed in Chapter 1, there are important senses in which they form the core of psychoanalysis in all its aspects, not just the therapeutic. The institutional structures, agreed concepts and practices, accepted canon of texts and methods of training are all infused with dynamics of authority and power. They also lie at the heart of the encounter between analyst and patient. There can be little argument with Masson on this point. All the energy of the consulting room centres on the asymmetrical, hierarchical relationship between the speaking patient and the listening analyst, between the one who reveals her or his distress and the other who finds a context and hence a meaning for it. Moreover, whereas in ordinary discourse and in some other forms of therapy the speaking person is assumed to have privileged knowledge of the self – knowing, for example, why she or he did something or what her or his thoughts and feelings might actually be – this backing to the validity of a patient's knowledge-claims is denied in psychoanalysis. If, in ordinary conversation, I tell you what I think, you may disagree with me but you would be unlikely to claim that I did not 'really' think that and that you know what I think better than I do myself. If you did make that claim I would be entitled to feel that my liberty as a human subject was being impugned: 'don't tell me what to think' is an important statement of the primacy of personal subjectivity and of the privileged access which each of us holds to our own internal processes. Only I really know what I believe; only I am entitled to say what I think and feel.

Psychoanalysis plays it completely differently. The patient speaks, the analyst listens and eventually – sooner or later – offers an interpretation which construes the professed thoughts and feelings of the patient in terms of other, more 'real', impulses. 'You may think you feel X, but actually you feel Y' is a common structure of such an interpretive reconstrual – usually, though unfortunately not always, phrased with more subtlety and care. The privileged access to our own subjectivity which is so central to our everyday humanistic understanding of individuality and of the boundaries of respect around the person is denied by the psychoanalytic assertion that the analyst can see further into the patient than the patient can her or himself. Surely, as Masson argues, this is a process of oppression, in which people who go for help to understand and deal with their distress find instead that they are being subjected to a re-education programme so that things they thought were true are disrupted and undermined, and their complaints are placed back on themselves? Psychoanalytic psychotherapy, in this reading, is nothing more than a struggle for power, with the analyst, backed by institutional authority which itself is supported by cultural acceptance of the knowledge claims of the 'psy-professions', holding all the cards.

This acknowledges the force of the claim that psychoanalysis trades in power, whether as a mode of understanding and education or as a method of therapy. However, is it reasonable to move from this acknowledgement to acceptance of the notion that because power and authority are so central to the psychoanalytic game, then it can be understood as *only* an opportunity for the analyst (perhaps acting in someone else's name, for example the medical establishment or the state) to abuse the patient? And is it always the case that through working in the arena of fantasy rather than reality, psychoanalysis hides the actual sources of people's distress, contributing to the obscuring of the social origins of trauma and unhappiness? Masson's alternative to psychotherapy appears to be a kind of advocacy procedure in which the perceptions of the client are clarified and confirmed, rather than challenged, and in which the focus is upon the external sources of her or his distress. Using the example of Freud's celebrated 'Dora' case,[10] Masson argues that therapy which calls into question the motives and character of the sufferer obscures the real external cause of suffering – these being, for Dora, the manipulations and sexual calculations of the adults surrounding her. Freud would have done better, in this example, to confirm Dora's perception (which in the case study he acknowledges as likely to be accurate) that her father was manipulating her to preserve his own liaison with another woman; at least then Dora would have been freed from doubt about what was really going on.

There are, of course, many reasons to think that the destructiveness of the external world is at the root of much or most psychological distress – whether it be the chronic privation of poverty, the trauma and dislocation of war, the cumulative strain of racist attacks or the betrayals of sexual and physical abuse. Psychoanalysts have never denied this even if they have not made it their principal interest. Indeed, as in Anna Freud's work in the wartime Hampstead nurseries or contemporary work with victims of sexual abuse[11] and disasters,[12] they have often engaged very actively with the consequences of external trauma, sometimes developing psychoanalytic theory and technique as a consequence. Still, the more general question here is whether the psychoanalytic process defuses awareness of social pathogenesis, blaming patients for their disturbance and consequently distorting their understanding and further undermining their mental health. Masson clearly thinks it does.

One does not have to be an adherent of psychoanalysis to see this as a rather peculiar account of the analytic and wider therapeutic process. Unless one is willing to postulate that psychoanalysis is a conspiracy in the service of the repressive social order, the notion that the function of the analyst is to confuse the patient so that she or he can no longer appreciate the true source of their disturbance seems very far fetched. Of course, that may be the unintended effect of the approach, making psychoanalysts themselves the dupes of deeper ideological forces, but before adopting that conclusion it might be as well to try to sort out what psychoanalytic therapy is supposed to be about and how it actually works.

One area of agreement with Masson can immediately be conceded: psychoanalysis does not focus on reality, at least not in the unproblematic way that Masson would have it. Psychoanalysis as therapy works with fantasy, with the internal version of the world through which individuals relate to one another and to external events. Psychoanalysts do not even, under normal circumstances, check out the stories told to them by their patients. They neither seek to validate them nor demonstrate their contradictions through appeal to objective evidence; they simply listen to what they are told and try to understand from what inner realm the story they are hearing arises. This presupposition that there is an internal, psychic world which is not immediately transparent marks out the radical difference between psychoanalysis and modes of advocacy or reality-oriented counselling. Psychoanalysis asserts that work is required before the relationship between what a person says and the complex of intentions and wishes from which it arises can be mapped. In psychoanalytic terminology, this is work on the unconscious, on the arena of mental functioning which is systematically hidden from the subject her or himself. This arena is complex and causal, and is not easily understood. For Masson, in contrast, the unconscious is a fabrication of psychoanalysis itself, and the only acceptable therapeutic work is of the kind that boosts confidence; because the external world disguises its own actions, the client might need help in learning to trust and act upon her or his perceptions. Interestingly, whether a client's perceptions can actually be *wrong* is left untheorised by Masson. Presumably, if a client suffers from the conviction that she or he is psychologically disturbed, it is the task of the Massonian to demonstrate that in fact it is the external world that is at fault. This might require analysis and interpretation, with the therapist as the one who knows – a mirror image of the psychoanalytic process which he so vehemently criticises.

The psychoanalytic view of psychological distress is that it may be caused by various factors – manifestly including environmental 'real world' events such as abuse – but that it is fundamentally a psychological phenomenon and needs to be addressed at that level. In a sense, psychological distress is a *relationship* to reality, a relationship which may be more or less rewarding and satisfactory. Despite all their divergences over matters of theory, technique and therapeutic aim, all schools of psychoanalysis share the belief that clarifying and resolving psychological issues will help the individual perceive the features of the external world more clearly – an aspiration which Masson would presumably also share. Inner conflict fuels the difficulty of dealing with what is outside, and more generally it is through psychological processes that events in the world are perceived and made meaningful. In the view of psychoanalysis, it is the fantasy underpinnings of distress that require analytic intervention, because what keeps the individual stuck in suffering is not just the event itself – the loss or abuse or continuing privation – but the way the event is inserted into a complex of meanings. Contrary to some popular representations of therapy, learning to live with the world does not have to be the same thing as tolerating its violence; becoming more aware of its impact on oneself and of the patterns of confusion and strength in one's own psychic response may in fact make one more sure of how damage is perpetrated. It may even allow one to become more unambiguously angry and upset. Freud's own famous early differentiation between the 'hysterical misery' of the neurotic and the 'common unhappiness' that is the limit of therapeutic optimism is just one statement of his sustained position that society produces suffering, and that psychoanalysis is a weak albeit important response to this state of affairs. An echo of this can even be found in the psychoanalytic radicals, for example in the idea that an outcome for therapy might be the capacity – in Marcuse's memorable phrase – to 'function as part of a sick society without surrendering to it altogether'.[13] Although this is framed as criticism of conformist modes of psychoanalytic psychotherapy, it does not seem such an unreasonable prospect.

Many questions are, however, begged in this account, questions of aim and procedure. The notion of the 'real' event seems to be unproblematic for Masson and has been used in a similarly undeconstructed way above, but in fact there is enormous debate about the extent to which events can be separated from their psychic registration. Throughout the human sciences, often in the name of postmodernism, moves to construe the world in terms of 'narratives' have been immensely powerful, so much so that it sometimes seems as if there is no reality left anywhere, only stories. In psychoanalysis this movement is just as strong as anywhere else, finding fertile ground already watered by the hermeneutic movement discussed in Chapter 3. One reply to Grünbaum, for example, has been to argue that the aspiration of psychoanalysis is not to produce cure, but to tell better stories:

> One of the central underlying objectives of clinical work is the joint construction of organised and interlocking narratives. . . . To the extent that the therapeutic process is successful – and we have to bracket the unsuccessful analyses – the analysand masters the pain and anxiety, overcomes the amnesias, and corrects the distortions, and thereby acquires a set of narratives that form a convincing and seemingly accurate biography.[14]

The incoherence of this is extraordinary. *Through* mastering pain and anxiety, overcoming amnesia and correcting 'distortions', the analysand 'acquires a set of narratives'. But how does she or he do this except through the process of narrative itself? What is a 'seemingly accurate biography'? Is it one which is sufficiently compelling to persuade the analysand that it might actually be true? If so, the issue is one of constructing a convincing narrative which either uncovers or mimics the 'truth' – a kind of parody of the traditional detective task of classical psychoanalysis. Moving to a narrative perspective means renouncing claims to be able to access the truth; the danger is that it will mean abandoning experience altogether.

Lest it be thought that this is a 'straw man' argument, here is an extract from Ricardo Steiner's warning editorial in the issue of the *International Journal of Psycho-Analysis* devoted largely to hermeneutics,

> Fragile and 'undoubtedly situated' as it is (and in this sense hermeneutics teaches all of us a lesson in humility) our reason and the values I mentioned are nevertheless the only instrument we have to make sense of constantly having to walk through the dark forest of our unconscious. We should, therefore, not give them up or allow them to be manipulated by all sorts of seductive narrative mermaids, especially today when our social, cultural and historical world seems constantly to remind us, behind the pluralism of various narratives, of the uncanny *basso continuo* represented by our repetitive personal and social capacity to destroy: which no relativism can avoid considering.[15]

Steiner is here not so far away from Masson in his awareness of the destructive potential of the world, however much he may be on the other side of the trenches with regard to the standing and authority of psychoanalysis. He is also well within the psychoanalytic tradition in drawing attention to the interweaving of personal and social issues and in warning against the collapse of psychoanalytic values into narrative relativity. Not all stories are the same and not everything can be encapsulated in a narrative. As Steiner also states: 'a person is not a text'.[16]

Nevertheless – and here is the tension in psychoanalysis – all the psychoanalyst has to go on is the particular 'text' produced by the discourse of the patient in analysis, and all she or he can do with it is try to find a new way of reading it, one which in some way produces a shift in the consciousness of the patient. In terms which are fashionable in family systems therapy circles, a new 'co-construction' of reality takes place whereby the stories told between the patient and the analyst reframe the former's experience so that it can be understood and felt differently. If this sounds arid, it is because it sounds too cognitive or perhaps too magical. What is it about this new 'co-construction' that might make a person feel different – hopefully, better? Psychoanalysis has a lot to say about this and scrutinising some of the various aims for therapy put forward within psychoanalysis might make this clearer.

PRINCIPLES AND PURPOSES OF PSYCHOANALYTIC PSYCHOTHERAPY

As noted earlier, a considerable amount of the problem in evaluating the standing of psychoanalytic psychotherapy lies in the difficulty of establishing clearly what it is trying to do. Certainly, it does not aim to alter reality in any straightforward way, yet it also follows from what has been argued above that enabling the patient to take up a more potent stance towards the external world may be an important positive outcome. Psychoanalytic psychotherapy is also not concerned with the establishment of some simple causal 'truth' because the notions of truth and reality are made problematic by the psychoanalytic emphasis on the disruptive yet inescapable operations of the unconscious – manifested in this context through fantasy. On the other hand, it is not just a 're-storying' procedure aiming to create new narratives which feel more comfortable. While the construction of new narratives might well be part of the analytic procedure, they are constantly made problematic by the same sites of disruption as operate upon any claims to truth. In other words, no narrative can be seen as stable, whether it takes the form of a claim to truth or 'simply' a story; everything is available to reinterpretation. Yet, sometimes this endless flow of meanings stops and the 'real event' takes precedence.

The divergence in psychoanalysis between different formulations of the aims of therapy reflect the terms of this debate. Freud's idea of the purpose of therapy was linked to his rationalist interest in strengthening the ego so that the power of the id could be more successfully managed. His famous analogy here was of the rider and his horse:

> the horse supplies the locomotive energy, while the rider has the privilege of deciding on the goal and of guiding the powerful animal's movement. But only too often there arises between the

ego and the id the not precisely ideal situation of the rider being obliged to guide the horse along the path by which it itself wants to go.[17]

Despite his minimalist ('common human unhappiness') position on therapeutic potency highlighted above and repeated at various times in his writings, Freud set an explicit task for psychoanalytic therapy, which he believed would make a real difference to the patient: 'The business of psychoanalysis is to secure the best possible conditions for the functioning of the ego; when this has been done, analysis has completed its task.'[18] This programme of strengthening the ego centres on a vision of psychological disturbance as produced by *repetition* – characteristically, repetition of an impulse, never carried into action but repressed in unconscious form, or of a trauma. The past, in this broad sense, constantly haunts the present; a ghost in action but unseen and usually unsuspected. We observe ourselves doing something and have no real idea why, and to cover this unsettling experience, we construct an account – in psychoanalytic terms, a rationalisation – which makes sense of our behaviour, a plausible story legitimating ourselves.

But this rationalisation does not remove the ghost. Like any haunting, the pretence that nothing is there can only be maintained with increasing violence to the perceptual system. Narrowing the range of vision so that the moving pieces of furniture are not noticed, constructing increasingly tenuous and laborious natural explanations, blaming others; these are the strategies of dissimulation employed both by neurotics and by non-believers who are plagued by poltergeists. Freud, who did not believe in ghosts and who had material explanations for every supernatural claim (including all forms of religion), nevertheless was relentless in his pursuit of the unconscious sprites responsible for fooling about with everyday life. The 'return of the repressed', a compelling phrase in the psychoanalytic vocabulary, refers to the refusal of the ghostly trauma or hidden impulse to stop repeating until it is brought out into the light; then it can be quizzed, given a name, put back into its history and put to rest. But first you have to catch your ghost. Shifting the analogy slightly, the parallels between the Freudian attitude and that of the detective have often been noted, particularly in relation to the convergence between Freud's methods and those of Sherlock Holmes.[19] The hallmarks of both the detective and the psychoanalyst are sharp observation, ruthless deduction, relentless perseverance in the face of disappointment and absolute assuredness of the value of the rational investigative method itself. Freud makes this explicit in various places, among the most eloquent of which is a short passage in the 'Dora' case history. Having made a particularly lewd interpretation of the meaning of Dora's 'symptomatic action' of inserting and reinserting her finger into the purse around her waist, he comments:

> When I set myself the task of bringing to light what human beings keep hidden within them, not by the compelling power of hypnosis, but by observing what they say and what they show, I thought the task was a harder one than it really is. He that has eyes to see and ears to hear may convince himself that no mortal can keep a secret. If his lips are silent he chatters with his finger-tips; betrayal oozes out of him at every pore.[20]

For both the detective and the Freudian psychoanalyst, the aim of this relentless deconstruction of the situation is to bring to light the causal factor in the case – the criminal, whether person or unconscious impulse. The parallel is strengthened by another feature: in neither situation, whether detective or psychoanalyst, is the identification of the culprit by deductive means the end of the story. While the plausibility of guilt may arise from observation, proof is something which can only be tested in court by appeal to the judgement of others – a situation which holds even in the case of confessions, as several notorious miscarriages of justice have revealed. For the detective, this means judge or jury; for the psychoanalyst it means – above all – the patient. How do these 'courts' make their decisions? Among other things, on the basis of the coherence of the investigative account, the production of documentary and eye-witness testimony, the statements of the accused (confession included) and in the case of a serial or repeated crime, its cessation when the suspect has been identified and arrested. When the patient observes her or his unconscious criminal elements at work and, with the help of the analyst, can shackle or channel them so that they cease to operate as they did before, the changes in the way she or he feels and acts should be strong testimony to the correctness of the analytic deductions.

Perhaps the analogy with exorcism is a stronger one, however. The criminal may be locked away, but the ghost has to be appeased. Hauntings only cease, it seems, when something left incomplete in the ghost's lifetime is finally dealt with. One way by which this is traditionally achieved is to call the ghost into existence and ask what it needs. Then the unfulfilled promise, the illegitimate act, the broken contract or unrequited love can be called upon and something can be done with it – the passion can be consummated or, more likely, defused. When this occurs to the ghost's satisfaction, it goes to where it belongs, now innocuous – lamented and mourned perhaps, but no longer disruptive and charged with pain. So too with the symptom-producing unconscious. What really troubles us are those chopped-off pieces of impulse and passion which are not linked into their proper place, which are not visible and resolvable, the claims of which are obscure but undoubtedly full of agony for their incomplete lives. They continue to create havoc because they are not connected with what is properly theirs – a place of rest, preceded by the consummation of their desire. Calling them forth from the depths makes it possible to interrogate them for what they want, to find a way of providing this or something like it (a substitute or a compromise), or to argue them out of the excess of their demand and then to find them a place in consciousness, as something perhaps regretted but no longer able to disturb. This is the Freudian approach: to find the ghost disrupting the patient's sensibility, to allow it voice so it can be understood and if necessary have its demands acted upon and to reinsert it into a historical progression that could also contain it. It is not just knowledge of the unconscious impulse or trauma which is the key here, but reconciliation with it. As Freud puts it, this involves releasing the energy which has been tied up with the unconscious impulse so that it can be put at the disposal of the ego and allow the subject better ways of dealing with life.

This model of psychoanalytic practice, involving uncovering the hidden impulse, examining it, resolving its uncertainties and finding ways of integrating it into consciousness, remains a very powerful one in contemporary psychoanalysis. In some ways, it represents the high point of psychoanalytic rationalism in that it displays a faith in reason which is most unfashionable at the moment. The Freudian mode – the so-called 'analytic attitude' – is one which recognises the existence of irrationality *as a problem* rather than as something to be sought after or escaped into. The Freudian revolution consists largely in articulating the decentring of the self, that is – as Freud noted in his famous portrayal of himself as completing the work begun by Copernicus and Darwin – it makes it clear that conscious selfhood is not the driving force of human subjectivity. It is that 'other site', the unconscious, which is at the source of action, and the unconscious does not obey the usual rules of logic. It is emotional, erratic, contradictory, impulsive, troubling and poetic. Nevertheless, recognition of the otherness within does not necessarily imply acceptance of the irrational as on a par with reason. The analytic aims enunciated by Sandler, Dare and Holder in their influential survey of psychoanalytic concepts makes this clear:

> [It] would appear that therapeutic change as a consequence of analysis depends, to a large degree, on the provision of a structured and organised conceptual and affective framework within which the patient can effectively place himself and his subjective experience of himself and others.[21]

Although the word 'affective' in the middle of this tempers its force, there is little doubt that the version of 'analysis' taken up in the Freudian community is one in which the capacity to think rationally about things – for example, to make a clear distinction between fantasy and reality – is crucial for the therapeutic process. This is why the possession of too fragmented an ego is a counter indication for psychoanalysis of this kind because it suggests that the self-reflective capacity of the analysand will be insufficient to conquer the forces of irrationality within.

All this is not much more than a restatement of Freud's classic dictum for psychoanalytic psychotherapy: 'Where id was, there ego shall be: it is a work of culture – not unlike the draining of the Zuider Zee.'[22] That it is a specific version of the psychotherapeutic process, however, has only become obvious in more recent, postmodernist times. The Freudian challenge, to take over the 'id' and colonise it, organising its energy so that it flows in the channels granted to it by the ego – so that it works in the service of what might be termed 'civilisation' – has now become problematic and tentative. The revolutionary excitement of Freudian psychoanalysis was its recognition of the existence of a causal area of irrationality within the subject, thus displacing the conventional reading of the Enlightenment subject as governed by the activity of rational thought. Subsequent theory, however, including recent postmodernist work, has pointed out that psychoanalysis stays within this same rationalist tradition by emphasising the taming of the unconscious as its therapeutic aim. Toril Moi, making an additional and important link between the unconscious and femininity here, summarises the tension as follows:

Psychoanalysis is born in the encounter between the hysterical woman and the positivist man of science. It is in this reversal of the traditional roles of subject and object, of speaker and listener, that Freud more or less unwittingly opens the way for a new understanding of human knowledge. But the psychoanalytical situation is shot through with paradoxes and difficulty. For if Freud's (and Breuer's) act of listening represents an effort to *include* the irrational discourse of femininity in the realm of science, it also embodies their hope of *extending* their own rational understanding of psychic phenomena. *Grasping* the logic of the unconscious they want to make it accessible to reason.[23]

One element in this is the acknowledgement of a genuine tension in the origins and history of psychoanalysis; it both allows for the existence of a discourse of irrationality and tries to make this discourse malleable. The debate over 'science' discussed in previous chapters is an element in this tension, as is the question of the purpose and procedures of psychoanalytic psychotherapy. In bringing the ghost to light, is its disruptive power to be denied?

Although most psychoanalytic procedures centre on the creation of channels of communication between unconscious phenomena and consciousness, the degree to which the colonising tendency dominates over the expressive tendency varies greatly. The alternative model of psychoanalytic practice ascribed to by the British Kleinian school exemplifies this difference. Klein argues that the fundamental task of analysis is to enable integration of the psyche to occur through overcoming splits which are perpetuated by unresolved primitive conflicts.[24] What is of great importance here, is that both (or all) sides of the conflict are unconscious 'id' phenomena. Whereas the Freudian emphasis is on the troubled relationship between unconscious impulses and consciousness, albeit mediated through unconscious ego defence mechanisms, the arena for Kleinian therapy is primarily unconscious. At the end of the affair, while consciousness should clearly be extended and the patient's relationship to the external world should have improved, the crucial point is that integration of the personality has occurred through the reconciliation of unconscious forces with one another.

In the Kleinian metaphor (the only safe way to regard it, as belief in the concrete reality of Kleinian concepts is a dizzying experience), psychic life is marked by the interplay between different modes of representation. Generally speaking, this fluctuation between what Klein refers to as the paranoid–schizoid and depressive modes is seen as a contrast between 'primitive' and developmentally more advanced mentation, identified as such because of the complexity of the psychological processes at work and also – perhaps jumping the gun – because depressive position functioning is perceived as ethically more advanced. In the paranoid–schizoid mode, anxiety is defended against by splitting linked to projection. Destructive impulses are divided from loving impulses and then each set is projected into the external object, resulting in a world perceived as comprising elements which are wholly good or wholly bad, at war one with another. By contrast, the mode of action in the depressive position is a containing one, capable of integrating conflicting tendencies into more complex and creative wholes. The paradigmatic instance here is the case of reparation, the 'variety of processes by which the ego feels it undoes harm done in phantasy, restores, preserves and revives objects'.[25] This is classified as a depressive position function because the capacity to engage in such reparation depends on acknowledgement of destructiveness and its linking with feelings such as regret and loss as well as an awareness that something can be done to institute new life into the object of one's destructive urges. Ambivalence and the acceptance of ambivalence are at the centre of this experience.

Traditionally, in Kleinian thought, reparation has been seen as a model of the creative process; what might have been shattered into pieces, in fantasy, is now constructed anew, imbued with feeling and with order. Clearly, this kind of imagery can also be employed to envisage an outcome for psychotherapy: that which was split and antagonistic might become integrated. Where emotion was rejected and projected into an external object, therapy could possibly offer the necessary containment for it to be taken back in and owned. Hence Klein's comment that 'the ultimate aim of psychoanalysis is integration of the patient's personality',[26] even if this can never be fully achieved. Importantly, although a strengthening of the ego is required as a prop to the process of tolerating the integration of ambivalent feelings, the key procedure in therapy is that of taking back inside what has been put out, at a level which remains to all intents and purposes unconscious. In the analytic relationship, the patient's aggression is projected into the analyst who then becomes a rejecting, punitive object. By the end of analysis, after interpretive work has ameliorated this representation, the fantasy figure of the analyst is taken in and identified with as a source of continuing nurture and goodness to be drawn on long after the therapy itself has ended. This is a model for mourning of all kinds, beginning with the first separation from the mother and extending throughout life.

What should be emphasised here is just how non-cognitive a process this is. Drawing benefit from psychoanalytic therapy does not depend on rational mastery of the unconscious. Instead, it requires the development of a capacity to do something rather irrational – to tolerate the existence of conflicting emotions and impulses and, through unconscious channels, to turn this tension to good effect. Moreover, even the developmental sequencing might be challenged. Kleinian thought does not propose that the paranoid–schizoid position is ever fully relinquished; there is too much evidence that under all sorts of stressful circumstances human subjects are all too prone to resort to splitting, denigration, idealisation and generally destructive projection and projective identification. The struggle to impose a depressive mode of functioning on this tendency to resort to primitive mechanisms is life long. In addition, the tension between paranoid–schizoid and depressive modes of functioning can also be seen as an encouragement to psychological growth. If one or other mode is shut off completely, there is stagnation, neurosis or psychotic dissolution. Anthony Elliott, writing about 'reflexivity' as a psychological and social imperative, draws attention to this aspect of Kleinian thought, portraying psychic life as a constant interchange between the depressive tendency to close things down – making them ordered and contained – and the opposing tendency to blow them apart. The argument is that while the psychotic components of paranoid–schizoid functioning might entice one into thinking of it as merely destructive, in fact it offers a necessary challenge to organised thought:

> Yet such changes from depressive to paranoid–schizoid modes of generating experience, and also from paranoid–schizoid to depressive states, are vital to creative living in the personal and social domains. . . . The paranoid–schizoid mode and the depressive mode fuse to produce a dialectic of experience: paranoid–schizoid turbulence breaks up the closures of thought and affect reached in the depressive mode, just as depression serves to negate the psychic dislocations of pure loving and pure hating.[27]

It should be noted that Elliott is not suggesting that the two modes of functioning are morally or psychologically equivalent. Indeed, he goes on to portray the difficulties involved when 'depressive modes of generating experience and managing psychological pain fully collapse into paranoid–schizoid defences of excessive splitting, omnipotent thinking, and denial'.[28] But he is arguing against the apparent closure of the more ethically advanced system; the sheer turbulence of paranoid–schizoid thinking, albeit mediated and refined by the containing structures of the depressive mode, contributes vitally to 'creative living'. A therapeutic programme, just like a political programme which wiped out this turbulence once and for all, would limit rather than enlarge the domain of subjective experience.

What is being argued here is that, despite the rather firmly normative formulations concerning mental health produced by Klein herself,[29] the Kleinian tendency has within it ideas which disrupt the allegiance of psychoanalysis to the triumph of reason. Where Freud seemed rather regretful about the impossibility of 'cure', post-Freudian developments of this kind seem to suggest that emotional turbulence – irrationality – is a necessary aspect of mental health. Psychoanalytic therapy might attempt to make these states tolerable, but should not try to do away with them. In a way, this approach offers a way out of the bind recognised by Philip Rieff, who in distinguishing between the 'analytic attitude' of Freudian psychoanalysis and the 'ecstatic attitude' of salvational or 'commitment' therapies, articulated a programmatic difficulty for contemporary lives.[30] The analytic attitude, based on the principle that irrationality enters into all aspects of human behaviour and has constantly to be examined in order to be managed, is never ending; even psychoanalysis itself, as an intellectual as well as an institutional edifice, has to be subjected to its scrutiny. Exhausting the capacity of the mind to self reflect, it produces at best the negative hope of escaping from hysteria, of 'living with one's ailments'. The commitment therapies, on the other hand, offer something which cannot be delivered – relief from conflict, the finding of salvation in a state of transcendence or otherness. That this 'ecstatic' attitude should have appeal is no surprise, but its intellectual vacuousness is less significant than the emotional confidence trick which it perpetrates on troubled lives.

Kleinian concepts offer one way forward from this, in which the analytic attitude has a limit placed upon it, found in recognition of the eternal tension between different aspects of the personality. Irrationality is a constant accompaniment of human subjectivity – indeed, subjectivity is forged out of it – and this has to be recognised in any psychotherapeutic process. On the other hand, this irrationality is not in itself a source of celebration, an ecstasy. Rather, it is an index of the troubled yet rich nature of the relationships which human subjects form with one another. The psychotherapeutic aim, therefore, becomes one of recognition or reflection upon the interweaving of inner tumult and its containing structures – of paranoid–schizoid pulsation and its mitigation through depressive modification. As the patient gains access to this tension, the capacity to live with and use it should be strengthened. In old fashioned terms, what this signifies is an acceptance of the disturbing force of imagination as it wells up, threatening dissolution but also promising creative living if it can be tolerated and owned.

It should be apparent that psychotherapy couched in these terms cannot easily be conceptualised as a procedure for reducing symptoms, nor for giving people more 'control' over their lives – a nebulous and contingent notion at best. The hope that this should be an outcome for psychotherapy still resides to some extent in the popular consciousness, the discourse of clinicians and the aspirations of patients. However, as clinical and theoretical work has developed over time, it has become clearer that the image of regulation of unconscious passion by the ego is a specific kind of cultural fantasy linked to a fast-decaying idealisation of reason at the expense of emotionality. The Kleinian development, while still adhering to much of the rationalist tradition, also articulates a startlingly different perspective in which the end point of therapy is an enhanced capacity to tolerate the crises of ambivalence seen as endemic to human subjectivity. Here, the to and fro of psychotherapy is not one in which the reasons for things get discovered so much as one in which emotional integration occurs in the context of an intense intersubjective encounter, some aspects of which can be spoken about, but others of which remain for all time inexpressible. The formula for psychoanalytic activity popularised by Bion, 'learning from experience', has come to imply a specific kind of personal transformation in which one is aware that something new is known, but cannot necessarily say what it is; one simply observes oneself being different, feeling differently and behaving in a calmer and more engaged way. Similarly, the model of mental health being pursued in psychotherapy is one in which the impossibility and indeed inadvisability of psychic peace is acknowledged. Psychoanalytic psychotherapy teaches that the fantasy of resolving all difficulties must be renounced in favour of an increased capacity to live in that tension which is a necessary component of human subjectivity. Behind the containing ('depressive') structures of feeling and responsible personal relationships lurks an awareness of something 'other' inside the self which can act, creatively or destructively, to subvert this containment whenever it threatens to become too cosy and closed.

The emphasis on the intersubjective transactions between analyst and patient to be found in the Kleinian literature produce some intriguing links with the 'narrative' turn in therapy, touched on earlier in this discussion. As was noted above, psychoanalysis has responded actively to the agitations of the cultural–political movement termed 'postmodernism' and particularly to the way it makes problematic ideas of 'expertise' and knowledge. Suspecting that the traditional Freudian interest in causality and cure might be an elitist attempt to keep the diversity of contemporary experience under control, some psychoanalysts – echoing therapists in other areas, particularly family systems therapy[31] – have attempted to introduce elements of postmodern thought into their therapeutic practice. This has taken the form of an increased interest in the contribution of the therapist to the therapeutic process (building on the Kleinian appreciation of the centrality of countertransference) and a focus on narrative and storytelling. The idea that constructing a new narrative to make sense of one's experience may be therapeutically beneficial derives from the realisation that language has constructive possibilities which materialise in interpersonal situations, as meanings are forged through the negotiations between one subject and another. In this respect, the 'talking therapies' are potentially very good examples of a general postmodern idiom in which alternative narratives – new identities, perhaps – are tried on for size, experimented with and developed or discarded as seems fit. As contact is made between one subject and another, new versions of the self (and hence, new interpretations of the world) take shape, always contingent and flexible, available to replacement as the generative process proceeds.

Among the most prominent features of this account as it applies to psychotherapy is the extent to which the construction of alternative versions of the self arises out of an active engagement between the patient's and the therapist's subjectivity. This is mediated through language, or rather it is a process which occurs *in* language. As each participant in the therapeutic interchange speaks, new positions of subjectivity are constructed, new points of view and arrangements of experience explored. In some contemporary therapeutic writing, this appears as a relativistic procedure, suggesting that a therapeutic narrative can be substituted for a self-damaging one in a rather schematic way and as such it has attracted considerable criticism from psychoanalysts and others.[32] However, as several writers have demonstrated, the promotion of 'new' narratives is a more subtle notion when taken into the framework of a possible postmodernist psychotherapy.[33] It should be made quite clear that postmodernism is not simply an encouragement to linguistic playfulness, to telling better stories. Rather, it works in the margins, with what happens in that space between what can be said and what cannot; there are limits, it suggests, to what can be known and particularly to what can be regarded as 'true'. In particular, postmodernist work draws attention to the manner in which every story is provisional – reflecting confusion, emotional investment and desire – and open to negotiation at each stage of its own development, whether this be in writing, ordinary conversation or psychoanalysis. Immersed in the intense experience of psychotherapy, there is no single discovery or shift in personality that can define change. Rather, there are moment-to-moment fluctuations, new perceptions, preliminary, provisional and partial modes of being.

Postmodernism, then, draws attention to the productivity of language and to the reflexivity of the therapist–patient relationship, understood as the emerging into mutual knowing of two sets of subjectivities. In addition, postmodernism's deconstruction of the position of the 'expert', in psychotherapy as in other arenas of the knowledge/power industry, is a matter of considerable importance for everyday work as well as for high theory. However, the principle discovery of postmodernism is that all truths are provisional and all stories can be better told because they all just miss the point.

What is this point? In relation to psychoanalytic psychotherapy, it is that the uncovering of any one 'truth' of the human subject – an identity, a cause for neurosis – is too restrictive. Rather, each of us is constituted as *process*, as a system of tensions and reconciliations, always on the move and in flux. The way this materialises in the therapeutic situation is in the to and fro between analyst and patient, that is in the intersubjective domain. What requires emphasis here is the active interpersonal work going on in the analytic encounter, the meshing of what has been called the 'de-translating' activity of the analyst with the 'joint construction–translation' of the analytic pair.[34] This is not simply a matter of conversation, of linguistic exchange. Instead, what is aimed at is a meeting of two sites of otherness, channelled through language but not reducible to it, a meeting of two unconscious structures. In terms of psychoanalytic aims there is here a return to the idea of making sense of experience, but focused within an intense intersubjectivity which retains a significant residue even after it has been put in rational form. In this residue, this otherness, much of the tension and creativity of subjectivity resides.

The significance of concepts such as 'otherness' and 'rupture' for contemporary psychoanalysis will be returned to, particularly in the context of their relationship to societal processes. But the increasingly abstract and threateningly idealising portrait of the psychotherapeutic project needs to be grounded at this point in a discussion of *practice*. What are the claimed components of psychoanalytic psychotherapy, and what legitimacy do they possess?

Chapter 5

The rules of the game

CONTAINING THE UNCONSCIOUS

Although Freud stated the 'fundamental rule' of psychoanalysis as that of *free association* – that the patient should speak whatever comes to mind, without selection or censorship – the rule of analysis is in fact even simpler than that. In reality, all that is required for analysis to take place is that the patient and the analyst should be in the room together. The patient might speak, but also might not; it is of little concern, as silences are treated in the same way as words. Nothing is what it seems, everything is open to interpretation on the part of the analyst, whose task is to listen and attempt to gain access to whatever is being communicated from below the surface of the patient's discourse. And the patient cannot fail to communicate, even if all this communication consists of is the proffering of a cut-off, non-communicating state.

This is one of the paradoxes of psychoanalysis, that the apparently free analytic situation is really one of the most constrained in existence. The patient is invited to speak of anything at all, given licence and indeed encouragement to use the setting in order to be reflective, to fantasise, to lie or dream, to be emotional or quiet. This kind of freedom is a scarce commodity: to speak without consequence, without being answerable for the effects of one's speech, without having to be sensitive to the listener and take the other into account. What one buys in therapy is permission to speak so that one can explore the resonance of one's own voice, safe from the danger of suffering hurt or antagonism as a result and without, on the face of it, having to consider the impact of one's words. Anything is possible: speak in any way, be silent when the mood arises, refuse to answer, make wild accusations, protest love or desire, tell stories, invent new identities and past histories, admit cruelties and criminalities, criticise, challenge, cry or laugh.

The invitation to behave in this way would be extraordinary in everyday life, but it is the stuff of the analytic situation. However, it remains so only for the fifty-minute 'hour', because one of the ironies or paradoxes is that this is a freedom made possible only by the very tight boundary which is drawn around it. The patient can say anything she or he likes and the analyst has to listen, but only while the session lasts. Before it begins and after it ends, there is nothing – no compulsion, no agreement to listen one minute longer nor even to hear the end of a sentence. The patient's freedom is limited to speech or non speech within the analytic hour; a boundary which is inviolate precisely because, if it were not so, the patient's freedom would not be in the context of a game but in 'real life'. Then it would cease to be play; it would be psychosis, a narcissistic disorder in which the patient labours under the belief that she or he need not take account of reality. Or else, if the analyst were to become actively involved in the patient's fantasy life, it would be abuse.

The constraints around analytic freedom are remarkably tight. Exact timing and frequency of the session is the rule, with agreed breaks and rates of pay. In addition, the patient is free only to speak, unless she or he is a child in which case play within certain established boundaries is also allowed. The patient can, of course, walk out, come late or refuse to come at all; all are further aspects of her or his freedom. But she or he is not free to invade the analyst's privacy or to establish any relationship outside the professional one. More significantly, the patient can demand anything from the analyst, but she or he has no right to expect any specific response. The patient is free to speak or to be silent; so is the analyst. The patient can say whatever she or he wishes; the analyst can take up any aspect of this discourse, spoken or unspoken and choose to comment upon it. The patient can make any claims; the analyst can dispute them. The patient can ask a question; the analyst can refuse to answer. In the meshing of these two strange freedoms, something very unfree occurs. The patient can speak or be silent as she or he wishes, but it makes no difference at all.

Psychoanalysts would argue that the major constraint in all this comes from the unconscious, that is that the apparent freedom of choice available to the patient is belied by the urgency of speaking of certain things in certain ways. This urgency is driven from the depths, from an area outside the control of the speaking subject. It is not, therefore, the analytic situation which places a limit on freedom, but the actuality of human subjectivity. At those moments when we believe ourselves to be free to make choices and to speak as we wish or act to determine our own direction in life, the unconscious trips us up via a little slip, a slight spilling or an unnoticed repetition. In the analytic environment, the exotic licence to dream and fantasise is heard in the patient's unconscious as an invitation to play pranks, making certain qualifying phrases necessary and common in any patient's vocabulary, phrases like: 'that's not what I meant', 'I didn't mean to say that' or 'I don't know where that idea came from'.

If it is the case that the psychic determinism characteristic of the unconscious places the freedom of the patient in jeopardy from the start, then the contribution made to this by the constraining circumstances of the analytic situation can be seen in a new light. If the patient were genuinely 'free', the artificiality of the analytic encounter would be an obstruction, a limit. This is, indeed, how it is often seen. As noted in the previous chapter, Jeffrey Masson's critique of psychotherapy is built around the idea that it distorts rather than bolsters the experience of the patient and that this happens in the context of intimidation and disingenuous 'truthseeking'. The freedom of the patient is impugned by the activity of the analyst. However, if the notion of the unconscious is accepted, the issue is turned on its head and the whole situation looks quite different. Now it is the patient who brings with her or him the internal constraints that produce suffering. What the analysis offers now is a containing rather than constraining setting for allowing the unconscious its head without losing control. It may be, as Freud suggests in the famous quotation, that the 'horse' of the id determines the path which is taken, but at least the ego/rider has a harness to stop it falling to the ground. A harness of this kind certainly restricts freedom, but it also makes it more likely that the rider will stay alive.

The language of 'containment' introduced here is widely used in psychoanalysis to describe the situation in which the analyst acts as a receptacle for disowned feelings and parts of the patient's self, holding them in trust until they can be tolerated. To a considerable extent, it is the entire 'setting' in which psychoanalytic psychotherapy takes place which has this function and the nature of this setting has become a significant concern of contemporary analysts. For some, it seems that a considerable portion of the effectiveness of psychotherapy derives from the provision of appropriate conditions. The usual requirements are a regular time and place for meeting, a time boundary around sessions that is rigidly adhered to (the fifty-minute 'hour'), freedom from interruptions, relative quiet and a reasonably stable and predictable analyst. Under certain conditions (for example with certain kinds of 'borderline' patients and particular therapists – notably those who are object relational) this might turn out to be *all* that the analyst offers. For example, in making a distinction between the kinds of patient who might benefit from classical analysis and those who might not, Winnicott suggested that with the latter, 'schizoid' group, 'the accent is more surely on management, and sometimes over long periods with these patients ordinary analytic work has to be in abeyance, management being the whole thing'.[1]

'Management' here means restricting interpretations to a minimum and, instead, focusing on the provision of a predictable and reliable analytic presence that is accepting and tolerant of regression. The idea is that this might offer to very disturbed patients an experience of having their most destructive and regressed impulses tolerated and contained, showing them that they are not capable of destroying the analysis. With this discovery, it is suggested, might come the feeling that something can be done, that an unbearable thought might be thinkable or a violent impulse survived. Like the infant discovering that her or his overwhelming anger does not, in the end, prevent the parent's love continuing, so the patient who finds the analysis *still there after all*, will feel relief.

What is offered in psychoanalysis is a severely bounded context for play and talk, not free – that much is clear even from the rudimentary outline of psychic determinism given above – but bursting with unconscious life of a kind which would normally be unacceptable, troubling or 'uncontainable'. However, the analyst is not just part of the setting, substitutable by an empty chair; he or she is its organising fulcrum and the degree of containment offered depends on the analyst's capacity to withstand psychic pressure. Psychoanalysts argue that rigorous adherence to boundaries is increasingly crucial the more a patient presses against them, demanding sympathy, change of session times or reduction of fees, or failing to attend at all,

[The] analytic treatment should be so organised as to ensure that the patient finds as few substitutive satisfactions for his symptoms as possible. The implication for the analyst is that he should refuse on principle to satisfy the patient's demands to fulfil the roles which the patient tends to impose upon him.[2]

Easing of austerity, which might under other circumstances appear to be no more than an expression of ordinary human understanding could, in the analytic situation, be taken as a sign of weakness or fear of what the patient has inside. So a patient who misses a session and then receives a letter from her or his therapist asking where the patient was and expressing concern might consciously feel cared about, but might unconsciously use this as evidence that the therapist is panicked by the patient's suicidal impulsiveness. The implicit message to the patient in the letter could then be that the analyst cannot be trusted to listen calmly as the patient talks about suicidal thoughts, or to maintain her or his separateness in order to be a safe person into whom the patient can project this feared aspect of the self. Better, perhaps, not to write, but wait to see what the patient says next time she or he comes.

If this seems extraordinary, as clearly it is, then it is worth considering the theoretical impulse behind it. The notion of 'containment' is wedded strongly (though not exclusively, as the example of Winnicott shows) to the Kleinian version of the therapeutic process. In large part, the vision here is of the patient releasing into the setting those aspects of her or his self which are felt to be dangerous, damaging and intolerable – the destructive energies of envy and hatred with which each human subject is held to grapple from the start of life. Activated in this way, they circulate and find a home 'in' the analyst, just as the infant's earliest paranoid–schizoid projections are fantasised as living 'inside' the mother's breast. The analyst's task here is twofold: to hold on to the projections and make sense of them; to then give them back in a more manageable form through the medium of interpretation. It is quite clear here that what is being described, from the point of view of the patient at least, is a process of being understood which in itself is therapeutically 'holding'. Even if the patient cannot understand what is going on, at least there is the hope that someone else does.

John Steiner, who has in some ways radically reformulated thinking on the power and limits of containment, describes the situation with very withdrawn patients who have escaped, psychologically and interpersonally speaking, into 'psychic retreats' from which they are unwilling to emerge:

> [The] patient who is not interested in acquiring understanding – that is understanding about himself – may yet have a pressing need to be understood by the analyst. Sometimes this is consciously experienced as a wish to be understood, and sometimes it is unconsciously communicated. A few patients appear to hate the whole idea of being understood and try to disavow it and get rid of all meaningful contact. Even this kind of patient, however, needs the analyst to register what is happening and have his situation and his predicament recognised.[3]

Steiner suggests a specific technique for communicating to the patient that the analyst has developed such an understanding, a technique which he terms 'analyst-centred interpretations', focused on what the patient believes the analyst to be thinking or feeling. He states: 'At these times the patient's most immediate concern is his experience of the analyst, and this can be addressed by saying something like, "You experience me as . . . ", or "You are afraid that I . . . ", or "You were relieved when I . . . ".'[4] Although the difference between this type of interpretation and a more classical one centred on what the patient is thinking or wishing might be slim, the subtle shift to registering what aspect of the analyst the patient has in mind and reflecting that back is held by Steiner to communicate (if it is accurately carried out) the willingness of the analyst to think about the patient's experience in an open way. Interestingly, the language Steiner uses here is much like that employed by the doyen of the previous generation of Kleinian analysts, Wilfred Bion, in outlining his notion of 'reverie' as the advisable attitude for the analyst to hold. Reverie, we are told, is 'that state of mind which is open to the reception of any "objects" from the loved object and is therefore capable of the reception of the infant's projective identifications whether they are felt by the infant to be good or bad'.[5]

This maternal imagery is translated directly into a model for the therapeutic situation, with the patient in the place of the 'infant'. In a similar vein Steiner explains:

> To be analyst-centred, in the sense which I intend to use it, the analyst has to have an open mind and be willing to consider the patient's view and try to understand what the patient means in a spirit of enquiry.[6]

What is emphasised is the communication of a state of mind on the part of the analyst in which any assault from the patient's destructive unconscious impulses can be withstood and tolerated. In practice, this means not only that the analyst should show her or his robustness by continuing to see the patient – by still being there, in one piece, at the appointed time each day – but that she or he should also demonstrate a capacity to continue thinking. For that, at least in the Kleinian model as developed by Bion and others, is the crux of the patient's handicap; an incapacity to tolerate thinking, to make links between one idea and another or – just as fatefully – between a feeling and a thought. With certain patients, the unbearable nature of the thought gets projected into the analyst, with the fantasy that she or he will be destroyed by it, just as the patient feels destroyed inside. If, on the contrary, the response is one of stability and an effort to recognise the thought, to preserve a thinking capacity, then the patient's disturbance is being 'held' and the distress is more likely to be managed. Referring to this process as 'containment' accentuates the way it mimics the desirable infantile experience of trusting that someone else can hold on to a thought or a feeling even when one cannot do so oneself. At its simplest, it recapitulates the infant's faith in the capacity of a parent to know what to do even when all the infant is aware of is a dangerous and bewildering confusion.

The important point here is the idea that this sensation of 'being understood' is the core of containment. In some quarters, containment of this kind takes the place of interpretive activity to become the central element in the therapeutic process. However, even though workers in the Kleinian tradition acknowledge that there is sometimes little that one can do with a particularly regressed patient other than to offer containment, they are generally dissatisfied with this as a therapeutic goal. Steiner is explicit here in arguing that containment is a necessary but not sufficient aspect of therapeutic movement:

> Containment requires that the projected elements have been able to enter the analyst's mind, where they can be registered and given meaning which is convincing. It does not require that the patient himself is available or interested in achieving understanding. If the patient is to develop further, he must make a fundamental shift, and develop an interest in understanding, no matter how small or fleeting.[7]

This process of moving beyond containment to an active engagement with understanding on the part of the patient is crucial for
analytic work of substance and depth. In Steiner's account, it is
dependent upon the capacity of the analyst to balance the open,
accepting attitude described above with more active, searching interpretive work. Otherwise, he suggests, what the patient comes to
believe is that the analyst is avoiding penetrating into the depths of
the patient's disturbance – and hence that it is truly something to be
feared:

> Interpretations may temporarily have to emphasize containment
> but ultimately must be concerned with helping the patient gain
> insight, and an analyst who is perceived as reluctant to pursue
> this fundamental aim is not experienced as providing contain-
> ment. Indeed, these two aspects of interpretation can be thought
> of as feminine and masculine symbols of the analyst's work.
> Both are required, and insight, which is so often disturbing, is
> only acceptable to the patient who is held in a containing
> setting.[8]

The relationship between containment and insight is here made
circular: containment is necessary for insight to be bearable, but it
also depends on the willingness of the analyst to pursue insight, so
showing the patient that the most feared thing – facing one's own
terror – can be confronted. Taking refuge in containment alone,
suggests Steiner, communicates to the patient that insight cannot be
borne, that knowledge will destroy. Paradoxically, therefore, pursuit
of insight through interpretation can lead to an increase in containment so long at it is not too ferocious, or built on too flimsy a basis
of already-existing therapeutic security.

Steiner refers to the analyst-centred (containing) and patient-
centred (insight-oriented) modes of interpretation as 'feminine and
masculine symbols of the analyst's work'. In so doing, he releases a
familiar genie from the bottle of psychoanalytic ideology, a
gendered play on the dichotomies of active/passive, instrumental/
expressive and knowing/feeling. The feminine symbol is the one of
holding and containing – the archetypal maternal notion. The
masculine symbol is that of driving forwards, penetrating the
patient's mind, creating disturbance. Both are necessary, but the
latter is more important than the former. This also raises a common
psychoanalytic distinction between pre-Oedipal narcissism and
Oedipal recognition of reality, the idea being that some ways of

relating to the world promote regression while others produce development. Containment is in the regressive, narcissistic mode, it provides the patient with the sense of being held and of safety in the face of a persecutory world. It promotes the fantasy of escape into the arms of the other (the 'mother'), who can do one's thinking for one. When contained, one does not need to struggle to understand, to make links, to face disturbance; every contradiction can be avoided and every wish indulged because someone else will take responsibility.

What this promotes is an illusory self fulfilment, a grandiosity that is in fact fragile, dependent on constant reassurance and the denial of difference. By contrast, Oedipal reality is built on recognition of the power of the symbolic father; it requires the individual to understand that her or his wishes may be thwarted by something outside, that contradiction exists and that the pain of renunciation cannot be wished away. The developmental argument here is a simple and potent one: that the cultivation of narcissism through supportive containment is necessary while the infant builds up the internal resources (basically, a secure ego or stable self) which will make it possible for her or him to manage the transition to an awareness of Oedipal reality. Without the preliminary narcissistic phase, the ego will be too fragile to cope with the assault perpetrated on the infant by contradiction and the demands of the social world – symbolised by the prohibitive, Oedipal father. But if narcissism is all that there is, this world will never be faced and the child will be condemned to an eternity of chasing after ideals, searching endlessly for the lost consolation of the mother's embrace. If containment is all that therapy provides, then the 'real thing' – the existence of contradiction and loss – is never faced, and patient and therapist become caught in the enticing web of narcissistic disavowal.

There are a variety of possible responses to this complex vision of the relationship between containment and insight. Returning to the issue of the analyst's responsiveness to the patient, from which this discussion began, there is a question of the extent to which gratification of the patient's demands is always contrary to the promotion of insight. In identifying a class of schizoid patients who could only tolerate 'management', Winnicott gave a positive gloss to the image of the analyst as mother. His argument was that the regressed state produced by the analyst's constant, non-interpretive presence allows such patients to relive their past and to find in the analyst a new 'mother' who can manage them, with all their fierce despair, making the emergence of a newly integrated self possible. For Winnicott, this could become an astonishingly active process on the part of the analyst: 'In the extreme case the therapist would need to go to the patient and actively present good mothering, an experience that could not have been expected by the patient.'[9]

Margaret Little, a psychoanalyst who was a patient of Winnicott's, describes his way of working with severely regressed states and evokes the beauty and disturbance of this approach:

> Literally, through many long hours he held my two hands clasped between his, almost like an umbilical cord, while I lay, often hidden beneath the blanket, silent, inert, withdrawn, in pain, rage or tears, asleep and sometimes dreaming. Sometimes he would become drowsy, fall asleep and wake with a jerk, to which I would react with anger, terrified and feeling as if I had been hit. . . .
>
> Early in the analysis, after a severe attack of gastro-enteritis . . . I went on feeling very ill and exhausted physically and deeply depressed. D.W. came to me at home – five, six and sometimes seven days a week for ninety minutes each day for about three months. During most of those sessions I simply lay there, crying, held by him. He put no pressure on me, listened to my complaints and showed that he recognised my distress and could bear with it.[10]

In the face of this poignant recollection, and of the general attestation by Little of how powerful and humane Winnicott's practice was, it seems somehow carping to criticise its absorption in the illusion that a new mother can ever be found or to argue, as the Kleinian psychoanalyst Hanna Segal does, that such a procedure 'interferes with the psychoanalytic process and the acquiring of insight'.[11] What Little emphasises is Winnicott's absolute presence for her, his continually renewed message to her that he could manage anything she might do, however extreme, and his judicious and very restrained use of interpretation until relatively late in the analysis. Truly a friend in need, demonstrating a mode of listening which is selfless and other-directed to an extent rarely found in human affairs. But is this what a psychoanalyst is for?

The debate here is a fierce one. On the one hand, there are therapists and analysts who argue that the healing process is dependent on the patient being met by a 'real' response, so that she or he can feel cared for and loved – *in loco parentis*, as the object relations therapist Harry Guntrip advocated.[12] If this is achieved, the patient's damaged self will be allowed to flex and grow, finding the strength gradually to face the world. Refusing to respond, being 'abstinent', will be experienced by such patients as a further repudiation, a rejection to add to all the early parental failures which have constituted them as borderline or schizoid individuals in the first place. A psychoanalyst who cannot depart from the rules to give a little tender loving care will produce more, rather than less, fragmentation and despair. On the other hand, the opposed argument goes, the flight to regression involved in provision of a 'corrective emotional experience' feeds into the patient's narcissistic fantasies in a way which might prevent insight occurring. This is because what is important in analysis is the development of a capacity to explore ambivalence, destructiveness and difference – to recognise the way the frustration of our desires provokes despair and hatred, and to find ways of understanding and working with this. The pretence that the patient need not face this but can be totally accepted and loved staves off the achievement of this more integrated state of mind. Moreover, the re-mothering scenario generates anxiety and encourages regression precisely because of the flexibility of its boundaries. As the boundaries do not remain stable, the patient is left uncertain of what can be managed and consequently is left uncontained. Believing that she or he is in a 'real' relationship with the analyst – that she or he has found a new mother – the patient feels abandoned when this illusion can no longer be sustained.

As ever, it is perhaps the polarisation of these views which prevents progress. This is fuelled by the simplistic feminine–masculine analogy adopted by Steiner as by so many other psychoanalysts before him.[13] The feminine is regressive and containing while the masculine is progressive and analysing; maternal versus paternal, pre-Oedipal versus Oedipal. As many psychoanalysts have pointed out, rather than representing a genuine engagement with reality, the fetishising of the Oedipus complex may be more accurately regarded as a juvenile fantasy, a repudiation of complexity. Dumping the feminine is as defensive as hiding in it because it denies the creativity embodied in the tension between these principles. Jessica Benjamin states this as clearly as anyone ever has:

Psychoanalytic theory has, until recently, been unable to think

beyond the Oedipal level. . . . The claim that the Oedipal achievement of complementarity represents a renunciation of
omnipotence and acceptance of limits – being only the one or the
other – misses another dimension, the one that gives depth to the
delineation of difference. It also serves to conceal the unconscious narcissism of Oedipal chauvinism – being the 'only thing'
– for which Freud's theory of the girl as 'little man' *manqué* was
exemplary.[14]

As Benjamin also notes, 'The tension between the omnipotent
wish for transcendence and the affirmation of limits has always
found expression in the domains of aesthetic and erotic pleasure.'[15]
Similarly in the therapeutic arena, it is not one or the other,
containment versus insight, nor even simply the progression from
one to the other (containment to insight, mother to father), but the
pleasure to be found in the tension between being safe and being
challenged, being looked after and being engaged with as an agent.
The analytic process resides in this tension; its staid regularity and
professional conservatism is continually undermined by the fire
with which it plays.

THE LIMITS OF INTERPRETATION

To be fair to John Steiner, it is worth repeating that he acknowledges and indeed draws attention to the circular relationship
between containment and insight. What produces containment in
his account is not just the 'holding' capacity of the setting, but a
certain type of interpretation. In focusing on interpretation, and
despite the protestations of those who would reduce it to a non-
specific mode of communication between analyst and patient,
Steiner is right at the centre of the psychoanalytic tradition.
Laplanche and Pontalis, reviewing the use of psychoanalytic terminology up to the early 1970s, state that 'Interpretation is at the heart
of the Freudian doctrine and technique. Psychoanalysis itself might
be defined in terms of it, as the bringing out of the latent meaning
of given material.'[16]

More formally, Laplanche and Pontalis define and describe interpretation as follows:

(a) Procedure which, by means of analytic investigation, brings
out the latent meaning in what the subject says and does.
Interpretation reveals the modes of the defensive conflict

and its ultimate aim is to identify the wish that is expressed by every product of the unconscious.

(b) In the context of the treatment, the interpretation is what is conveyed to the subject in order to make him reach this latent meaning, according to rules dictated by the way the treatment is being run and the way it is evolving.[17]

Similarly, writing from within the British context and at about the same time, Joseph Sandler and his colleagues define interpretation as 'all comments and other verbal interventions which have the aim of immediately making the patient aware of some aspect of his psychological functioning of which he was not previously conscious'.[18] Although these definitions are both rooted in the non-Kleinian, classical Freudian tradition, they point to some consistent considerations which are central to all psychoanalytic under-standing and practice. At root, psychoanalysis is formulated as a discipline and practice of uncovering latent meanings, of reaching below the surface of action and consciousness to reveal the disturbing elements of unconscious life. Whether this is seen as a mode of causal truth seeking (the trauma, fixation or drive consti-tuting the wish and its necessary repression) or as a hermeneutic enterprise (the network of unconscious meanings which can be accessed through analysis of the confused patterns of emotion and thought experienced by the person), the enterprise shares this crucial characteristic. Interpretation implies an active process of unravelling or, rather, of reaching below. It says, categorically, that things are not as they seem.

Both the definitions given above stress the interpersonal elements of interpretation, at least as constituted 'in the treatment'. Interpretation is not for the analyst alone, rather it is 'what is conveyed to the subject in order to make him reach this latent meaning'; it is a verbal communication with the 'aim of immedi-ately making the patient aware of some aspect of his psychological functioning of which he was not previously conscious'. It is impor-tant to hold onto this perspective, for it differentiates the psychoanalytic use of 'interpretation' from a more general, looser hermeneutics, applicable to all texts. In the broader sense, interpre-tation is simply a method of understanding the constituting meaning of a text of any kind – a film, the transcript of an inter-view, a literary work, an advertisement, the response of a crowd to a football match, a political event. These things need interpreting if one is to go further than merely describing their outward form. How they are interpreted depends on many things, most notably the explanatory framework adopted by the interpreter – social, psychological, even 'psychoanalytic' in the sense of employing notions of unconscious force or fantasy. But where full psychoanalytic interpretation is specific is in its adoption of this 'psychoanalytic' intellectual frame in the context of an evolving relationship between two individuals (or between more individuals, in the case of group analysis). This relationship confers reflexivity on the interpretive process, that is the interpretation has effects which result in changes in the thing interpreted, making the original interpretation immediately out of date. Something is communicated between interpreter and interpreted, between analyst and patient, making it possible for the latter to share and engage with the interpretation which has been offered. Something occurs, therefore, which is more than just revelatory; it is also constructive and transformative. The analyst gives an interpretation, the patient hears it and works on it, absorbing it and making it her or his own. In the process, the patient is changed and something new appears in the place of what was previously an absence, a failure to own or understand the voice which was speaking from within. In this newness, there is more material for interpretation because it is in the nature of human subjectivity that the unconscious is never exhausted and that fantasies keep on pumping away, reimagined and continually active. So, in the language currently fashionable in psychotherapy, constructing new narratives to make sense of the patient's experience is always a provisional process – the very act of articulating a new narrative makes that narrative inadequate because it attempts to pin down something which is fluid and untameable.

One of the great discoveries of psychoanalysis is that human subjectivity is inexhaustible, because it is in the nature of the mind to constantly *work*, to produce new imaginings, desires and fantasies in response to, and in anticipation of, the moment-by-moment encounters each of us has with other people and with the material world. This idea has been given particularly cogent expression in recent work by Cornelius Castoriadis who argues that the Freudian unconscious is a site for constant production of imaginary representations of self and other, that is for fantasy as a constructive and ever-transforming basis for all psychic activity. He claims two 'characteristic features of the human psychism' that mark human versatility (through symbolism and representation) as distinct from the instinctual regulations dominating animal behaviour. These two features are given by Castoriadis as:

1 The autonomization of the imagination, which is no longer enslaved to functionality. . . . There is unlimited, unmasterable representational flux, representational spontaneity without any assignable end . . .
2 The domination, in man, of representational pleasure over organ pleasure.

'There is, therefore,' writes Castoriadis, 'a bursting of man's animal psychism under pressure from the inordinate swelling of the imagination.'[19] If this is correct, if the 'characteristic features of human psychism' derive from the endlessly playful and creative activity of imagination, then no interpretation can ever be a final one, none can be a 'truth'. Instead, interpretation – like language in general – is performative; it is defined in terms of its effects.[20] What interpretation does is to reach below the surface of the patient's consciousness to communicate a message about the relentless flow of fantasy, a kind of shaft down or window into it or, perhaps, a still camera taking a photograph, representing something that was there at that moment; 'true' in an approximate kind of way but never quite to be the same again.

There is a sense, however, in which even provisionality of this degree misses the point. What is being argued here is that interpretation is never truth interpretation. Hence, the assumption of some psychoanalysts that they might be able to 'know' the cause or explanation of a patient's suffering, and particularly that they might offer a 'correct' interpretation of a dream or an impulse or emotion must be misplaced. Psychoanalytic interpretation can never produce this kind of absolute knowledge, partly because human subjectivity is not like that – it is fluid, not fixed – and partly because of the performative nature of interpretation itself. As the word is spoken, so something new comes into being, making what was said obsolete. On the other hand if this lesson is learnt, then a critique of psychoanalysis for its apparent mastery, its ostensible claim to know the patient better than the patient can ever know her or himself, is also redundant. Psychoanalysis is an activity in which the moving target of the patient's subjective experience is sighted and resighted, but never completely pinned down. Although there is a body of claimed knowledge, this acts as a set of guidelines or an heuristic for action; it helps the analyst locate the target – gives the general direction in which to aim – but the atmospheric conditions, the idiosyncrasies and specificities of the individual patient make it impossible ever to know in advance exactly what to do. In any case, once you have done something – made an interpretation – the target shifts and changes shape and you have to start again.

The degree to which the interpretive encounter is *intersubjective* is still not fully expressed in this account. Psychoanalysis is not something which one person does to another. It is, rather, a special kind of *relationship*, something which happens between people; it operates in the interpersonal, communicative domain. 'Psychoanalytic interpretive understanding achieves its full, complete and unique aim when it serves communication between one unconscious and another, through a conscious awareness and understanding of symbolic expressions.'[21]

Some notions of intersubjectivity, particularly those inspired by Kleinian theory, sometimes seem to have an element of mysticism in them, in the sense that they imply that one person might have privileged understanding of another without that understanding being mediated through language or any other explicit symbolisation process. The consequence of this position can be a potentially oppressive practice in which the knowingness of the analyst takes the place of a detailed examination of the symbolic products of the patient – in which, fundamentally, there is no grounding of the relationship between one and the other in anything material happening between them. When interpretation arises from this perspective – the 'automatic' knowledge that the analyst has of the patient, given out by her or his unspoken unconscious emanations (for instance projective identifications) – there is plenty of room for the kind of patronising, precious or moralistic judgements which the more cynical critics of psychoanalysis see as characteristic of the whole approach. Opposing this, however, does not mean discounting the entire interpersonal position and suggesting that one person can never know another or, more to the point, that what happens in psychoanalysis is not interactive and intersubjective. Quite the contrary. The point about interpretation made above is that in its most powerful form it emerges out of the fluid meaning states which cross the boundaries between people, making it possible to explore something new occurring in the interpersonal space – something happening in the area between one subject and another. The correct 'object' of psychoanalytic study and influence is not the individual human psyche, but what happens between people. More precisely, this 'what happens between' is given as something very specific: in the analytic relationship, what happens between patient and analyst, that which is worked on as the focus of analytic activity, is known as the transference.

At the beginning of a famous paper on transference in Freud's 'Dora' case, Jacques Lacan comments as follows on psychoanalysis as a whole:

> What needs to be understood as regards psychoanalytic experience is that it proceeds entirely in this relationship of subject to subject, which means that it preserves a dimension which is irreducible to all psychology considered as the objectification of certain properties of the individual. What happens in an analysis is that the subject is, strictly speaking, constituted through a discourse, to which the mere presence of the psychoanalyst brings, before any intervention, the dimension of dialogue. . . . Briefly, *psychoanalysis is a dialectical experience*, and this notion should predominate when posing the question of the nature of the transference.[22]

Both Freud and Lacan emphasised the strangeness of transference as a phenomenon emerging in the analytic situation.[23] In a professional setting, a staged encounter between a patient speaking of anything she or he wishes and an analyst listening and occasionally commenting, becomes charged with intense emotions and fantasies. The analyst's being, in the mind of the patient, is exaggerated, eroticised, made persecutory or divine, idealised, denigrated, loved or hated. The sober analyst is in most countries dressed in an unremarkable (perhaps shabby) suit if a man or, if a woman, a modest, unrevealing dress (probably not trousers – the whole thing is like a gender-conventional religious order). Yet this nonentity, this anyone, becomes the focus of intense feeling, desire, despair. It certainly is strange, if it can be believed.

One of the features of the psychoanalytic experience to which Lacan draws attention in the quotation above is that it is concerned with a human subject who speaks in analysis. Even if one does not want to accept as a general truth the Lacanian slogan that 'the unconscious is structured like a language', this must be the case within psychoanalysis itself – which is, after all, the only thing that analysts can claim to have any specialist knowledge about. The unconscious appears in the form of the patient's speech – including her or his silences – and nowhere else. Or rather, it appears in the spoken and silent space between analyst and patient, in what the analyst calls forth in the patient and vice versa. 'Psychoanalysis is a dialectical experience'; something new happens in analysis through the speech which passes between patient and analyst. Known as transference, it is a particular form of a general attribute of human relations – that they are infused with imagination, fantasy and desire, and that they are constantly on the move, creating and recreating forms of encounter which stagnate only when they die. Indeed, as Lacan notes perspicaciously in his discussion of psychosis, the refusal to enter into the symbolic order in which one becomes a cultural and linguistic subject – in which one can appreciate the interchange of 'I' and 'you' positions that defines the social order – is what marks out the psychotic state of mind.[24] Not being able to tolerate intersubjectivity, the psychotic patient turns only to the most rigid and repetitive of imaginative scenes, in which what comes from the other has no effect. Kleinians, particularly those using Bion's ideas,[25] read this as a process of fragmentation of the self so that an external environment fantasised as purely persecutory cannot demolish it, but the effect is the same as with the Lacanian view: psychosis allows no access to the intersubjective dimension, to the pooling of feelings and ideas out of which something new and unexpected might emerge.

If the analytic process is understood as a dialectic in which the subjectivity of the patient is created anew through its immersion in an intersubjective space ('the subject is . . . constituted through a discourse'), then transference is the name given to this space and it should no longer be so surprising that it is filled with fantasies, paranoid anxieties and regressive longings. What else could it be filled with, given that these are the stuff of human unconscious functioning? But this view of the transference does stand in opposition to the understanding put forward by some analytic schools. Most significantly, the classical Freudians are not so keen on the imagination as they are on reality. Transference, Sandler and his colleagues write, is 'a *specific illusion* which develops in regard to the other person, one which, unbeknown to the subject, represents, in some of its features, a repetition of a relationship towards an important figure in the person's past'.[26]

The feeling or attitude expressed is 'inappropriate to the present', that is it is unreasonable and does not belong here at all. Clearly, this is in some respects an unexceptionable claim. As noted above, the idea that any particular analyst should deserve the intensity of

feeling lavished upon her or him by many patients is usually ludi-
crous – most people, including most analysts, are not that special.
To some extent, the position or role inhabited by the analyst
explains the discrepancy. Lacan's formula for the analyst as 'the
subject supposed to know' recurs here.[27] As such, the analyst might
be related to with hope, anxiety and dread by the vulnerable
patients seeking out healing or help. But still, it does not usually
take long for a patient to discover that the analyst's virtues do not
lie in what she or he knows, and indeed that the analyst may know
very little of direct relevance to the patient's needs. Yet still they
persevere, these patients, sometimes for years on end, often full of
complaints, sometimes financially impoverished by the analysis,
investing the encounter with this other person with a magical
capacity to transform their lives, even when this is manifestly not
what happens. Certainly, in this sense, the 'specific illusion' developing in the transference is 'inappropriate'.

In another sense, however, it is not. Returning to the quotation
from Castoriadis given above, if the human psyche is characterised
by 'unlimited, unmasterable representational flux, representational
spontaneity without any assignable end', then the invitation to
untrammelled speech which constitutes the analytic encounter is
bound to produce imagination, fantasy and play. 'Representational
spontaneity without any assignable end' is not a mistake, an illusion
about reality; it is what constitutes *psychic* reality from beginning to
end. Despite its origins this notion is akin to, or at least more
consistent with, the Kleinian understanding of transference. Arising
out of the practical considerations of her work with children and
the theoretical implications of her understanding of the ubiquity of
unconscious 'phantasy', transference came to be understood by
Klein as a process in which *current* emotions and parts of the self
were externalised (projected) into the relationship with the analyst
in order primarily to deal with anxiety, but also enabling therapeutic
activity to occur:

> Transference, already regarded as an enactment in the consulting
> room, was now regarded as a re-enactment of current phantasy
> experiences in the way the child's play is a re-enactment of his
> phantasy elaboration of his traumas. . . . The practice of Kleinian
> psychoanalysis has become an understanding of the transference
> as an expression of unconscious phantasy, active right here and
> now in the moment of the analysis.[28]

This does not mean that Kleinians ignore the historical dimension of transference activity. For one thing, Klein stated explicitly that the mechanisms on which transference is based are fundamental aspects of human mental functioning which themselves have origins in infantile psychological processing – projection, paranoid–schizoid functioning, projective identification and so on. Klein states: 'I hold that transference originates in the same processes which in the earliest stages determine object relations.'[29] Just as the infant projects into the mother's breast her or his terrifying destructive phantasies, so the patient uses the analyst as a receptacle for split-off feelings and bits of the self. Moreover, Kleinian technique also stresses a historical, developmental dimension:

> A full transference interpretation should include the current external relationship in the patient's life, the patient's relationship to the analyst, and the relation between these and the relationships with the parents in the past. It should also aim at establishing a link between the internal figures and the external ones. Of course such an interpretation would have to be long and is seldom made fully, but for a transference interpretation to be complete at some point or other those elements should be brought together.[30]

What becomes apparent in the Kleinian mode of understanding and working with the transference is that the Freudian conceptualisation of the transference as a kind of irrational error – a misreading of the present in terms of the past – gives way to a more fluid and fertile understanding in which current emotions and self representations, infused of course by past experiences but nevertheless alive and growing *now*, take precedence. Seen in this way, transference becomes an expression of the impregnation of the analytic relationship with fantasy and desire, with the imaginative flux that constitutes human subjectivity. What transference does is position patient and analyst as elements of the patient's fantasy, externalisations of the inner world of objects and relationships. The boundaries of selfhood dissolve, allowing the analyst direct access to the inner life of the patient.

None of this can be fully understood without considering the other side of the famous therapeutic couplet, transference and countertransference. Freudian psychoanalysis viewed countertransference as the equivalent of the patient's transference. From this perspective, it is a fantasy relationship born out of the 'baggage' carried by the analyst and hence is an interference in the analytic task of introducing a rational appreciation of reality into a version of the world distorted by unconscious, irrational wishes. In terms of technique, the task of the analyst would be 'to reduce manifestations of countertransference as far as possible by means of personal analysis so that the analytic situation may ideally be structured exclusively by the patient's transference'.[31] Interestingly, elements of this view survive in the object-relational claim that a 'real' relationship between analyst and patient is to be aspired to so that fantasies on both sides can be punctured and removed. Winnicott, for example, is quoted as seeing countertransference as the analyst's 'neurotic features which *spoil the professional attitude* and disturb the course of the analytic process as determined by the patient'.[32]

Kleinians, on the other hand, have been much clearer that countertransference is a specific mechanism of therapeutic activity. It is the analyst's guide to what is happening in the fantasy dimension of the therapy and hence is the source of her or his understanding of the patient's emotional and unconscious state. The clearest early formulation of this position can be found in some seminal work by Paula Heimann. Recognising that any specific patient will produce a response in the analyst peculiar to that patient, she argues that by 'comparing the feelings roused in himself with the content of the patient's associations and the qualities of his mood and behaviour, the analyst has the means for checking whether he has understood or failed to understand his patient'.[33] Here, the understanding is that the analyst will have feelings called up by the analytic process, that these will relate to the analyst's own state of mind but that they will also be connected to the patient's mental state, and that it is a possible and important analytic task to distinguish between these two sources of the analyst's response. In tracing the history of the Kleinian focus on countertransference – which, it should be noted, took place despite Klein's own opposition to the idea that the countertransference might be a central tool for understanding the patient – Hinshelwood identifies the following steps:

> (1) The importance of the analyst's feelings as an indicator of the patient's state of mind; (2) the discovery of a normal form of projective identification which is used as a method of *non-*

symbolic communication; (3) cycles of introjective and projective identifications as the basis of an intrapsychic understanding of the interpersonal transference/countertransference situation between analyst and patient; (4) the idea of 'normal' counter-transference; and (5) the importance of the analyst's mind above all else as the significant aspect of the patient's environment.[34]

Without developing all the technical aspects of this scheme, the central ideas can nevertheless be described. The space between patient and analyst is not a gap, but a meeting place into which unconscious feelings, thoughts and wishes are poured and drawn upon. This is an active interpersonal process with contributions from both analyst and patient, but given the structure and intent of the psychoanalytic situation it is the intense unconscious emotions of the patient which are of dominant concern. However, from the point of view of the patient (and much as Steiner describes in his work on 'psychic retreats' described earlier), the capacity of the analyst to hold on and respond to the projections of the patient is of crucial importance. Impacting on the analyst, the patient's projections – whether emotions or parts of the self – become the central sources of feeling, reflection and interpretation. What the analyst does with these, how she or he infuses them with parts of her or his own self, is thus crucial to the progress of the analysis. The technical concern of this orientation to the work is:

> To allow oneself to be guided, in the actual *interpretation*, by one's own counter-transference reactions, which in this perspective are often not distinguished from emotions felt. The approach is based on the tenet that resonance 'from unconscious to unconscious' constitutes the only authentically psycho-analytic form of communication.[35]

Now there is no real distinction between transference and counter-transference, although there are differences of emphasis. The fluid process of encounter is one which has a structure of 'not knowing', that is each unconscious emanation is met with a response, itself partly unconscious, and each response feeds a new emanation. Something happens between patient and analyst and it is certainly strange for it never stands still long enough to be fully known.

This image of the interpersonal encounter embedded in the transference–countertransference cycle is very influential and can be found in some contemporary Freudian as well as Kleinian work. Its implication is that there is a mode of knowing that operates at the unconscious level and is perhaps acting outside of language – although this is a point of dispute between Lacanians and Kleinians, for example. Whether coded symbolically or not, this notion of countertransference suggests that there is an intimate link between patient and analyst centred on the capacity of the analyst to feel unconscious resonance with the patient. The analyst's task becomes that of acting as a receptacle for the patient's unconscious fantasy while remaining anchored in the analyst's own self, so as not to enact the patient's disorder. The analyst is both in and out of her or his self, connected to the patient yet never quite one with her or him. It is in this borderline, this 'hinterland' of unquiet experience, that the resources for analytic activity have to be found.

What has been stressed in the past two chapters is the way psychoanalytic psychotherapy centres on a fluid encounter in which outcomes are of necessity unstable. Psychoanalytic psychotherapy comes to be best understood as a mode of work in which the relationship *is* the effect. No distinction between 'process' (what happens in therapy) and 'outcome' (the changes it produces) can be formally sustained. As patient and analyst move 'in' and 'out' of their selves, new constructions of meaning are continually produced. Looked at this way, psychoanalysis is a process of discovery rather than a treatment. Yet this interpretation still leaves hanging a troublesomely banal but insistent question: if this is the case, how can one ever know if psychoanalytic psychotherapy works? Except for the classic reason of a wish to 'explore the unconscious', why should anyone who really wants help take up this peculiar form of relationship at all? Does it become impossible to find any way of evaluating the worth of psychoanalytic therapy, and if so does this mean that it should be regarded as a medium for spiritual growth rather than as a mode of treatment for psychological distress? In the next chapter, these questions will be explored through a brief encounter with a remarkably unwieldy beast, the literature on psychotherapy research.

Chapter 6

The outcome of psychoanalytic psychotherapy

The complexity of the psychoanalytic treatment project should make it obvious that any simple approach – perhaps any approach at all – to the question of whether psychoanalysis 'works' is doomed to provoke dissension and controversy. This is not just to do with vested interests or with the fact that psychoanalysts are trained to do only this one thing, so that telling them it does not work would not be welcome news. It also represents a genuine epistemological, psychological and social debate: what is the 'cure' in psychoanalysis? Is it really, as some Lacanian work seems to suggest, the repeated asking of questions, the discovery of a voice in which these questions to no one can be pronounced?

> Each time the analyst speaks, interprets in the analytic situation, he gives something asked of him. What he gives, however, is not a superior understanding, but a reply. The reply addresses not so much what the patient says (or means), but his call. Being fundamentally a reply to the subject's question, to the force of his address, the interpretive gift is not constative (cognitive) but performative: the gift is not so much a gift of truth, of understanding or of meaning: it is, essentially, a gift of language.[1]

This is poetic; provocative. It fits with the emphasis on intersubjectivity described in the previous chapter and is congruent with the modern appreciation of the constituting, performative nature of language, within and outside psychotherapy. It emphasises the meaning centredness of psychoanalysis and the way the analyst acts not so much as a healer but as a 'lure', a space or position into which the patient can project her or his distress, receiving back some recognition but no advice. This image of analytic work is intellectually compelling to a considerable degree, but it does nothing for attempts to measure outcome. Does psychoanalysis help people in distress or just reveal to them the impossibility of any cure?

As noted previously, Freud expressed pessimism in some places and optimism in others – a lot will be gained if the ego has more control over unconscious impulses. Is this sufficient, and if so how does one know when it has been achieved? Should analysts be satisfied if and when patients are released from their symptoms or is it crucial to establish improvements in a patient's sense of self, or dream life, or in the arena of 'mature relationships'? Or else, returning to Lacan's provocative critique of psychoanalytic aims, does the patient benefit from the discovery that such mature relationships are impossible? Is the desired outcome measurable in the capacity to tell different stories about experience, or in the achievement of cognitive 'insight', or the acknowledgement that insight is always limited, or the realignment of developmental pathways, or the attainment of creativity, or acceptance that one will never become a psychoanalyst, or acceptance *as* a psychoanalyst? The range of cures and repudiations of cure to be found in the psychoanalytic literature is enormous, making it possible to argue for and against every conceivable position. While this may be reassuring for those who are not looking for simple answers to complicated questions, in a period when publicly funded treatments are increasingly required to be 'evidence based', it poses a host of intellectual and professional problems.

It should be quite clear from all that has gone before that the psychoanalytic process is an interactional one, specific to each analyst–patient pair in their immediate personal encounter, the effects being subtle and not necessarily easily observable. Traditionally, however, outcome studies of psychotherapy have assumed homogeneity in the treatment process across different analyses and have focused on the measurement of changes in patients on a number of observable or rateable clinical criteria. Many such studies of psychoanalysis are difficult to evaluate because of their reliance on symptom checklists and their use of only short-term treatments carried out by inexperienced therapists, conditions which are neither appropriate to nor characteristic of ideal applications of psychoanalytic psychotherapy. All this means that psychoanalysts can quite easily dismiss most empirical research into the effectiveness of their work as misleading and insufficiently grounded in what they actually do or strive to achieve. Nevertheless,

there have been a number of studies, often carried out by psychoanalysts or researchers working within psychoanalytic clinics, in
which attempts have been made to use measures more attuned to
the usual therapeutic aspirations of psychoanalytic psychotherapists. In general, the results of these have been disappointing
enough for one to ask whether the game is worth the candle. Here is
a summary from Judy Kantrowitz:

> There have been six systematic clinical-quantitative studies of
> terminated analyses over the past three decades. These studies
> have involved 550 patients treated in supervised psychoanalysis,
> four or five times a week, by 370 candidates at four different
> psychoanalytic institutes. . . . While these outcome studies varied
> in degree of comprehensiveness and rigour, their findings have
> been strikingly similar. Taken as a group, these studies found: (1)
> given a population preselected as suitable for psychoanalysis, that
> is patients evaluated as having primarily neurotic difficulties who
> were motivated for analysis, almost all patients attained some
> therapeutic benefit following psychoanalysis; (2) only 40 per cent
> of these patients demonstrated an analytic result, that is develop-
> ment and at least partial resolution of the transference neurosis;
> (3) it was not possible to predict in advance either which patients
> would have a successful analytic result or which patients would
> retain their therapeutic gains over time.[2]

As will become clearer below, this is quite a modest statement of
a position of some despair. Looking at the major studies of the
outcome of psychoanalytic psychotherapy carried out by
researchers sympathetic to the aims of such therapy, there is
precious little to suggest that it works. There is, according to
Kantrowitz's review, evidence for *some* therapeutic benefit for
'patients evaluated as having primarily neurotic difficulties who
were motivated for analysis' – that is for those who were not too
disturbed and who believed that psychoanalysis could help them,
and who were compliant with the treatment. However, these
patients did not necessarily improve in the way or through the
means postulated by psychoanalysis, and anyway it was not clear at
the assessment stage who would benefit and by how much.
Extending this last point, a slightly earlier review by Bachrach *et al.*
which criticises the research methodology employed in most studies
but which nevertheless seeks to confirm the effectiveness of psychoanalytic psychotherapy, also notes the impossibility of prediction of

therapeutic effects and the nebulousness of explanations of the impact of therapy when effects are observable:

> The studies . . . suggest that it is necessary to wait until a case is terminated before a true, meaningful assessment of analysability can be made. In fact, it could reasonably be argued that important elements of the desired results of psychoanalysis, such as capacity for self-analysis or enduring shifts in pathological compromise formations, cannot be determined until many years after termination. . . .
>
> The extent and quality of therapeutic benefit and analysability is relatively unpredictable at initial consultation for cases considered suitable for analysis.[3]

From these reviews – which, it should be emphasised again, are *sympathetic* to the project of psychoanalytic psychotherapy – it is quite clear that the empirical evidence leads to discounting analysts' claims either to be able to select patients who might be able to benefit from analysis or to understand why they do change when they do. Indeed, Bachrach *et al.* seem to imply that the only safe measure of 'analysability' is retrospective. Those who benefit from analysis are those who should be seen as analysable; a tautology to delight the heart of the most virulent critic of psychoanalysis.

Whither the three-to-five-times-a-week treatment, stretching sometimes over several years at considerable cost to the public or private purse, totalling hundreds of hours and thousands of pounds or dollars? Here is another view, covering similar ground but perhaps slightly more desperate, arising from a commentary on a symposium devoted to some of the most substantial empirical studies of the outcome of psychoanalysis:

> Although each of the outcome studies reported here has significant problems, we must be struck by the consistency of the findings among the authors, using quite different methodologies. Our capacity to select cases for analysis is poor, with less than half of carefully selected patients ever experiencing an analytic process, however that is defined. Patients show improvement, but it cannot be demonstrated that the improvement is the result of the specific psychoanalytic components of the therapy, and there is excellent evidence that the reverse is true. Patients who see therapists more often and for longer periods do better, but this may only reflect the fact that the patients whom the therapist

likes and feels gratified by and are getting better are the ones he keeps in treatment, or perhaps that there are no clear endpoints to treatment, that we can all get better than we are, and therapeutic relationships are helpful.[4]

Increasingly, reading this material, it seems that psychoanalysis genuinely has nothing to do with cure. This is not only on philosophical grounds antagonistic to the idea of cure ('we can all get better than we are' perhaps being the optimistic version of the broader idea that all psychoanalysis can do is help us live with our ailments), but also on pragmatic grounds: analysis seems to have no specific, predictable effects. All that time and money, all those complicated words and painful silences – and it does not even work.

It is worth spending a little time on the major studies which, even with their 'significant problems', give rise to these conclusions. Perhaps the best known is the Menninger Foundation study of patients seen in analysis, which explored what happened to them over a period of up to thirty years.[5] This cohort of patients was seen initially in the 1950s and each patient was allocated on clinical grounds either to psychoanalytic psychotherapy, 'expressive psychotherapy' or 'supportive psychotherapy'. Unlike many studies the patients were seen for as long as was deemed necessary (in fact, between six months and a dozen years for their initial treatment) and were formally assessed during that period and subsequently. All the patients were followed up after two or three years, many of them remaining in contact with the research project for periods ranging from twelve to twenty-four years beyond termination, and four of them were still in ongoing treatment after thirty years. The most striking finding of this remarkable and honourable study was that there was no evidence of any superior effect of psychoanalytic (or of 'expressive') psychotherapy over supportive therapy. In fact, psychoanalytic psychotherapy had poorer outcomes than expected, while supportive psychotherapy had better effects. In addition, when improvements did occur it was not possible to observe any qualitative differences between changes brought about through and by psychoanalysis, and changes brought about through more supportive means. Wallerstein notes that this contradicts the psychoanalytic expectations that the resolution of unconscious conflicts is necessary for therapeutic improvement and that purely supportive work will have limited effectiveness:

Effective conflict resolution turned out *not* to be necessary for therapeutic change. An almost overriding finding was the repeated demonstration that a substantial range of changes was brought about via the more supportive therapeutic modes cutting across the gamut of declared supportive *and* expressive therapies, and these changes were (often) indistinguishable from the changes brought about by typically expressive-analytic means.[6]

A psychoanalyst he may be, but Wallerstein is too honest to engage in special pleading: 'Just as more was accomplished than expected with psychotherapy, especially in its more supportive modes, so psychoanalysis, as the quintessentially expressive therapeutic mode was more limited than had been predicted.'[7]

Although there have been attempts to reanalyse the Menninger data to identify subgroups of patients who did benefit more from psychoanalysis than from the other treatment conditions,[8] the clear finding from the Menninger work is that there is no evidence for the superiority of psychoanalytic psychotherapy over other forms of psychotherapy, at least for the kinds of therapy carried out in the 1950s and 1960s by relatively inexperienced (but, as time went on, increasingly established) therapists working with fairly needy clients. Moreover, contradicting the claims of this form of psychoanalysis to have very specific effects, particularly in the area of resolution of unconscious conflicts, it seems that a good proportion of the efficacy of psychotherapy was due to its 'supportive' components.

Other similar studies have produced findings broadly in line with those of the Menninger Foundation; that patients generally benefit from psychoanalysis if they are the right kind of patient, but that they also benefit from non-analytic modes of therapy. On the whole, these studies have lacked control groups and should therefore be seen more as 'audits' of the activity of various psychoanalytic training centres than as rigorous research studies. In addition, as has been frequently pointed out,[9] many of these studies rely on the judgement of the treating analyst in assessing degree of change in patients – a judgement which clearly might be biased. While some researchers claim that analysts are more conservative in their willingness to ascribe improvement to their patients than are the patients themselves or outside observers,[10] the opposite seems to be the case where this has been looked at in detail. For instance, in the Boston study of twenty-two patients seen in four-or-five-times-a-week supervised psychoanalysis, analysts were more positive than the patients themselves in their evaluations of outcome, and the patients were in turn more positive than the research team.[11] Making sense of these discrepancies in this particular study is complicated by the fact that the different judges (analysts, patients, researchers) were using different measures and time points for their assessments (analysts making judgements at termination of therapy, patients a year later and researchers on the basis of pre- and post-treatment psychological test data). Nevertheless, it is clear that over reliance on any one method – particularly, perhaps, judgements by analysts – may give only a very partial picture of change.

There has been much interest in the research literature on the question of 'analysability' mentioned earlier (which, translated, means an interest in what kind of patients benefit from psychoanalytic psychotherapy) and the means by which patient benefit is achieved. Basically, the conventional research studies throw very little light on this question other than to confirm the Menninger finding that 'supportive' elements of psychotherapy are more important than is traditionally acknowledged. The Boston study examined four variables 'most commonly agreed upon as essential qualities for analyzability'. These were 'reality testing, level and quality of object relations, affect availability and tolerance, and motivation for analysis'.[12] None of these four variables, assessed prior to analysis either alone or in combination, were predictive of degree of improvement in psychoanalysis: 'neither the initial level of psychopathology nor the number of years in analysis was related to the outcome of treatment'.[13] Following up seventeen of these patients ten years after the end of therapy, it was clear that several of them had retained their treatment gains or had improved further, but there again seemed to be no reliable bases on which to predict who might improve. In particular, there was no evidence to support the psychoanalytic idea that resolution of the 'transference neurosis' might be important nor that the attainment of a 'self-analytic function' was what carried them through. Rather, positive outcome was connected with a host of factors, different from one case to another,

> For some former patients, continuing self-analytic work and accruing insight were of great emotional benefit; for some, the sense of well-being and comfort gained from re-evoking their former analyst in fantasy at times of stress seemed far more important. For others, benefit came from a combination of acquiring insight into unconscious factors and maintaining a

mental representation of a supportive relationship, though there were few patients in this study who described this total process as having occurred.[14]

On the other hand, ten of the seventeen patients who were followed up had returned for further psychotherapy in the intervening period, though it is a moot point whether this should be regarded as success or failure.

In contrast to the Boston finding of no relationship between length of therapy and outcome, the Columbia records project, which looked at '295 analyses, 172 analytic psychotherapies, and 114 psychosomatic patients treated by psychotherapy conducted between 1945–1961', identified treatment length as the only variable associated either with what was termed 'analysability' (judged from a questionnaire completed by the treating analyst at termination) or therapeutic benefit. There was also a relationship between analysability and therapeutic benefit, but as less than half the analytic patients were judged to have developed an 'analytic process', this effect was weak.[15] Basically, this large sample of relatively young, neurotic, middle-class, well-educated patients did well if they stayed in therapy.[16]

Kantrowitz comments that the patients treated by psychoanalytic psychotherapy in the Boston study had improved on all measures, but that it was not possible to establish how this improvement had occurred. It should be added that, as there was no control group, it is also not possible to establish whether they improved more than they would have done without treatment or through some other means of therapy. The results of the Menninger study suggest that the answer to this question is likely to be that other forms of psychotherapy would have been just as effective. In their review, Bachrach *et al.* state that the research literature is:

> consistent with the accumulated body of clinically derived psychoanalytic knowledge, e.g. patients suitable for psychoanalysis derive substantial therapeutic benefit; analyzability and therapeutic benefit are relatively separate dimensions and their extent is relatively unpredictable from the perspective of initial evaluation among seemingly suitable cases.[17]

It should be apparent that even this rather conservative claim reflects an over-optimistic reading of the literature, particularly as it is not at all clear *in advance* which patients are 'suitable for psychoanalysis', other than that they are probably just as suitable for other types of therapy. However, the failure of the resounding research 'no' to psychoanalysis to penetrate Bachrach *et al.*'s review is characteristic of most responses from psychoanalysts. It seems quite clear that very few people have ever given up psychoanalytic practice because the research evidence suggests that it is an unreliable procedure, although it is probable that some at least have stopped because they could not make it work. Still, the point is that despite this failure of researchers wedded to psychoanalysis to demonstrate its effectiveness, the profession grinds on, its fees charged and paid, its training institutes still in demand. What is going on here?

As many others have done, Bachrach *et al.* point to endemic weaknesses in the research, which reduce the power of its findings. These weaknesses include failure to ensure that what is being investigated is good quality therapy (most of it, in studies, is carried out by trainees of varying degrees of experience), use of inappropriate patients, or over-reliance on measures of change based on the judgement of interested parties, such as the treating analyst. In research on long-term therapy, there are additional problems generated by the relative lack of a clear, predetermined focus (work in, say, the fourth year of therapy might be carried out on different issues from those which dominated at the beginning) and the difficulty of finding appropriate comparison treatments.[18] For these reasons and others it is not difficult for analysts to argue that the research misrepresents their activities – especially as, in the nature of things, the large outcome and long-term follow-up studies outlined here involve analyses carried out two or three decades ago, using techniques rather different (it is said) from those which might be employed today. In reply, one could suggest that if psychoanalysts are so convinced that what they do is worthwhile and is not properly evaluated by this research, then it is about time they carried out a study without these methodological weaknesses. However, as they tend to be busy making a living, this is perhaps a forlorn hope. Unfortunately for psychoanalysis, public purchasing decisions concerned with psychotherapy provision look more rather than less likely to be directed by evaluative evidence in the future and there is a limit to the length of time (almost a century, in the case of psychoanalysis) for which a therapy can be deemed 'insufficiently researched' yet still promising.[19]

Even with its important methodological limitations, the outcome research literature is clearly damaging to the claims made by psychoanalysis that it is an effective treatment for psychological problems. Research carried out by people sympathetic to psychoanalysis – who are often psychoanalysts themselves – has generated very few findings which support the efficacy of psychoanalytic psychotherapy, its superiority to alternative treatments or its capacity to select appropriate patients. As a 'treatment' – something aimed at relieving symptoms with minimum dose and maximum efficiency – psychoanalysis can be judged a failure. It is expensive, drawn out and unreliable. It must be admitted that other forms of therapy are not much better at 'treating' many problems, but with some they clearly are.[20] Analysts, immersed in their day-to-day work, and impressed with the poignant and powerful material which faces them all the time, often seem to believe that they 'know' that what they do works, so they do not need to depend on – or even take note of – empirical research findings. However, one could just as easily, and with more justification, argue that everyone 'knows' it does not work, so all the case studies in the literature can be ignored, written off as instances of believers talking to one another. When one steps back and really looks at it, a hundred years of therapeutic endeavour has established very little indeed.

There is obviously something seriously amiss here. The theory and practice of psychoanalytic psychotherapy has such verve and complexity, it addresses the subtlety and diversity of psychological conflicts with such unusual inventiveness and it holds the 'person' in mind in such a principled manner, that one feels it must be doing something more than the outcome research suggests. Even if the scientific claims made by psychoanalysis (for example that therapeutic improvement is a function of increased insight) are unsupported, one might think that the remarkably provocative interpersonal structure by which psychoanalytic psychotherapy is constituted must itself have effects. That is, even if (for example) the theory of neurosis is 'wrong', acting *as if* it is meaningful must surely do something? Psychoanalysis may not be an effective 'treatment' in conventional terms, but it could still have significance and be effective as a way of 'treating' people and of forging a relationship which produces difference, making something new happen.

The argument here is a tense one. Is it so unreasonable to ask for evidence of effectiveness when counting symptoms, measuring changes in mental health and looking for improvements in adaptive functioning? On the other hand, if the paucity of data supporting psychoanalysis as a mode of treatment led to it being written off altogether, would not a unique and precious procedure for making sense of disturbance be lost? Perhaps the problem lies in trying to couple the investigatory, analytic stance with any expectation of therapeutic improvement; understanding may not have anything to do with change after all. This would support the idea that the complex, interpersonal nature of the psychoanalytic enterprise leads both to a variegated and unstable notion of improvement or cure and to a version of the psychotherapeutic process which is radically at odds with attempts to measure quantity of change, with or without controls. But turning the argument back on itself again, if this is the case – if psychoanalytic psychotherapy has little to do with 'outcome' as usually discussed and more to do with the enrichment of people's lives through involvement in a new type of relationship – perhaps it should cease claiming a place in the industry devoted to treating psychological disturbance. Something is in the wrong place. Either it is psychoanalysis, pretending to be what it is not; or it is psychotherapy research, asking the wrong questions and getting meaningless answers. Or possibly, of course, it is both.

PROCESS AND CHANGE

Staggering under the weight of uninterpretable and disappointing outcome findings, psychotherapy researchers have turned their attention to questions of 'process'. A way into this discussion is offered again by Kantrowitz's review of the Boston study, in which she describes a finding she regards as crucial, but which emerged incidentally and hence could not be formally claimed as a research outcome nor properly explored,

> The most striking finding to emerge from the Boston study was the impact of the interface of personal characteristics of the analyst and the patient on the outcome of the analytic process. . . . The descriptions offered by patient-analyst pairs suggest that the impact of their similarities and differences over time is likely to be more important in terms of the outcome of analysis than characteristics of either patient or analyst which are recognisable at the outset.[21]

Kantrowitz is particularly interested in aspects of the patient–analyst match which might impinge on the transference–countertransference cycle to promote or impede the progress of psychotherapy.[22] This is obviously an important issue that gives the lie to claims of complete analytic neutrality; actual characteristics of the analyst matter and may have differential effects on different patients – a finding unlikely to surprise any but the most doctrinaire of practitioners. More to the point, however, is the ground this opens out in research terms. Acknowledging that what occurs in psychoanalysis is something worked on between (for sake of argument) two people struggling together to communicate and produce meaning, implies that research has to be mounted at a level sensitive to the nuances of language and the idiosyncrasies of particular therapist–patient relationships. In the language of earlier chapters, this demands the development of an informed hermeneutic approach to psychotherapy research which attempts to describe, model and explain the operation and impact of psycho-analytic psychotherapy as an intersubjective process. This is not a licence to say that research is irrelevant. Rather, it is an attempt to identify the sort of research which might actually bear witness to psychoanalysis, making it possible to evaluate its strengths and weaknesses in ways more subtle than are available through the conventional outcome research literature.

There is a tradition of 'process research' in psychotherapy, in which the focus has been on those aspects of therapist and patient personality, behaviour and interaction which are related to outcome. The underlying assumption of much of this research is that, since evaluative studies have shown a generally modest positive impact of psychotherapy of all kinds, it is far fetched to imagine that the effective components are the unique property of any one 'brand-name' psychotherapy. Instead, there is likely to be a set of common elements ('active ingredients') which cut across all schools of psychotherapy and are the source of therapeutic improvements. The differences between psychotherapies then reduce to differences in the languages employed to code these active ingredients; that is to the extent that they are effective, psychotherapies differ mainly in their packaging. There is a range of findings in this area, mostly connecting outcome with aspects of the patient's attitudes to the therapist,[23] but the most influential account of them has been that of Orlinsky and Howard, published in the third edition of Garfield and Bergin's *Handbook of Psychotherapy and Behavior Change*. Reviewing thirty-three published studies on the topic, they found five treatment processes which were apparently, in their language, 'effectively therapeutic'. These were:

1 'The patient's and therapist's therapeutic bond';
2 'Certain therapeutic interventions, when done skilfully with suitable patients';
3 'Patients and therapists focusing their interventions on the
   patient's feelings';
4 'Preparing the patient adequately for participation in therapy
   and collaborative sharing of responsibility';
5 'Within certain limits, having more rather than less
   therapy'.[24]

This is a summary statement of the strongest effects found in a
voluminous literature on process-outcome relationships. It has been
an important contributor to the argument that psychotherapy
works and that it can be understood to work through specifiable
and stable interpersonal means. By the time of the *Handbook*'s
fourth edition in 1994, a vast number of studies on process-outcome
relations were available for the updated review. Orlinsky *et al.* list
these as generating '2354 separate findings' and claim that these
represent 'a new stage of development in research-based knowledge
about psychotherapy'.[25] Orlinsky *et al.* argue that there are some
consistent findings from the research which need to be taken seriously by all clinicians. In summary again, these are taken under a
few generic headings as follows:

1 **Therapeutic contract**   Findings 'strongly imply that if an appropriately prepared patient who is viewed as suited to the form of
   the treatment in question becomes actively engaged in talking to
   a therapist who is seen as skilful, the result of therapy will be
   viewed as beneficial'.
2 **Therapeutic operation**   Evidence supports a focus on life problems and core personal relationships, experiential confrontation
   and interpretation.
3 **Therapeutic bond**   'The strongest evidence linking process to
   outcome concerns the *therapeutic bond* or alliance.'
4 **Self relatedness**   'Equally strong evidence links outcome to
   patient openness versus defensiveness.' Therapists should therefore
   work at enhancing the patient's capacity to 'make a constructive
   contribution to their own treatment'.
5 **In-session impact**   'A consistent relation of *therapeutic realiza-
   tions* (patients' positive in-session impacts) to outcome is
   evident from every process perspective except that of therapists.'

6 **Sequential flow** 'A large body of findings already indicates that longer *treatment duration* is very generally (though not linearly) associated with better outcome.'[26]

On the face of it, this review material provides some compelling evidence for the importance of a number of process variables in psychotherapy, broadly defined. Several of these might apply to psychoanalysis, particularly those branches which stress the importance of the therapeutic alliance. Psychoanalytic therapy tends to be relatively long-term, to focus on core personal relationships, deal directly with the patient's attitude to therapy and change, and work in the 'here and now' so that 'in-session impacts' are maximised. However, there are some caveats to take into account. First, there remains considerable controversy among psychotherapy researchers about the status of the claims made in reviews of this kind. For example, in a recent re-examination of the studies on which Orlinsky and Howard based their conclusions, Shapiro *et al.* concluded that there was in fact a very small 'effect size' (a statistical measure of the relative impact of a variable) of therapist interventions on outcome. They comment:

> Although some interventions appeared more effective than others, these differences were virtually abolished by statistical control for methodological features of studies, several of which were significantly related to the effect size obtained. These findings suggest that traditional methods of conducting and aggregating process-outcome studies have not yielded strong evidence for the efficacy of therapist interventions.[27]

In the case of *psychoanalysis*, the evidence concerning effective process variables is particularly weak, even though there are numerous studies (many of which seem not to go much further than the 'preliminary' stage) and some very sophisticated measurement instruments such as Lester Luborsky's 'core conflictual relationship theme' approach to transference, or Mardi Horowitz's extensive research on 'configurational analysis' for psychodynamic formulations.[28] For example, reviewing the empirical studies of transference interpretations for the Bergin and Garfield *Handbook*, William Henry, Hans Strupp *et al.* reach what they describe as 'the following tentative conclusions':

1 'There is little sound evidence linking the frequency of interpretive activity to superior outcomes. In fact, several studies have

linked greater frequency of transference interpretations to poorer outcomes.'

2 'Transference interpretations do not necessarily repair poor alliances and may damage the existing alliance.'

3 'Transference interpretations do not elicit differentially greater affective response or necessarily increase depth of experiencing when compared to nontransference interpretations or other interventions.'

4 'Interpretations are more likely to elicit defensive responding than other types of interventions.'

5 'The average level of therapist accuracy may be much lower than assumed.'

6 'Transference interpretations followed by affective patient responding do seem related to positive outcome.'

7 'Therapist skill may make a difference.'

8 'The effectiveness of transference interpretations is a function of numerous interacting variables.'[29]

There is little here to gladden the eye of a psychoanalyst, with the possible exception of items six and seven. Transference interpretations, the meat of psychoanalytic technique, are – if anything – linked to poor outcomes. They do not have a beneficial effect on the relationship between analyst and patient, they are not superior to other interventions in terms of their affective impact, they are likely to produce defensive responses and they are frequently inaccurate. Once again, a great deal of research work seems to produce at best lukewarm findings, with plenty of fodder for those who wish to pick psychoanalysis apart.

It seems apparent that, as with the general outcome studies outlined above, and despite an enormous amount of research endeavour, traditional methods of process-outcome research have not supplied any convincing demonstrations of links between aspects of the therapeutic process in psychoanalysis and change. Why might this be? The simplest explanation, of course, would be that no such links exist, that psychotherapeutic practice has no significant bearing on the results of therapy, which depend upon non-specific features of the therapeutic setting or – more probably – the life circumstances of individual patients. Psychoanalytic psychotherapy, with its complex mode of theory and practice, is an expensive way of accompanying a suffering individual along their life trajectory while they do or do not sort themselves out.

Variations in the process of psychotherapy might conceivably make a difference to the likelihood that a patient will continue coming to see her or his analyst, with attendant benefits for the analyst, but there is little evidence to suggest a specific relationship between anything that the analyst does or any attribute she or he possesses, and the eventual outcome. The extensive training and supervision regimens, the debates and splits over points of doctrine and minutiae of practice – these characteristic attributes of psychoanalytic institutions all merely inculcate knowledge of ritual, of how to pray to the Unconscious, but they do not actually have any material effects.

There is much force in this cynical argument. Of course, it is possible for analysts and other psychotherapists to query the extent to which alternative modes of treatment have established good outcomes, in the treatment of psychopathologies but also in wider medical treatments. The 'hit rate' of general medicine in many areas is not that high and the research which has been carried out on physical treatments is in many instances neither as substantial nor as convincing (even) as the psychotherapy outcome research. It is in this context, and only in this context, that the following claim from Howard *et al.* makes sense: 'It seems that psychotherapy is the best documented medical intervention in history. No other medical intervention has anywhere near the empirical scientific support that psychotherapy enjoys.'[30] Given what has gone before, this should make any rational person even more cautious than they are at present about taking medical advice, but it is not really an argument that can be taken seriously in defending psychotherapy. Just because no one knows sufficiently well when and how treatment X works, it does not justify adoption of the equally unsupported treatment Y – although there is an interesting sociological and psychological question to be asked about why treatment X should continue to be prescribed in an unchallenged way, while treatment Y is abused by anyone who cares to enter the fray.

There is another approach to all this, however, which is perhaps more illuminating of the endeavour to make rational judgements about the strengths and limitations of psychoanalytic psychotherapy. As argued above, the large-scale audits of the effects of psychoanalysis on patients have indicated that many patients benefit but that they do not do so markedly more than patients receiving other forms of psychotherapy. There are, in addition, no strong empirically established guidelines for predicting which patients will improve as a result of psychoanalysis, nor is it really known how and why they change when they do – although theorising on this is one of the major preoccupations of the analytic literature. Traditional process research has not helped either. Correlating the behaviour and attributes of groups of therapists with the outcome of psychotherapy for groups of patients has produced very meagre and unstable findings – little more, in fact, than the suggestion that patients who get on well with their therapists and who (therefore?) stay in therapy for a reasonable amount of time, do better than those who do not. However, what is being lost sight of in this is the operation of psychoanalytic psychotherapy as a specific encounter between one person and another in and through which the significant meanings dominating the patient's life can be reconstructed. That is, what is much harder to track through the kinds of group-based research represented so far in this chapter, is the 'hermeneutic dimension', the way psychoanalysis acts to offer re-readings of subjectivity in the heat of an intense personal relationship. This does not mean that it is free from the requirement that it should be of benefit, but it does suggest that large-scale correlational studies might not be the best way of gaining access to an understanding of what, in the analytic situation, is going on.

Elliott and Anderson voice this familiar complaint in the context of a critique of traditional research philosophies:

> As therapists, we know that psychotherapy is a complex process. For example, we know that some events are more important than others, that many very different things happen in therapy, that context is absolutely crucial, that communications usually have more than one meaning, and that clients often surprise us with what they find important or helpful. We also know that we have learned far more about how to do therapy from descriptive accounts (by writers, supervisors and clients) than from the quantitative results of psychotherapy research. However, when we act as therapy researchers, we typically ignore this knowledge, following instead the simplifying assumptions we learned in graduate school as part of our positivist research tradition.[31]

The emphasis, seen in this quotation, on the complexity and context dependence of psychotherapy is now rapidly becoming characteristic of psychotherapy process research. Continuing in a cynical vein, one might suggest that this is because the research has failed to support psychotherapy, particularly of a psychoanalytic variety, and so those with a vested interest in it are trying to find alternative ways around the problem. However, this really would be not just unfair, but neglectful of some very significant points about both the research process and the nature of psychoanalytic psychotherapy. In particular, it would entail accepting at face value the mechanistic modes of research traditionally employed in the psychotherapy arena, when what has become increasingly clear over recent years is that a new, meaning-driven set of research interests and methodologies is required in this and related areas if important questions about psychology are ever to be satisfactorily addressed.

In Chapters 2 and 3, it was argued that psychological research has to take much fuller account of subjectivity, of reactive and reflexive processes, and of hermeneutics if it is to escape from the reductive and trivialising procedures and models by which it has been characterised for far too long. Movements towards narrative and discursive work within social psychology were compared with psychoanalysis and it was argued that the congruence to be found there is not accidental, but reflects a shared concern with interpretation, textual construction and discovery orientation. In psychotherapy process and outcome research, the same argument holds. The mechanistic model of research, in which attempts are made to identify simple contributing variables that impact on outcome, misreads the very complex and circular input–output relations which dominate the psychotherapeutic encounter. Therapy of the psychoanalytic kind does not reduce to the application of specific techniques with separable and measurable effects. Rather, as has been argued in this chapter and the last, it is a complex and recursive process of meaning generation, taking place in a very fluid linguistic and interpersonal environment. 'Process' of this kind cannot be captured by the static, decontextualised measurement procedures of conventional positivist research paradigms. As Elliott and Anderson note in the preceding quotation, this is obvious to anyone who works clinically in this way, but seems to be forgotten when they become researchers.

Employing an influential metaphor, Stiles and Shapiro describe the dominant approach to psychotherapy research as adopting the 'drug metaphor', in which it is assumed that the treatment package is made up of stable and specifiable active and inert 'ingredients', with the task of the researcher being to identify which are which in order to maximise the former and remove the latter.[32] The clearer one can be about which ingredients are 'active', the clearer will be one's prescriptions about what should go into effective psychotherapeutic interventions. If, for example, the optimal balance of transference versus non-transference interpretations could be established as X to Y, then that could be incorporated into the training manuals which are beginning to proliferate in this field. Stiles, Shapiro and colleagues have devoted a considerable amount of energy to articulating the components of the drug metaphor and then demonstrating its fallaciousness. They argue that at least one of the following assumptions is to be found in the vast majority of process-outcome studies of psychotherapy:

> (a) that process and outcome are readily distinguishable from, and bear a simple cause–effect relationship to, one another; (b) that component names refer to ingredients of consistent content and scope; (c) that the potentially active ingredients are known and measured or manipulated; (d) that the active ingredients are contained in the therapist's behaviour, with the patient in a correspondingly passive role; (e) that the dose-response curve is ascending and linear in the range being examined; and (f) that the best way to demonstrate a psychotherapeutic procedure's efficacy is by controlled clinical trial. Finally ... the common methodological assumption that a process component's efficacy is shown by its correlation with outcome.[33]

In fact, all these assumptions are highly questionable. 'Process', as a measure of what happens in the psychotherapy session, may itself be an aspect of 'outcome' or a product of 'outcomes', as where a patient begins to feel benefits and consequently invests more in the sessions, or where a therapist sees that a particular patient responds well to a trial interpretation and so increases the frequency with which these interpretations are given. 'Component names' are not unequivocally linked to 'ingredients' which are always the same and 'dosage' issues are very difficult to specify in psychoanalytic psychotherapy. A transference interpretation on the part of one therapist may be milder or longer or more comprehensive than that by another and may vary greatly from one patient (say, a compliant one) to another (a hostile, paranoid one). Consequently, statements about what the constituents of a therapy might be can only be made in specific contexts, not in any general way. As Stiles *et al.* also point out, what is an 'active' ingredient may be impossible to know. While measuring one class of behaviours (to follow the example, transference interpretations), one might miss innumerable other utterances and behaviours of both therapist and patient, without having any empirical means of establishing which of those could be of significance:

> A crucial assumption in the clinical trial of a drug is that the investigation is manipulating or at least measuring the biologically active ingredients. Therapists and clients emit an enormous variety of verbal and nonverbal behaviours within psychotherapy sessions, and researchers have no assurance that those aspects not measured in a given study are inert.[34]

In addition, studies focused only on the 'input' of the therapist tend to ignore the contribution of the patient, thus missing the interpersonal element which is central to all psychoanalytic approaches. More generally, psychoanalytic (and many other) modes of psychotherapy are to a large degree custom built, organised around the very specific interaction between a patient and a therapist, whose usual procedures may be specifiable in outline but will also vary in form, intensity and focus as a complex product of the evolving relationship with that particular patient. Treating this multi-layered process as if it was a drug, a treatment to be administered or 'given', knocks the life out of it and makes the research studies devoid of any meaningful content.

In Chapters 2 and 3, the argument proposed for a psychological 'science' was that it should be based on a discovery-oriented approach in which what is made primary is the search for meanings, for interpretable patterns of order and understanding. Again, this applies equally to research into psychoanalytic psychotherapy. The process of change is too slippery to be pinned down by gross categories of therapist behaviour and patient response; as has often been noted, the only reliable finding to derive from such work is that our understanding of how change in psychotherapy occurs is meagre.[35] Tighter observation linked to moment-by-moment changes across therapies described in great detail is needed to make more sense – one is tempted to say, more literary sense – of what happens in the analytic situation. To use a much-abused term, this requires a more 'exploratory' approach, less constrained by the search for unique and stable outcomes consistent with some pre-given theory. Howard and Orlinsky argue in a related manner in a paper which seems to represent a renunciation of their earlier process-outcome review work:

No matter what the methodology, clinical research has to be judged ultimately on the basis of its informativeness. It is clearly self-defeating to espouse a methodology that we must always fail to properly implement. . . . Instead, we recommend the adoption of more exploratory methodology and a greater emphasis on the generalisability and constructive *replication* of findings.[36]

Exploratory methodology will be descriptive and will not attempt to link arbitrarily isolated 'process variables' with equally arbitrary outcome assessments, but instead will attend to tracking the in-session and out-session interactions and changes occurring in individual cases at a level of complexity which is clinically meaningful. Flinging data around does not solve any problems, even if it gives work to computer programmers.

At the centre of much of this debate is the issue of language and its functions in the therapeutic encounter. 'Empathy', 'transference interpretations' and other therapist activities are essentially linguistic in the way they appear in the therapeutic situation; traditional research methods deal with these in a decontextualised way. Research that treats therapist interventions as stable and regular inputs to patients who are not distinguishable from one another is based on a version of language as transparent and mechanical. What this means is that the words used by the therapist are viewed as the carriers of ideas – 'inputs' – which always have the same meaning and which consequently can have regular effects across different circumstances and different patients. What this misses is the contemporary understanding of language as productive and constructive – as having 'performative' properties – so that something new comes into play every time an utterance is made. In this way of understanding things, the play of speech on speech that constitutes psychoanalytic psychotherapy and other 'talking cures' is something creative and unpredictable, its meaning constructed as it goes along, fluid and non-replicable in its form. The following quotation, taken from an appeal for a more theory-based, more contextually subtle mode of researching psychotherapy, expresses this idea clearly:

It is hard to see how the therapist's meaning in using a particular utterance could be discerned without the use of contextual information – at a minimum the immediate sociolinguistic context of the patient–therapist discourse! Treating the therapist's utterance as a statistical unit would seem to entail the unit be considered in terms of its structural, situationally invariant features such as its grammatical form, or in terms of its situationally invariant semantic meaning (e.g., 'Yeah, what a truly brilliant guy' could not mean in any context 'What an intellectual rogue!'). In other words one would at best be studying the meaning of isolated utterances, rather than the meanings intended by the speaker, since the latter intended meanings are always constrained by – as they define and are embedded in – the discourse situation and all of its protean particularities.[37]

Psychoanalysis acknowledges and even privileges the constructive and variable properties of language through its emphasis on fantasy and, in the therapeutic situation, transference. The analyst speaks, the patient speaks and what they say can be inscribed, transcribed, compared with other statements, classified and counted. But the meaning of the speech is utterly dependent on the context at a large number of levels: the fact that the encounter is defined as 'therapeutic', the position of the particular session from which the speech is drawn in a continuing therapy (whether at the beginning, middle or near the end, for example), but most importantly and most elusively, the patterns of fantasy which surround the analyst–patient relationship. As every utterance is made, it impacts upon and contributes to the restructuring of the relationship and it is also understood only in the context of that relationship – this context being mainly not its 'real' characteristics but those which are unconsciously ascribed to it. So, taking Russell's simple example, 'Yeah, what a truly brilliant guy' might mean virtually anything, depending on its context – not just what has gone before, but the whole structure and standing of the fantasy web in which the transference is inscribed. 'I wish I was brilliant', 'You are brilliant', 'You are useless', 'He's a charlatan', 'You're a charlatan', 'I am attracted to him', 'I wish I were like you', 'I wish I were you' – these are all plausible interpretations of this one, apparently transparent sentence. A potential response from the analyst might be: 'I wonder if you think I am clever enough to understand you?' This is clearly a transference interpretation but it only makes sense in the context of an analyst's idea that a patient may be struggling with the question of who is 'brilliant' and who is not, and that his possibly ironic previous statement should be met with an acknowledgement that it includes derogation of the therapist. In another situation, the words might mean something else and how they are heard by the patient is an altogether more complex issue.

None of this means that recording and classifying analyst interventions is a useless activity. For example, looking at the frequency of transference interpretations may be a way of characterising the practice of different analysts or of establishing something about the differing demands made by different patients. But it does show the futility of relying on that kind of research for an understanding of the analytic process and hence the impossibility of moving from it to any clear measure of the relationship between therapist 'intervention' and 'outcome'. Psychoanalytic psychotherapy is not a beast of that kind; it is a way of exploring a semantic space, constructed and reconstructed in every move made by patient and analyst, deeply complex, multilayered, heavily contextualised, obscure and performative. Its effects are clearly unpredictable and its process in some ways even more so, not because of huge variations in what individual analysts do – they probably behave in a fairly standardised way, given the training regimen – but because the meanings of these actions, these statements, are fluid and multiple. Moreover, they are inexhaustible. As a patient reflects on what has been said, it could change shape; the fantasies around it could alter and apparently trivial comments become significant, meaningful interpretations lose their bite. Understanding that psychoanalytic psychotherapy is a performance, an interpersonal event, means giving up the idea that input–output research will ever satisfactorily contain or explain it.

This leaves us with a deep and uncomfortable conundrum. There is little evidence supportive of psychoanalytic psychotherapy's effectiveness as a treatment approach and equally weak data on the components of psychotherapy which may be related to outcome. This can be read, with some justification, as an indication that psychoanalysis should be renounced as a therapy. Alternatively, there are also strong grounds for arguing that no meaningful data could be expected from the kind of research which has dominated the field and that the strengths of psychoanalysis will only become evident when much more subtle, idiographic and discursive research procedures are more widely employed. One could say that until then psychoanalysis should continue; after all, it is so thoughtful and full of such integrity that it can do no harm. Or one could say that it is about time that psychoanalysts stopped hoodwinking people into believing that their fancy language and arcane practices have a rational basis – if psychoanalysts believe they have an effective method of therapy, the onus is on them to demonstrate it. On the other hand, if they do not do so and we throw psychoanalysis away, will we not have lost one of the most inventive and fertile procedures to have emerged out of modern psychology? Is it all a game, this endless conversation between patient and analyst, the one wallowing in fantasy, the other pretending to understand but both knowing they are merely keeping each other in business? Or is it that, as one person touches the other through thoughts and words, the results are unpredictable but that this is as it should be – that psychological 'treatment' is not a pill but a multifaceted, unreliable, moral and intimate contact which might produce change, but then again might not?

Part III

Society

Chapter 7

Psychoanalysis and the politics of identity

Up to now, the concern of this book has been with the standing of psychoanalysis as a body of theory and as a clinical discipline. This has very often represented the limits of formal attempts to evaluate psychoanalysis: how well do its theories stand up to logical or empirical scrutiny, how effective is it as a mode of therapy? What is equally important is to develop an evaluative stance towards the engagement of psychoanalysis with the world outside the consulting room – its non-clinical 'applied' aspect. Such applications have been part and parcel of psychoanalysis from the beginning, ranging from Freud's explorations of art, culture and society,[1] through the political, literary and psychobiographical writings of critics such as Lionel Trilling, Herbert Marcuse and Erich Fromm during the 1950s and 1960s, to contemporary psychoanalytic explorations of art, literature and politics. On the way, psychoanalysts and psychoanalytically informed writers have concerned themselves with questions of artistic creativity, destructiveness, war, femininity and feminism, social policy, geography, political theory – and virtually every other element in the firmament of the humanities and social sciences.[2]

The tradition of psychoanalytically informed social theory has been lively and productive, generating some of the most challenging and innovative thinking in psychoanalysis. Its relationship to the clinical sphere, however, has been an awkward one. Some writers, such as Michael Rustin, identify the clinical as the most important arena from which to draw insights and theories which can then be used to make sense of social phenomena. Others, like Marcuse and Russell Jacoby, have rejected clinical psychoanalysis, seeing it as a place of compromise and defeat in which the radical potential of psychoanalytic theory becomes defused by the familial ideology of bourgeois culture. Clinical psychoanalysis has, on the whole, gone its own way, neglecting or ignoring what is often seen as the wild speculations of political and cultural theorists, especially if they are not themselves actually psychoanalysts. Or rather, what is visible in the operations of the psychoanalytic 'establishment' is a process of paternalistic approval for applications of psychoanalysis congruent with already existing orthodox psychoanalytic theory, with little engagement with the implications of disjunctive theory – in much the same way as empirical findings supportive of psychoanalysis are recycled endlessly, while contradictory findings are often ignored or interpreted away.

There are, however, a number of areas where the encounter of psychoanalytic theory with social practice has profound and unavoidable consequences for the activities of psychoanalysts in the consulting room and for the standing of psychoanalysis in the wider world. Characteristically, these are marked by a dual relationship between psychoanalysis and society in which psychoanalysis is looked to for accounts of social phenomena which need explanation, and also, conversely, in which the adequacy of its treatment of these phenomena is subjected to social scrutiny. At various times, depending on the state of the social order, different types of social phenomena come to the fore, for example war, delinquency, family breakdown, prejudice, authoritarianism and, of particular significance now, racism, homosexuality and gender politics. One thing that these and other similar issues have in common is that they are resistant to explanatory processes derived solely from the social sphere, because as well as existing on the social level they are also part of the lived reality of individuals. Michael Rustin, in discussing the potential contribution of psychoanalysis to understanding and combating racism, makes this point well. Approaches to racism which deal only with the (undoubtedly important) social and economic features of racist practices, not only neglect an important dimension of racism (its inhabitation of individual psyches), but also fail to explain the tenacity with which racist beliefs and practices are held. Rustin argues that this is because racism serves ends which are profoundly irrational yet which have important psychological and social functions. Ignoring this aspect of racism leaves one open to repeating it even as one attempts to develop an oppositional practice. Rustin writes:

It is not, of course, being argued that these social and political levels of oppression have no reality. The point is rather that a crucial means by which such structures are upheld is through irrational mental process, and that this dimension needs to be recognised and confronted as such. Above all, it is vital for those opposed to racist definitions not to fall victim to similar delusional and wilfully untruthful systems of thought as those which dominate the worlds of their oppressors.[3]

Some of the details of this argument as it applies to racism will be considered more fully later on. What is being suggested here is that racism and the other social phenomena in which psychoanalysis is involved as an explanatory theory demand this treatment because they cannot be reduced to terms which might make them amenable to the discourses of the more formal social disciplines such as sociology, politics and economics. Rustin expresses this as an issue of rationality, which he regards as a rule of functioning of a good society and something amenable to definition and pragmatic observation:

> It is hard to imagine a distinction between good societies and bad ones, or tolerable ones and intolerable ones, which doesn't turn on the pervasiveness or otherwise of rational, well-informed and intelligent ways of thinking, and their opposites – irrational, ignorant and stupid ways. . . . These distinctions do not follow merely from arbitrary cultural and ethical preferences. Consistency and inconsistency in thought, respect and disrespect for contextually known facts, are empirically observable attributes of practices and beliefs about the social world, as well as about the natural.[4]

Perhaps ironically in the light of our earlier discussion of its own 'disrespect for contextually known facts', psychoanalysis is taken as the science of the irrational – that is, as that approach and set of ideas which can make rational, narrative sense of the investment of individuals and societies in the 'irrational, ignorant and stupid' ways of thinking which are observable throughout the world but which might otherwise remain inexplicable. Psychoanalysis is called into play when questions about the social order are phrased as 'What (on earth!) do people want?', when their actions are in the arena upon which psychoanalysis has always been focused: the wilful, the unexpected, the uncanny, the irrational.

This is not all, however, for the discipline of psychoanalysis has a more specific area of functioning than the whole irrationality of humankind. In previous publications I have argued that the particular terrain of psychoanalysis is that of *subjectivity*, defined loosely as that which gives intentionality to human psychology, as the internal experience of being. In contrast to the major project in academic psychology of describing patterns of psychological activity from the outside, psychoanalysis struggles to develop a language and set of concepts that do justice to the 'inside' of the psyche, to the mental contents that constitute each of us as subjects in the dual sense of 'agents' of our actions and 'subject to' the workings of the unconscious.[5] It is legitimately called into action, therefore, when what is demanded is a theory which can make sense of the subjective determinants or impact of a set of phenomena – the 'meaning' of an event for people, its resonance or its threat. If, for example, a country explodes into internecine warfare, 'ethnic cleansing' (that is, genocide) and vicious aggression over apparently trivial land claims, it is unlikely that the explanations for this will be found solely in political and social history or economic advantage (which is not to say that they will not be found there *at all*). Something else is bound to be operating here, some excessive factor which reverberates subjectively for people, into which their fears and desires are channelled, generating and sustaining the bloodletting and mutual persecution. This is what is meant by excess; the desperate and rigid self defining of whole communities in terms of 'nationality' and the demonising of almost identical other communities (Freud might have had this in mind when he referred to the energy produced by the 'narcissism of small differences'), the desperate clinging on to some notion of identity bearing small relation to any real attribute of the individual or group, but nevertheless enormously powerful as an organising principle for people's lives. Without social, economic and political analysis, it would be impossible to understand the context and effects of phenomena such as these. But without the addition of an investigation of subjectivity, the social explanations fail to give an account of what drives people on, when no objective, rational interests are perceivable.

The language of the previous paragraph should provide a pointer to the exact terrain of the potential influence of psychoanalysis. Narrowing it down still further, we are not here dealing even with subjectivity as a whole, but with dreams and nightmares. More fully, we are dealing with fantasy. This, it is clear, is the proper topic for the psychoanalytic trade. In individual psychoanalysis, the object of study is the unconscious, explored through its penetration of consciousness and its capacity to twist and turn every trick of being. 'Subject to' the unconscious, the analysand finds her or his own subjectivity riven with excess, with that which cannot be pinned down or controlled. Going through our everyday lives, we are dominated by fantasy. To take the most obvious example, sexuality is nine-tenths imagination and at best one-tenth deed, taking its form from and providing its enjoyment by the investment of the imagination in the act. Indeed, as is testified to by the ubiquity of pornography, most of sexuality takes place in the mind, willed to some extent but beyond control much of the time. Here is an advance of Kleinian thought over Freudian. Whereas Freud describes fantasy as occurring in the space between the wish and the lost object so that it is always a substitute for reality, Kleinians present it as simply what the mind does: 'Phantasy is not merely an escape from reality, but a constant and unavoidable accompaniment of real experiences, constantly interacting with them.'[6] In addition to the constructive operations of the perceptual apparatus, attested to by the researches of cognitive psychologists, whereby we build up pictures of the world on a moment-by-moment basis through our expectations and active grasping of part perceptions to make them whole, psychoanalysis asserts – in this area, perhaps, demonstrates – that unconscious fantasies are constantly playing in our minds. Nothing is 'only' real; it all connects with other thoughts and ideas, other wishes or dreams, other anxieties. This is also true in political as well as individual life.

The Slovenian cultural critic, Slavoj Žižek, communicates this exactly in a piece on Eastern Europe published shortly after the demise of the Soviet Union and the collapse of Yugoslavia, in which he articulates the way fantasy might govern the relationship of individuals and collectives to themselves and others. Writing about the new nationalism to be found operating virulently in ex-Yugoslavia, he employs the notion of 'enjoyment' in a shocking and unexpected way to convey the emotional investment that might be sucked into any symbolic position. Indeed, the argument runs that it is *only* through use of this notion of enjoyment that the power of these apparently ('rationally' speaking) arbitrary categories of self definition and social definition can be understood:

To explain this unexpected turn [the self-destructive new

nationalism of the ex-communist states], we have to rethink the most elementary notions about national identification – and here, psychoanalysis can be of help. The element that holds together a given community cannot be reduced to the point of symbolic communication: the bond linking its members always implies a shared relationship to a Thing, towards Enjoyment incarnated. This relationship towards a Thing, structured by means of fantasies, is what is at stake when we speak of the menace to our 'way of life' presented by the Other; it is what is threatened when, for example, a white Englishman is panicked because of the growing presence of 'aliens'. It is this eruption of 'Enjoyment' which explains what is happening in the East.[7]

Rustin comments about the stress on fantasy identifications in this piece, that Žižek's 'argument, consistent with Freud, is that such phenomena need to be acknowledged as substantive dimensions of any actual political process'.[8] More precisely, accounts of social phenomena which neglect detailed examination of the investment ('enjoyment') of fantasy, will remain abstracted from the activities of the people – seen as individuals or collectives – who are involved. In a slightly later publication, by which time the Bosnian war had taken full hold, Žižek spells out the complex relationship between fantasies of survival and destruction, which have the effect of perpetuating the fear of the other in the very moment in which that other is attacked and destroyed. Arguing that 'hatred is not limited to the "actual properties" of its object' but is instead targeted at what the other represents in fantasy – its 'real kernel', in Lacanian language '*objet à*' – he comments that 'the more we destroy the object in reality, the more powerfully its sublime kernel rises before us',

> This paradox, which has already emerged apropos the Jews in Nazi Germany (the more they were ruthlessly exterminated, the more horrifying were the dimensions acquired by those who remained), can be perceived today apropos of Muslims in Bosnia: the more they are slaughtered and starved out, the more powerful is the danger of 'Muslim fundamentalism' in Serbian eyes. Our relationship to this traumatic-real kernel of surplus-enjoyment that 'bothers us' in the Other is structured in fantasies (about the Other's omnipotence, about 'their' strange sexual practices, etc.). In this precise sense, war is always also a *war of fantasies*.[9]

What is excessive is what the other means. This cannot be explained in terms of ordinary war aims or of personal or political interests, nor can it necessarily be articulated by the protagonists. It can, however, be observed or deduced from observations: what, if there is no element of fantasy involved, can explain the frenzy, the willingness to demolish the self as well as the other, and the escalating hatred so evident on the contemporary political scene? Whether the language employed here is derived from Klein (paranoid–schizoid functioning, the term given to the state of mind characterised by intense projection of destructive fantasies into the outside world, which is then experienced as persecutory) or Lacan (*objet à*) or elsewhere, something has to be said about this excess, this astonishing psychic energy which leaves rationality staggering behind.

Psychoanalysis comes into its own here, at least potentially, as a method and language for exploration of these fantasy investments without which social meanings cannot be pursued. Jacqueline Rose, arguing that fantasy should be 'at the heart of our political vocabulary' comments:

> There is a common assumption that fantasy has tended to be excluded from the political rhetoric of the left because it is not serious, not material, too flighty and hence not worth bothering about. My starting premise works the other way round. Like blood, fantasy is thicker than water, all too solid – *contra* another of fantasy's more familiar glosses as ungrounded supposition, lacking in foundation, not solid *enough*.[10]

Like Žižek, Rose identifies the material nature of fantasy, the way its processes as well as its effects can be seen. Moreover, the issue is not just one of 'acknowledging' fantasy and taking it into account when piecing together a full picture of an event; Rose states that it should be 'at the heart of our political vocabulary'. It is the fantasy that fuels the politics as well as the other way around; indeed it may be that the former is in operation even more than the latter. As psychoanalysis attests in the clinical sphere, there is always something excessive about psychic functioning – this is the precise nature and definition of the unconscious. Social events build on this and exploit it, and may also provide some of its contents. However, just as 'ideology' can no longer be reduced to false consciousness but is seen, following Althusser, as a medium through which the social is articulated and experienced, so the psychological dimension cannot be mapped unproblematically onto the social – always, something extra remains. This does not, of course, mean that there is no relationship between the social and the psychological. The entire heritage of social psychoanalysis has demonstrated exactly how much the structure of the individual psyche is infiltrated by the structure of society – a point which will be returned to particularly in relation to racism. However, it does suggest that a very specific conceptual apparatus is required to spell out the psychic attributes – the functioning of fantasy – that interdigitate with the social; purely social categories will not suffice. While there might be a range of possible languages for delivering an account of fantasy, particularly those of literary criticism, psychoanalysis is the most elaborate and the only one that takes fantasy as its prime object, irrespective of the products or actual content of the fantasy in question, removed from all aesthetic considerations and from moral judgement or remonstrance.

At least, that is the way it might be. The main concern of this chapter and the next is to examine whether psychoanalysis can deliver on this promise, whether its exploration of fantasy in the social domain can indeed be liberational and constructive or whether, as its many critics aver, it has succumbed to the particularly strong normative values of the cultures in which it has its home. What has been argued so far is that psychoanalysis has a privileged place in social theory because of its unique capacity to articulate the fantasy structures of social and political forces and to do so in a manner that respects the specificity and variety of every individual's 'excess'. The evaluative point is whether and to what extent psychoanalysis lives up to this idealised portrait – can it deliver on this promise? – for there is a profound danger here, one which parallels the dangers of ineffective psychotherapy. In the latter case, it can be argued that if psychoanalysis claims a place as a therapy (using up private and public resources) but is ineffective, then it is not only wasteful but also actively destructive. The hopes of individuals looking to psychoanalytic psychotherapy for help will be dashed and their belief might become that nothing can help them; by that point in time, this might indeed be the case. In the political sphere, the worry is not so much ineffectiveness as conformity. Psychoanalysis stakes a claim to be able to interpret the wildness of political and social processes in terms of the fantasies which inhabit them, but it can do so in numerous different ways. Some of these might have the effect of challenging the received wisdom of political thought, introducing a new way of reading and understanding social phenomena that generates activity and empowers people to move towards more productive modes of consciousness. Other ways of reading the world, whether in the consulting room or in the 'public' arena, may be no more than dressed up and obscured recapitulations of the existing ideology – for example, bourgeois familial ideology – calling people back to their 'common sense' understanding of the world and thus failing to offer them the kind of 'strangeness' which is the hallmark of truly incisive analytic work. Psychoanalysis then functions as a way of reconciling people to their current social reality, rather than as a critical, searching exploration of things which are not at that point known.

There are clearly numerous assumptions present in this argument, for example that it is possible to differentiate between retrogressive and progressive uses of psychoanalytic theory, that the former is a bad thing and the latter a good one, and that the grounds for the distinction might be between 'sameness' and 'strangeness', that is between repetition of assumed common sense (ego function) and the surprise of unexpected discovery and new awareness (the unconscious breaks through). The most famous debate around these issues is that between the Frankfurt School 'critical theorists', particularly Marcuse and Adorno, and the so-called 'revisionist' psychoanalysts, notably Fromm, Horney and Sullivan.[11] This dispute, retold energetically by Russell Jacoby in a slightly later context,[12] centred on the attempt by the revisionists to make of Freudianism a *humanistic* theory and practice which would separate out the needs of the person from the activities of the social order. This would make it possible to specify which social conditions are damaging to the individual and, conversely, those which might enable each individual to reach her or his full potential. However, the price for this is that it requires the postulation of a *non-social subject*, an essential being existing pre-society or contra to it, developing in its context but not fundamentally formed by it. Against this image, the Frankfurt School argued that what we take to be the individual is already a social product, that, for example, those aspects of our functioning which we take to be 'natural' are in fact the consequences of an historical process. Marcuse comments about the revisionists:

> In shifting the emphasis from the unconscious to the conscious, from the biological to the cultural factors, they cut off the roots of society in the instincts and instead take society at the level on

which it confronts the individual as ready-made 'environment' without questioning its origin and legitimacy.[13]

Jacoby gives a still sharper comparison, alerting us to some of the productive tensions in the critical theory account: 'The revisionists introduce history, a social dynamic, into psychoanalysis from, as it were, the *outside* – by social values, norms, goals. Marcuse finds the history *inside* the concepts. He interprets Freud's 'biologism' as second nature, petrified history.'[14] Without reviewing the details of this well-documented debate, it is worth noting its most provocative element which can be coded as a dispute about closure. What is at stake here is a contrast between a 'positive' account of what psychoanalysis can offer to social values – prescribing particular ways of organising society which will produce social and individual health (a position that certainly can lead to progressive policies but can also be sucked into normative prescriptiveness of the 'right way' to be) – as against what the Frankfurt School referred to as the 'negative' characteristics of psychoanalysis; its capacity to sustain a critical attitude constantly exploring the underpinnings of the individual and the workings of the social order. This debate is continued in many forms, for example in Lacan's scathing critique of 'American' psychoanalysis and of the tendency of object-relations theorists to talk about 'mature object relations'. What this is opposing is any idea that conflicts can be resolved rather than laid bare; more precisely Lacan rejects the implication that, even in principle, the ego can become whole, untroubled by the dislocating violence of the unconscious.[15] The trade of psychoanalysis, in this vision, is tension. It is oriented towards the fissures in experience and all apparent closures are to be interpreted as ways of avoiding or defending against these fissures. No narratives are to be taken as given or as finished; the more seamless and convincing they appear to be, the more we are invited to doubt them and to ask what split or anxiety is being renounced at their core. In his characteristically Lacanian way, Žižek draws on this idea to criticise any assumption of authenticity, any belief in the efficacy of narrative explanations:

> Herein resides the ethical attitude of psychoanalysis, the reversal baptized by Lacan 'la traversée du fantasme', going-through the fantasy: in the distance we are obliged to assume towards our most 'authentic' dreams, towards the myths that guarantee the very consistency of our symbolic universe.[16]

Pushing towards the limits of its sphere of activity, psychoanalysis in this mode explores the fantasies which give rise to, and rebound from, social structures. Its 'ethical attitude' is simply to do this – to make us stare at those things which we would rather not recognise. When psychoanalysis itself looks away, when for example it adopts normative assumptions of health or relationships as its goal and prescription, it betrays its own task and it becomes no more than another narrative, consoling or repressive as the context allows.

POSTMODERN IDENTITIES

The argument developed in the previous section is that psychoanalysis has a potentially privileged position in regard to social commentary because of its focus on unconscious fantasy, on that 'excessive' aspect of human subjectivity which cannot be contained within sociological or economic theory. However, psychoanalysis is variable in its capacity to stay with this position, to use its insights in such a way that understanding is opened out rather than closed down. In particular, it has a tendency to slip back into normative assumptions, dressed up as expert psychological understanding, and to back away from the anxiety inherent in facing the unconscious directly. One way of assessing this is to ask how much psychoanalysis, when confronted with social phenomena, articulates the tensions and disturbances perceivable within them, rather than prescribing solutions.

In the 1950s and 1960s the primary concerns of politically oriented psychoanalysts and theorists of psychoanalysis were with the politics of social class ('Freudo–Marxism'). Included in this was an honourable tradition of work on prejudice, anti-Semitism and fascism, work which has had a lasting impact in arguing for the importance of unconscious as well as sociopolitical elements in these phenomena.[17] More recently, however, some new critical forces have come into play which make problematic the positions taken by the classic radical Freudians. These have their origins in what has come to be called the 'identity politics' of the past twenty years, which have questioned the grand narratives of oppression and liberation put forward by previous generations on the political left and which have argued for the centrality of specific configurations of power and resistance to be found in different, often fluid forms, in a range of individuals, groups and situations. The most

powerful discourses here surround feminism, gay and lesbian politics, and the black and anti-racist movements, all of which either
dispute or supplement the economic and class-based analyses of
inequality which previously dominated the scene. The idea of a
monolithic state as the source of all power, to be opposed through
alliances of workers brokered by their shared class interests, has
given way in the face of theoretical developments (notably by
Foucault)[18] and – much more significantly – the articulating
consciousness of women, black people and gay and lesbian groups
as they recast themselves as political agents. The struggle for political and social theory here is to find a way of comprehending this
new phenomenon without falling back into reductive, economistic
explanations that miss the point of identity politics altogether.

For psychoanalysis, the task is to grapple with a way of theorising unconscious investments in wildly divergent patterns of
being, which can be fragmented and contradictory and which cut
across the traditional fault lines of class, sexuality, 'race' and
gender. In a way, this is a golden opportunity, for the new identity
politics is explicitly organised around patterns of identification and
personal investment which are recognisably multiple and unstable,
with visible contradictions in individuals' personal locations
(witness the multiple identity positions contained, for example, in
the complex location of an individual as a white lesbian woman or
a black heterosexual man). Moreover, there is a newly focused
understanding of the *constructive* nature of the process undertaken
socially and personally as people find their place in an identity
grouping and explore the understanding of themselves and the
social order which this can bring. In principle, therefore, psychoanalysis is perfectly attuned to the needs of the time: as politics
becomes more concerned with subjectivity, it more than ever needs
a language in which to talk about the interrelationships between
consciousness, fantasy and social positioning. Psychoanalysis could,
again in principle, supply such a language; it could make sense of
the complex business of creating and recreating 'identities' and of
filling these out with content as well as exploring the intense investments which people hold in them and the deep aggression (for
example, as racism or homophobia) to which they often give rise.

The new identity politics is related to a further term, that of
postmodernism. This is certainly an arena in which psychoanalysis
has had a voice. Indeed, a considerable portion of the language of
postmodernism has been borrowed from psychoanalysis, again

because of its concern with subjectivity and the influence of the fracturing of the modern world on personal status and consciousness.[19] Anthony Elliott comments,

Psychoanalysis has made significant contributions to these theoretical debates on modern and postmodern identity, providing methods of analysis for thinking through the connections between these cultural trends and new patterns of self-organisation. In these debates, psychoanalysis has been used to trace the fragile and precarious structures of psychic interiority engendered by the cultural conditions of our late modern age.[20]

Postmodernism stresses the fragmentary nature of social being, its lack of cohesion and direction, and the way discourses arise out of this fragmentary existence to organise consciousness. That is to say, the postmodernist vision is one in which stable absolutes cease to exist, even as a possibility. In their place come a swirling multiplicity of subject positions, fluid in their nature, destabilising and at times interchangeable, relativistic and reactive. Out of these, certain structuring lines of being are constructed through symbolic procedures so that the categories of identity can be held onto. 'Race', gender and class are among the most powerful such categories because the social order as a whole employs them as organising principles; but they are not absolute, either in their meaning or in their constitution. How they are invested in by people and what they come to mean in practice are complex questions demanding analysis of the way social categories and personal structures of desire interweave.

It should be clear from this that identity politics is a primary site for the testing of any theory of subjectivity and hence is a crucial arena in which to assess the claims of psychoanalysis to be able to offer a way of thinking about the engagements of subjectivity with social processes. Elliott concludes his book with the warning that,

If psychoanalysis is to remain effective as a critical theory, it must necessarily step back from the tendency to see the self solely in terms of the 'psychic', and instead confront head-on the issue of the construction of the unconscious in the field of the social and political.[21]

In the light of the earlier discussion, it is useful to add to this the related demand that psychoanalysis examines the *fantasy* structures of the 'social and political', recognising them for what they are rather than appropriating them as its own, normative values. To what extent can it do this? As will become apparent from the discussions of gender, homosexuality and racism in the next chapter, psychoanalysis has had enormous difficulty in sustaining a critical vision in the face of the immensely powerful pull of conformist, normalising tendencies. Whether there is any possibility of this situation changing remains to be seen.

Before examining these specific instances of identity politics, there are some important contributions to the rethinking of the notion of 'identity' which arise from psychoanalysis and which warrant exploration, for in them lie seeds of a strikingly critical social analysis.[22] Here, the strength of psychoanalysis lies not in that part of its tradition which has dealt explicitly with 'identity' in the past, such as in the well-known work of Erikson,[23] but in the alternative tradition which continues to question the *function* of identity – that is, which refuses to accept it as an unproblematic concept but instead 'deconstructs' it to ask what it is doing. The contrast here can be seen in a comparison between the common-sense notion of identity as an act of self recognition, in which one understands what one really is, and the postmodern but also psychoanalytic idea that identity is – or, rather, identities are – constructed actively as a search for something, as a way of becoming something or staving something off. In the former way of seeing things, growing into or discovering an identity entails constructing a relationship with the world which is compatible with one's inner self – ideally, allowing what one is to reach fulfilment in what one can come to be. Even if it is recognised that the term, psychologically speaking, should be in the plural as 'identities', the assumption is still of something to be achieved in order to align oneself with the truth of one's experience. 'My identity as a man', 'my identity as an academic', 'as a father', 'as a white person': these are slogans often put forward unproblematically, as if what they mean is clear. In truth, they are formulae which cover something more complex and uncertain. Not only do they tend to hide a process of struggle and incompleteness – my identity as a man is something which I can never feel to be completely and authentically achieved, only worked at every day in a range of contradictory situations – but they also obscure a more radical sense in which identities are constructed rather than found.

The most striking claim relating to the issue of identities to have come from the general postmodernist stable is the following: that identities do not refer to the inside but to the outside. That is, notions of identity – like notions of self or 'ego' – are misleading because they suggest the existence of an inner essence with form and substance. Instead, the 'truth' of the human subject, such as it is, is one of incoherence, constituted either by emptiness and lack (the Lacanian view) or by contradiction and disorder. The apparent stability of self and identity is a way of fleeing from the affective impact of this inner chaos, of taking refuge in fantasies of containment suggested by external features of the social world. Lacan, in his commentary on Freud's famous dream of 'Irma's injection', makes this point particularly eloquently and influentially:

> [The] ego is the sum of the identifications of the subject, with all that that implies as to its radical contingency. If you allow me to give an image of it, the ego is like the superimposition of various coats borrowed from what I will call the bric-à-brac of its props department.[24]

This is the familiar Lacanian idea of the speciousness of the ego as a unified entity: what in ordinary life we take as the core component of selfhood is revealed under analysis to be 'bric-à-brac', bits and pieces placed together or on top of one another more or less by chance, covering up an emptiness beneath. Moreover, the ego is 'the sum of the identifications of the subject'. Identification is that process whereby the ego takes the object and makes it *subject*, incorporating each object as part of itself. For example, in Freud's developmental account, as the growing child has to give up desired sexual objects, so in fantasy does the ego take them in, internalising them and changing as a result. The ego thus comes to be a home for lost desires and forsaken objects; its character is formed along the line of these objects which are introjected and absorbed, accompanied by the id-originated psychic energy invested in them. In Freud's words, this 'makes it possible to suppose that the character of the ego is a precipitate of abandoned object cathexes and that it contains the history of these object choices'.[25] It is worth recalling that the ego is the part of the mental apparatus in which consciousness resides, but it is also home to unconscious defence mechanisms and hence is more extensive than just what is available to the subject's awareness. If one is to know who one is – a reasonable, if undoubtedly approximate, definition of possessing an 'identity' – then this can be achieved only by the process of more-or-less conscious reflection on the activities of the ego. However, given that identification, out of which the ego is formed, is itself a largely unconscious procedure, then the ego – the centre of the conscious subject – is ripped open by the subject's fantasised perceptions of others. The ego is formed out of 'abandoned object cathexes', that is identity comes from the outside.

In all this, it is clear that subjectivity is more than just what is symbolised or known and that there is a process of construction going on to make one's identity or identities coincide with the demands of this subjectivity. This process involves the taking in of material from the outside, that is, it is a process of *adoption* undertaken by every human subject as part of the search for a structure through which the complex multifariousness of subjectivity can be made stable and grounded in something apparently safe and under control. One insight which has been stressed by many postmodernists, including some contemporary psychoanalysts, is just how much subjectivity is a contingent and fluid phenomenon. Some ideas on this from Cornelius Castoriadis were described in Chapter 5. He argues that the Freudian unconscious is a site for constant production of imaginary representations of self and other – that is, for fantasy as a constructive and ever-transforming basis for all psychic activity. Fantasy overwhelms biological need and in this sense, symbolic activity is the essence of the human subject. Castoriadis' emphasis on the primary status of the imagination – the way representations are produced endlessly by the human subject – is an important marker of a view of the psyche as indefatigably active and creative. New forms are continually brought into existence then displaced by newer ones as the mind goes about its task. As each moment is met, so new associations are produced. Moreover, the dizzying excess of fantasy is not just an accompaniment to perception – and still less a substitute for reality; rather it is a primary nexus out of which perception and thought emerge.

However, the state of effervescence is necessarily unstable, perhaps at times unbearable. In response, society is instituted in a state of 'closure', offering structure and constraint to the radical wildness of the imagination. This constraint is experienced as necessary, but it works like a strainer through which travels the multiplicity of the human psychic flux, leaving behind the excess from which taste derives:

> [Through] this social fabrication of the individual, the institution subjugates the singular imagination of the subject and, as a

general rule, lets it manifest itself only through dreaming, phantasying, transgression, illness. In particular, everything occurs as if the institution had succeeded in cutting off communication between the subject's radical imagination and its 'thought'. Whatever it might imagine (whether it knows it or not), the subject *will think* and will make/do only what it is socially obligated to think and make/do. We see here the social-historical side of the process that, psychoanalytically speaking, is called repression.[26]

What Castoriadis refers to as 'the institution' or 'society' is here taken to refer to those external reference points which are turned to with relief by the subject, as they offer to pin down the otherwise uncontainable emergence of representations of one impulse after and alongside another. When we struggle to find out what it might mean to be such-and-such a person, to have this or that identity, we are engaged in an act of self labelling and self construction which is essentially static, a 'prop' out of which an imaginary stability can be made. We do this by inserting ourselves in a social-symbolic order, by what might be thought of as 'seeking out a name'; when we have found it we try to rest content, although frequently we are faced with a sense that there is something missing, something which our identities have not been able to express. This is because identities can never be whole, full expressions of the stream of subjectivity whose flowing fantasies always push at the boundaries of what we allow them to be. There is no 'natural' identity, according to this way of reading the world. Instead, all identities are adopted and none will ever satisfy. It is in the nature of things because identities are not found; they are made.

THE AMBIGUITY OF THE MIRROR

In Lacan's famous exposition of the mirror stage in development, he captures something of the sense of being 'misrecognised' which is possibly characteristic of contemporary culture. In contrast to Winnicott, who uses the idea of mirroring to convey the importance of a developmental process in which the child sees her or himself accurately and thoughtfully reflected back by a concerned mother (that is who enters into her or his true self/identity through this interpersonal process),[27] Lacan emphasises the impossibility of identity as related to a 'true' self. In his view, the ego is used to create an armour or shell supporting the psyche which is otherwise experienced as in fragments. Lacan emphasises the *exteriority* of this process – that which appears to us as our 'self' is in fact given from the outside as a refuge, an ideal ego, a narcissistically invested image:

> The fact is that the total form of the body by which the subject anticipates in a mirage the maturation of his power is given to him only as a *Gestalt*, that is to say, in an exteriority in which this form is certainly more constituent than constituted, but in which it appears to him above all in a contrasting size that fixes it and in a symmetry that inverts it, in contrast with the turbulent movements that the subject feels are animating him.[28]

Here, Lacan is arguing that the subject gains relief from the intensity of fragmenting internal impulses through the boundedness and apparent stability of the mirror image – something external but connected to the subject, holding a promise of future 'power'. Whereas Winnicott portrays the mirroring function as one which allows the child actually to grow into her or his self (to genuinely find the 'maturation of his power', one might say), for Lacan this is a specious process in which the subject is hoodwinked, or hoodwinks her or himself, into taking on the image as if it were real. The mirror suggests that the subject is integrated, but 'in fact' there is to be found a multiplicity of drives and desires. Moreover, as with the rather different understanding put forward by Castoriadis, there is here an image of the external, social world as operating both reassuringly and antagonistically – in a sense, guilefully – to divert the subject away from its terror of dissolution. The message given to the infant 'in the mirror' is that the ego has integrity and wholeness, but this message is a socially constructed one, legible in the reflecting surfaces and faces of an order stressing the autonomy and psychological independence of individuals.

Identity fades away as an issue here. According to Lacan, the structure of human knowledge and ego functioning is a delusional one, finding in the spectral image a misleading promise of integrity. This is read by Lacan as a paranoid sensation. The negativity and persecutory associations of the paranoiac are to do in part with the aggressiveness of the drives, threatening to burst the image apart – a notion akin to those worked on by Klein in her description of paranoid–schizoid functioning.[29] But it is also connected with the haunting of this satisfying image of the integrated self by the spectre or memory of something else: somewhere inside, each of us knows that we are not really whole, that this seeming self is a bare cover for something disturbing. As we look in the mirror, we catch a glimpse of something in the corner, just moving out of sight, running away before we can see what it is.

The mirror is a source of reassurance and threat, its seemingly smooth surface containing unexpected ripples caused by that which can be seen yet not quite named. In contrast to the generative and creative sense of the unconscious evoked by Castoriadis, Lacan emphasises the threat to be glimpsed at the corner of the visual field. Using the ebullient disintegration to be found in the paintings of Hieronymous Bosch as an emblem, Lacan focuses on what happens when the veneer of integrity shatters:

> This fragmented body ... usually manifests itself in dreams when the movement of the analysis encounters a certain level of aggressive disintegration in the individual. It then appears in the form of disjointed limbs, or of those organs represented in exoscopy, growing wings and taking up arms for intestinal persecutions.[30]

The mirror stage reflects the impossibility of becoming a self without taking on the meanings of the other – without becoming *identified* with another's gaze, with the pre-existing desire of the other that one should be some one thing and not anything else. In the mirror stage, the terrible struggle to hold the forces of dissolution at bay is repressed in the face of a manic optimism that 'identity' will solve the problem, fixing what is fluid in us as a meaning expressible in an easy sentence: 'I am this and not that.' Looking in the mirror, we see what we wish for: a home for our hopes and impulses, a surface to bind our inner fragments together. As an image of the adoption of identity, this is excruciatingly painful. We leap into the other's gaze to escape the turmoil inside.

In Lacanian terminology, the imaginary wholeness promised by the mirror is shattered by another step of alienation – the move to the symbolic order of experience in which the structures of language interfere with the image-making process, revealing that it is already organised by a law indifferent to the emotions and desires of the individual subject. Lacan expresses this idea most economically at the end of his seminar on Edgar Allen Poe's story, *The Purloined Letter*. Having traced in masterful detail the structural interconnections between the different characters in the Poe story as a consequence of the movement of the eponymous letter, Lacan comments as follows on what constructs the identities of the individuals concerned:

> Everything which could serve to define the characters as real – qualities, temperament, heredity, nobility – has nothing to do with the story. At every moment each of them, even their sexual attitude, is defined by the fact that a letter always reaches its destination.[31]

All is determined by the movement of the symbolic order. The position of each one of us, our sensations, feelings and actions, are given by our place in the system; it gazes on us irrevocably and we struggle against it at our peril. Lacan has no time for, or patience with, claims of the significance of character and selfhood. He consistently debunks the notions of affect and of mature relationships used by object relational theorists. Instead, he evokes an empty subject, constituted through lack and marked by the impossibility of fulfilment or of recognition of the actuality of the other. For that is the register of 'identity' in the Lacanian scheme: it is an aspect of the fantasy of fulfilment which is split apart by the discovery that the subject is produced by, rather than generative of, the signifying chain. When we find an identity we believe we have found something with substance, but the order of causality is the other way around; it finds us. That is, the symbolic order positions the subject in relation to other subjects, marking us as incomplete, only present through our relationship with what lies outside.

It should be clear from this that the notion of identity is a deeply problematic one, particularly if viewed through the Lacanian prism of the imaginary and symbolic. Whereas Castoriadis, in his own destabilisation of the ego, at least envisages a positive resonance in the incurable psychic flux of the unconscious, Lacan sees the whole thing as a distortion, a defensive structure. As has been pointed out numerous times by Castoriadis and others, there are many difficulties with Lacan's account, including the central issue of 'misrecognition'. Who misrecognises what is in the mirror? Yet, there is also a way in which the Lacanian scheme captures something deeply expressive of the contemporary experience of being lost, of searching for who one is in the semi-awareness that one is running away from something else. Perhaps one problem in the literature is that the Lacanian description of the imaginary and symbolic orders is often discussed with only passing reference to the third Lacanian order, the 'real', yet it is here that the origins of the anxiety which sends subjects tumbling towards 'identity' is most troublingly and powerfully located.

The finest extended meditation on the place of the real in ordinary life (specifically, in popular culture), can be found in Žižek's *Looking Awry*. Here, the real is portrayed as that which erupts from the borderline between inside and outside – in the terms used above, that which is just at the edge of the mirror, in the out-of-sight margin. It is catastrophic in its threat, in its impact as reminder or return ('it erupts in the form of a traumatic return, derailing the balance of our daily lives').[32] Yet it also offers substance to life, representing that contingent element which makes life worthwhile:

> For things to have meaning, this meaning must be confirmed by some contingent piece of the real that can be read as a 'sign'. The very word *sign*, in opposition to the arbitrary mark, pertains to the 'answer of the real': the 'sign' is given by the thing itself, it indicates that at least at a certain point, the abyss separating the real from the symbolic order has been crossed, i.e. that the real itself has complied with the signifier's appeal. In moments of social crisis (wars, plagues), unusual celestial phenomena (comets, eclipses, etc.) are read as prophetic signs.[33]

The real resides outside the registers of imaginary and symbolic. It is the order of the leftover, that which is bubbling under the surface – rhythmic, uncertain, disruptive – but it is not a mystical order outside of the realm of experience. Rather it is what our psychological and social devices keep at bay. At certain times, it breaks through to link us with everything we have left out, and this is what Žižek refers to as 'the answer of the real'. Much of the time, however, it pulses away as a threat, as that which can demolish all our attempts at identity construction. It is this threat of the real against which the imaginary bulwark of identities defends the subject. The real stalks its prey at times of radical challenge – when the social-symbolic order breaks down, when, for example, death is on the streets, when change is intense and uncontrollable. The ambivalence with which the subject confronts its destiny is then apparent. That which is left over, that which cannot be contained, is terrifying but also exhilarating; just as war disturbs and excites, so the breakdown of identities is devastating but can also be felt as an illumination, a kind of freedom. Hence, perhaps, the otherwise incomprehensible mythic attraction of madness. Symbolising the ultimate state of deindividuation and escape from formal identity, psychosis has frequently been romanticised (in contrast to its banal and miserable actuality) as the way through or out, as that which might put the subject back in touch with her or his essence. Lacanian theory does not romanticise psychosis in this way, but it does tell us something about this urge towards self destruction.

Examining the literature of postmodernism, what is continually reiterated is something present both in Castoriadis' idea of representational flux and in the Lacanian real, as well as in some other contemporary psychoanalytic ideas such as Julia Kristeva's notion of 'the abject'.[34] This is an idea, or perhaps just an image, of *rupture*, of something that breaks through and unsettles any set identities. Even multiplicity is not an answer: simply accepting the existence of more potential identities does not prevent them all from being rattled by the force of this rupture. Nevertheless, people's multiple adoptive identities are taken on as a way of trying to keep that force at bay, of holding themselves together in the face of the continuing and possibly escalating suspicion that something utterly unknowable might be just around the corner.

There is an invitation in this to look more closely at something very central to psychoanalysis, the notion of 'otherness'. Strikingly, Kristeva uses this as a motif for her meditation on the contemporary condition, *Strangers to Ourselves*:

> To discover our disturbing otherness, for that indeed is what bursts in to confront that 'demon', that threat, that apprehension generated by the projective apparition of the other at the heart of what we persist in maintaining as a proper, solid 'us'. By recognising *our* uncanny strangeness we shall neither suffer from it nor enjoy it from the outside. The foreigner is within me, hence we are all foreigners. If I am a foreigner, there are no foreigners.[35]

In postmodern times, the condition of strangeness is forced upon us, but this is no new thing, only a possible increase in intensity and scale. Psychoanalysis, indeed, places something strange and unknown at the centre of every human subject. This is the unconscious, whether theorised as affectivity, as lack, or as self-generating imagination. By definition, the unconscious is the not known, the strange. In addition, it is disruptive. It sets one's teeth on edge; one never knows when and in what language it will speak. Writing about the Biblical Book of Ruth, Kristeva points out how essential strangeness is to sovereignty – how King David's origins in the outsider (the Moabite Ruth), while endlessly problematic for him, grant him that edge that propels him towards greatness. 'If David is *also* Ruth, if the sovereign is *also* the Moabite, peace of mind will then never be his lot, but a constant quest for welcoming and going beyond the other in oneself.'[36] The home born, the settled one, the never adopted and never strange: these are not the material for royalty. Denial and repression of the stranger within, the site of otherness from which creativity emerges, is a sign of failure. For each one of us, encountering our own strangeness is the only way to go.

If the strangeness within is linked to the unconscious and if the unconscious is linked to nameless dread and excitement, then each of us harbours a place of rupture to which we have constantly to return. Calling this 'the real' only marks out its area of activity, it does not sum it up or moderate it. Unlike the adoptive identities with which we console ourselves all the time, the place of rupture does not respond to a name, it simply keeps acting, surprising us and keeping us in contact with that from which we turn. Faced with the external stranger, we may be both curious and afraid, we may find the strangeness exotic and erotic but also abrasive and shadowy. All these responses are appropriate, too, to the strangeness within; they suggest, along with the whole thrust of psychoanalysis, that what exists in the margins is perhaps the most intense source of meaning in people's lives.

Psychoanalysis is usually, and correctly, understood as a product of modernism, committed to the idea that it is possible to identify latent meanings behind even the most confusing and fragmentary of phenomena. This can be seen not only in its classical theory, but in its practice. Faced with the obscurities of personal conflict, whether over identity or more circumscribed neuroses, the analyst pursues an interpretive path committed to meaning construction on the grounds that this will allow the analysand more control over her or his everyday life. As was discussed in Chapters 2 and 3, it makes a difference here whether one adopts a hermeneutic or more traditionally causal attitude towards psychoanalysis, with the former having far less confidence in the possibility of uncovering any 'fixed' or absolute meaning at work beneath the analysand's discourse. Nevertheless, both approaches trumpet the possibility and meaningfulness of the interpretive project, even if it is never possible to achieve the closure of a final answer to the analysand's discursive question – that is to articulate a complete statement of the unconscious wish lying behind the analysand's conflict. This is in line with the general modernist view that it is in principle possible to identify the causal underpinnings of any personal or social product (any text, in the literary version of this), even if in practice this task might be extraordinarily difficult.

Freud was profoundly addicted to this position, with the whole thrust of his form of psychoanalysis being to take hold of the apparently irrational and inexplicable – the outpourings of hysterics, his own dreams, the mistakes and symptoms of everyday life – and to show that they had meaning and significance, that they could be understood through the operations of the mind. This rationalist model is intellectually colonising in the sense that, in the same movement with which it allows irrationality its voice, it makes available to inspection orders of experience which might claim to be immune to logical formulation. The analyst, standing outside the phenomenon she or he is exploring, examines it and gives it name and significance – a prime example of what Foucault has called the 'medical gaze'.[37] In this guise, psychoanalysis acts to defuse the unconscious and to make it less a creature of the night; understood through intellectual activity, it holds fewer terrors and surprises.

Much psychoanalytic endeavour and, indeed, much intellectual work in general still maintains the honourable traditions of modernism, in which it is an ethical project to struggle to understand the world and to bring order to it. In its more progressive forms, it does so with an awareness of the critique of rationalism which has flowed from the postmodernist and identity politics positions described above; specifically, that in privileging reason, post-Enlightenment thinking discounts the voices of those who do not 'buy into' its power structure – notably women but also all those regarded in this vision as 'primitive', including colonised ethnic and 'racial' groups. Holding to a vision of the world in which reason is not all, these groups then get written off as 'irrational/superstitious/emotional' by the proponents of reason, resulting in a construction of knowledge owing most of its rhetorical power to a privileging of Western and 'masculine' (instrumental, 'active', controlled) modes of being. As discussed in many recent writings, the consequences of this are become increasingly apparent as the Enlightenment vision of rational progress breaks down under the pressure of the fragmenting forces operating in late modernity, with crises appearing in science, ecology, masculinity and identity – all those areas which modernism appeared to have sewn up.[38]

It is possible, in the face of this critique, to discount rationality altogether as a purely ideological product of capitalist society. Then nothing has general significance; the world consists of local and temporary contingencies, with no pattern and no comparative value – everything is interchangeable. However, those critics who wish to argue for the maintenance of rationality as an ethical criterion and hence for the continuation of the interpretive project have suggested instead that it is possible to employ judgements of reason in each particular area so that, for example, the capacity of a society to maintain caring relationships among its members or to empower women or combat racism is not made subservient to its technological progress or its economic 'efficiency'. Michael Rustin, again, is eloquent on this:

> It is important to retain the criterion of rationality as discriminating between different kinds of individual and social behaviour, if there is to be any ground for making moral judgements, whether of acts, individuals or societies. If one recognises that the categories of 'rational' and 'irrational' are separately applicable to many different spheres of life, it is possible to avoid the privileging of 'Eurocentric' and 'Western' world-views which has followed from post-Enlightenment faith in reason, and has made Western rationality sometimes seem like one ideological face of imperialism. [39]

One can see the workings of this book and many others in similar ways. Any attempt to employ critical judgement depends to some degree at least on the exercise of rationality; one can only hope that one's capacity to maintain awareness of the 'many different spheres of life' which might be relevant is not lost in the process. In psychoanalytic terms, sustaining an ability to think even in the face of troubling impulses and confusions, instead, for example, of acting them out, reveals a belief in the saving power of reason, however partial its actual functioning might be.

Even with this defence, however, acceptance of moderated rationality as a way of approaching the world is not a complete answer either to the critique of reason or to the revelations of postmodernism. In the long discussion above of the postmodern deconstruction of identity to which some forms of psychoanalysis have contributed, it was argued that what this has revealed is the need for an approach to identity politics – and, indeed, to subjectivity in general – capable of understanding what happens when the 'real' breaks through, when we are faced with the failure of symbolisation, with what is left behind when all interpretation is over. Maintaining a model of rational activity in which thinking about difficult things is highly valued, we can see that the specific contribution of psychoanalysis to the examination of postmodern social processes lies in its capacity to examine the productivity of fantasy and, as a part of that, to maintain an awareness of the way fantasy constantly disrupts all assumptions about the stability of identity or identities. Looking for the points of emergence of the real – the moments and spaces of rupture – enhances one's capacity to refuse the normative coercion of everyday social life. This is not just a matter of playfulness, but a project of political resistance. In recognising the endless productivity of unconscious imagination and the forceful anxieties that it produces, along with its excitement, it might become possible to articulate the 'excessive' nature of social and political phenomena described earlier in this chapter. The measure of psychoanalysis' standing here is, therefore, the extent to which it can stand apart from the ideological structures in which it is embedded and maintain an analytic attitude – an attitude of exploration focused on the desires and anxieties feeding into, and arising out of, problematic social identities.

The next chapter looks at three crucial arenas for identity politics and asks questions about the attitude of psychoanalysis towards them. If the contribution of psychoanalysis to the formulation of postmodern identities is impressive at the level of general theory, its concrete understanding and activity when faced with the demands and needs of particular subject groups is much more uneven. The story to be found in the 'case studies' of gender, homosexuality and racism is not an entirely pretty one, but it does at least say something about where to look for the construction of a form of psychoanalysis which might deliver on its promise of knowing something about the social effects of fantasy and desire.

Chapter 8

Psychoanalytic agendas
Gender, homosexuality and racism

The subject of this chapter is the contribution made by psychoanalysis to three crucial areas of identity politics: sexual difference, male and female homosexuality, and racism. The general question governing this study arises from the arguments of the previous chapter: how well does psychoanalysis articulate an understanding of the fantasy dimensions of these personal and social positions, refraining from normative assumptions and allowing expression of those aspects of experience usually left out from – or occluded as 'excessive' – in social discourse?

I will of necessity use a different method of presentation and analysis for each of the three areas under discussion. There is a vast literature on psychoanalysis, gender and sexual difference, beginning with debates in Freud's lifetime and taking on enormous energy in the period since the emergence in the late 1960s of 'second wave feminism'. This literature, in which are represented all political positions and all conceivable evaluations of psychoanalysis (from patriarchal-coercive discipline to potential liberator and vehicle for feminism), is too voluminous and too well known to be subjected to a comprehensive review and general evaluation here.[1] Suffice it to say that the language of feminism has been deeply informed by psychoanalytic ideas, and the language and practice of psychoanalysis has been challenged – and to a lesser, though still substantial degree – transformed by feminism. However, tensions between the two approaches remain. Quite frequently, these are translated into personal attacks: psychoanalysts who see feminist critics as dominated by envy; feminists who see psychoanalysts as misogynistic and oppressive representatives of a patriarchal order committed to keeping women 'in their place'. On the other hand, feminists of many persuasions have turned, usually selectively, to psychoanalysis as an approach that might enhance understanding of the infiltration of patriarchy into personal and interpersonal life. The focus of discussion here will be the extent to which psychoanalysis has shown itself capable of offering such an enhanced understanding, articulating a subjective dimension to the operations of patriarchy and hence to oppositional practice. And so the question to be asked is: where, in psychoanalysis' encounters with gender, can anything radically innovative be found?

No such short cut to the potential contribution of psychoanalysis can be taken with regard to its treatment of lesbianism and male homosexuality. Even though the literature here also begins with Freud, it is not only more sparse than the general literature on gender, it is also more troublesomely unequivocal. With disappointingly few exceptions, psychoanalysis has promoted accounts of homosexuality which are, in political terms, reactionary. This has had a powerful impact on psychoanalytic practice, including training (many training institutions have routinely excluded homosexuals from becoming psychoanalysts or psychoanalytic psychotherapists). It has also meant that as the gay and lesbian identity movement has developed over the past twenty years, psychoanalysis has largely been perceived as an enemy, not as a potential contributor to its literature and self understanding. This is particularly ironic given the focus of psychoanalysis on sexuality: if it cannot say something worthwhile here, there must be an argument for dispensing with it altogether. In my 'case presentation' I will briefly outline this sorry story, drawing especially on the critical accounts of psychoanalysis which have begun to emerge from psychoanalysts and others trying to develop a new dialogue between psychoanalysis and gay and lesbian politics. I will also ask whether anything can be found in the psychoanalytic edifice to enrich rather than obstruct our understanding of male and female homosexuality.

Third, the area of 'race' and racism is one which has exercised social critics greatly in recent years, but psychoanalysts only slightly. Psychoanalysis has always been pilloried for its eurocentrism and for its earlier, Freudian vision of 'savages' as akin to children in their mental functioning – that is to say, simple, direct and under the sway of unconscious impulses. Freud's own speculative prehistories of humankind, notably in 'Totem and taboo',[2] are embarrassing to almost all sympathetic readers of psychoanalysis; their direct application to 'other' cultures was contested early by Malinowski,[3] but their racist dimension has had relatively little attention paid to it. Basically, with few significant exceptions, psychoanalysis has stood back from an active engagement with the politics of race. This it can no longer afford to do as, under contemporary conditions, it is vital for a discipline trading in the irrational and the erratic, the aggressive and the libidinal, to make sense of the phenomenon of racism which holds so much of the globe to ransom. In this section, then, rather than reviewing the depressing paucity of previous psychoanalytic work on racism, I will examine in some detail some recent thinking to ask whether psychoanalysis' elaborate notion of 'otherness' can be used provocatively to enrich our understanding of how fearful and destructive the actual face of the 'other' can make us feel.

NEW SEXUAL AGENDAS[4]

Since the publication in 1974 of Juliet Mitchell's book, *Psychoanalysis and Feminism*, psychoanalysis has been drawn upon by many theorists attempting to articulate a new vision of gender and sexual relations – a 'new sexual agenda'.[5] This does not mean that Mitchell's defence of psychoanalysis has gone unchallenged. Indeed, the conservatism of psychoanalysis in this area is well documented: in theory and in clinical work it has rarely supplied convincing recruits to the radicalisation of gender politics or to the ranks of sexual revolution. Those who have tried using psychoanalysis in this way – for example, Herbert Marcuse – have usually been outsiders to the movement itself; while the exceptions – most obviously Wilhelm Reich – have risked exclusion. Where feminists have become psychoanalysts, the conservatism of the institutional structures have been difficult to combat – although there have been important exceptions to this rule with, for example, Jessica Benjamin, Nancy Chodorow and Juliet Mitchell herself continuing to produce theoretical work of remarkable quality.[6] More importantly, however, there is now a sense of banality about many of the psychoanalytic claims about gender and sexual difference. Freud's phallocentrism and misogyny, as well as his confusion over feminine development and sexuality, is so clearly documented as to require no detailed repetition.[7] The issue of 'penis envy', so long a stick for one side to beat the other with, has passed into history without much trace, and given Melanie Klein's revelations of the degree of envy existing in every individual subject, male or female, a little bit more or less, attached or not, does not seem likely to make much difference. The influential object-relational idea that girls, because of their close ties with their mothers, struggle with issues of autonomy and separation while boys trip up over intimacy can now be seen both as a truism and as a tautology, describing a socially induced state of affairs without grasping hold of the complexities of the psychological mechanisms at its root. To say that girls reproduce feminine stereotypes because of their identification with their mothers and boys become 'masculine' because of their repudiation of their mothers is not a specifically psychoanalytic formulation. It could just as easily have been derived from social learning theory.

If psychoanalysis is to offer some kind of significant challenge within the context of gender politics, it is important to hold on to something new and provocative in the psychoanalytic project, something off centre enough to make us look awry at ourselves, and at our gender and sexuality. It is fascinating to observe how many of the attempts to do this in recent years have centred on the work of Jacques Lacan (in Britain, at least, since the publication of *Psychoanalysis and Feminism*), if among feminists in particular this has been with considerable ambivalence.[8] It will be argued below that this is in part because of a genuine contribution by Lacan to the project of understanding sexual difference, but there can be little doubt that it is at least as much because of the 'effect' of Lacan, his constant disturbance of existing ideas. Undoubtedly, as Luce Irigaray has several times asserted, Lacan's work is confused, phallocentric and in many respects arid.[9] Yet it also seems to convey something of what one might look for in psychoanalysis – a theory and practice which keeps producing surprises, which never stands still and which couples every assertion with a question. Slavoj Žižek, whose book *Looking Awry* is subtitled, 'An introduction to Jacques Lacan through popular culture', follows a similar line of argument to the one developed here.[10] For Žižek, Lacan's appeal seems to be only partly because of the content of his theory; it also arises from the dizzying style of the work, its 'idiotic enjoyment' – a phrase Žižek uses about popular culture but which might easily apply to his own rendering of Lacan. Trying to look awry at psychoanalysis and the new sexual agenda, Lacan's maddening intervention has been a constant irritant, a voice announcing something unexpected.

Of particular interest in this respect has been Lacan's insistence that the true concern of psychoanalysis is with symbols and that the symbolic dimension of experience is always deeply infiltrated by the construction of sexual difference. In this apparently abstract argument there is an opportunity to focus on the way fantasy operates at the heart of gender, for the 'symbol', as it moves across its terrain, is something which codes and expresses fantasy rather than being a straightforward representation of 'reality'. Lacan emphasises the way the symbol works; that is, the material impact of the letter or the word is given priority over the intention of the subject who speaks it. Individuals are, therefore, better understood as *effects* as opposed to sources of meaning, positioned by the movement of the 'signifier' rather than (as in liberal theory) having language and meaning under control. While, again, this might in its abstraction appear to scale the heights of intellectual self abuse (what was Lacan himself if he was only an effect, not a cause?), it also reminds us that the consciously intentional aspect of human subjectivity – how we think of ourselves as masculine or feminine, for example – is a small and misleading part of the story. Behind every such conscious thought there is a fantasy called into being by the symbol as it slips into and out of existence. In this effect can be found the much-sought-after 'enjoyment', the excess that makes experience so rich and unbearable, which in this context means making gender such a central yet mystifying concern.

One argument to be developed below is that evoking Lacan in this way might lead to a more rigorous, less sloppy and sentimental use of psychoanalysis than can be derived from, for example, object relations or even Kleinian theory. Not everyone agrees, however, and it is worth noting that the opposition to the Lacanian influence comes not just from more traditional schools of psychoanalysis, but also from feminists who once worked with him or who derive their critical perspectives from a more activist politics or approach to social theory.[11] To some extent, this critique derives from a dislike of Lacan's famous 'ladies' man' masquerade – his coquettishness, his mystifications, his certainties which evoke uncertainty. They are also, however, built upon a more marked antagonism towards the content of Lacan's theory, to the extent that it seems to demonstrate an authoritative and unequivocal allegiance to patriarchal (usually expressed as 'phallocentric') orthodoxy. Lacan's reference, for instance, to the phallus as 'master' or 'privileged signifier' around which all sexualities and issues of sexual difference circulate seems to place him firmly in the hall of Freudian phallocrats, although it is worth noting that he is more slippery than most, evoking both a feminine counter to masculinity through the playfulness of his

notion of 'jouissance' (it is never fully clear whether this is a masculine or feminine form of ecstasy) and denying that the phallus has
any positive content outside its effects.[12]

The question of whether Lacanian theory does offer something
innovative and constructive to a 'new' and by implication non-
phallocentric sexual agenda is the focus of the latter part of this
section. However, one suggestion to make here is that criticism of
Lacan's apparent certainty may be part of the whole muddle in and
about psychoanalysis – the muddle of where something so slippery
as an exploration of the unconscious can be understood to be.
There are many *claimed* certainties in psychoanalysis, but none of
them can actually be certain, given that the procedure of psychoanalysis reveals so clearly that everything, even its own theories and
'findings', is imbued with the seductions and irrationality of
emotive, flamboyant, unconscious impulses. When psychoanalysts
start to believe in their knowledge they become ossified and drawn
into the ideologies of their social context; the history of psychoanalysis' treatment of homosexuality demonstrates this only too
well. More than anyone except Freud, Lacan succeeds in holding
open the terrain of 'truth', in constantly posing it as a question.
'Truth' is part of the effect of the signifier, linked into a shifting
chain which produces it as a kind of side effect. It is, therefore,
constantly on the move.

So the suggestion here is that there may be something in psychoanalysis which can still be a challenge to gender theory. In part this
lies in the idea – present in much psychoanalytic work but formulated most insistently by Lacan – that the organisation of our
sexuality comes in an important way from outside; that the agenda
of sexuality and sexual difference writes us, rather than the other
way around. This leads to an insistence on the social dimension as
primary in the production of gender. More generally, this mode of
psychoanalytic thinking is a challenge because it refutes certainties
– pre-given categories or complete understandings, fixed ways of
being or final acceptance. Lacan reveals this in some of his work,
but he is not the only source. Indeed, there is a sharp question mark
hanging over the Lacanian and post-Lacanian enterprise, concerned
with the degree to which the abstractions of these theories make
sense in relation to the concrete contents of gendered patterns of
being. In this respect, it is no accident that the deconstructive capac-
ities of Lacanianism have had their strongest impact on theory, not
clinical work. Detailed description and analysis of the patterns of

development and interpersonal relationship which lead to specific organisations of gender is not the Lacanian school's preferred way of working. Yet there has been very important work in this area and it may well be that it is in this more empirical approach that an account of gender relations which is both intellectually sound and 'user friendly' might reside. Lacan unsettles everything, which is well and good and postmodernistically correct, but if the received vision of gender development is to be challenged, it might be useful to have something more substantial to feed off. For example, if we have a good theory of gender identity formation, do we need Lacan at all?

Polymorphous identification

In a recent paper, the American psychoanalyst and feminist Jessica Benjamin makes an appeal for a more complex understanding of gender development than is available either in psychoanalysis or in contemporary gender theory. Criticising what she sees as the tendency to continually reproduce masculine identity and feminine identity as two opposed poles, she suggests that the psychological mechanism of *identification* is one which makes it possible to incorporate loving relationships both with those with whom we are ostensibly the 'same' and those from whom we are 'different'. Openness to the plurality of available identifications is a way of transcending or transgressing the conventional rigidity of masculine *versus* feminine. Benjamin writes: 'If sex and gender as we know them are oriented to the pull of opposing poles, then these poles are not masculinity and femininity. Rather, gender dimorphism itself represents only one pole, the other pole being the polymorphism of the psyche.[13]

The 'polymorphism of the psyche' is an appealing notion suggesting that, psychologically speaking, it may be possible to take up multiple positions, built around fluid identifications with others, in the areas of sex and gender as well as elsewhere. Benjamin, basing herself on recent psychoanalytic theorising and observational work,[14] offers a developmental account of how this might come about, emphasising the significance of identificatory love (particularly, in children of both sexes, for the father) and criticising traditional psychoanalytic renderings of the Oedipus complex as contributing to a focus on difference at the expense of what might be termed 'connectedness' or, in Benjamin's words, 'commonality'.

Her general moral, political and psychological stance here is to hold that while the acceptance of difference is an important developmental achievement, *by itself* it is merely a formula for the preservation of rigid dimorphism. She lays out the general point elegantly as follows:

> The implicit assumption in differentiation theory is that acknowledging difference has a higher value, is a later achievement, is more difficult than recognising likeness. The neglected point is that the difficulty lies in assimilating difference without repudiating likeness; that is, in straddling the space between the opposites. It is easy enough to give up one side of the polarity in order to oscillate towards the other side. What is difficult is to attain a notion of difference, being unlike, without giving up a sense of commonality, of being a 'like' human being.[15]

In Benjamin's version of things, the classical account of the Oedipal father as a prohibitive force produces a gender dimorphic theory (and practice, one might add) in which paternal and maternal principles are opposed. The only way forward with such a theory is to emphasise difference, eventually validating one pole (usually masculine) over the other. By contrast, exploring multiple identifications, particularly in what is conventionally termed the pre-Oedipal period, leads to a recognition of the existence of a plurality of subject positions out of which each human subject is built. This serves to undermine any claims to fixedness in identity, here specifically and particularly gender identity. Benjamin suggests that it is to the degree that the pre-Oedipal child has 'lovingly incorporated through identification' the characteristics of the other, that loss can be managed and the Oedipal child can avoid repudiating or idealising the other.[16] That is, if cross-sex identification based on love has been possible early on, later absolute differentiation from the other need not occur; theories and practices based on such absolute distinctions are consequently markers of failed identificatory processes, not descriptions of necessary or even healthy development. Such theories and practices also lead to a rigid vision of gender identity as something fixed, stable and homogeneous, when in fact the prospects for decent human relationships rely on it not being like that – on, for example, it being possible for a man to imagine what it might be like to be a woman, in the sexual relationship as well as in parenting and other aspects of life.

Benjamin's description of recent psychoanalytic work on gender development and her critique and revision of Oedipal theory offer an important and empirically grounded route into the study of gender polymorphism. In particular, her emphasis on the fluidity of subject positions is one which is commensurate with much contemporary feminist thought and with the insights of postmodernism. If there is a challenge to be found in this it is to any approach that marks out the terrain of difference as something fixed, with opposed elements (such as masculine and feminine) which are incommensurable or incompatible with one another. Careful thinking about and observation of the way infants develop – how identifications occur and make available objects which can be taken in to form the infant's mental world – suggest that the widespread configuration of sexual difference as something compelling and irrevocable need not be maintained. In terms of psychoanalytic and political theory, Benjamin's paper suggests that much of our brow beating about the difficulty of taking up the position of the 'other' is itself in the service of preserving that difficulty – it emphasises what holds people apart and represses that which links them together.

The great value of Benjamin's work is to draw together observational material and psychoanalytic theory to question traditional analytic assumptions (particularly about the 'reality' orientation of the Oedipal stage versus the 'narcissistic' orientation of the pre-Oedipal) and to show their affiliation to wider imperatives towards gender fixity. That is, Benjamin manages to re-examine and rework traditional psychoanalytic theory and to show the implications of this for a more general (feminist and other) understanding of gender positions. Moreover, she achieves her critique of psychoanalysis' (and society's) Oedipal vision (the idea that the paternal Law necessarily fixes gender identity for all time) without bolstering an alternative valuation of the same vision by idealising the pre-Oedipal relationship with the mother, as object-relations theorists do. Staying within the terms of psychoanalysis, with a commitment to the uncovering of unconscious mental structures, Benjamin shows that it is possible to historicise the opposition of pre-Oedipal and Oedipal in psychoanalysis and to show how it has been part of a wider social process of polarising gender. In so doing, she explicitly articulates a psychoanalytic theory to contest this polarising, dichotomising tendency – one based on fluid and multiple identifications cutting across traditional 'paternal' and 'maternal' positions.

Benjamin is an unusually complex and sophisticated psychoanalytic theorist who rarely loses sight of the interpenetration of subjective and social processes. Nevertheless, without displacing her critical vision, it is worth laying the alternative Lacanian one over it. This is of particular interest in relation to the psychological mechanism of identification, which Benjamin places at the centre of her account. It seems logically and empirically likely that identification might be the crucial psychological process out of which identity – including gender and sexual identity – is constructed. But what exactly does 'identification' mean here? Is it, for example, a love relation between a pre-existent ego and a nominated object, or a process of taking in and transforming aspects of the other so that they are experienced as elements of the self? Is it something interpersonal or social–structural? More fully, what is the relationship between identification as something operating between one actual individual (for example, a child) and another, and between the socially sanctioned symbolic aspects of each of their positions? (This is akin to the thorny old chestnut, does a boy without a father have an Oedipus complex? If so, with whom does he identify – a real alternative father or a symbolic position: the social Law?) What structures the fantasy space in which identifications move? Is it the empirical encounter between self and other or something outside this which already prompts the identifications to take a certain form? Here, filling out these questions, Lacan makes some pertinent points.

Neutrality and the letter

One way into the question of what lies behind or beyond identification is through one of Lacan's most famous seminars, the 1955 discussion of Edgar Allan Poe's story *The Purloined Letter*.[17] On the face of it, Lacan uses this story to project a vision of the psychoanalyst as master investigator, able to enter into and then release himself from the circuit of desire at will, with profound self consciousness and some humour. However, there are a number of complications which call into question Lacan's integrity here – but which also highlight the problematic aspects of identification and investment, particularly as they drift across sexual difference.

Poe's tale is told by a narrator, a Watson-like figure who is foil to the investigator/analyst Dupin and who extracts from him his philosophical musings and his account of how he outwitted the Minister who had stolen – in broad daylight – a potentially compromising letter from the Queen. Reading the Poe original with a psychoanalytic but not-yet Lacanian eye, the issue of identification stands out as a crucial theme. The police fail to find the stolen letter because their ludicrously exact investigation is couched at the wrong level; they can only act according to their own beliefs about how a thief might behave. Dupin, on the other hand, imagines himself inside the mind of the Minister, identifies with him and thus comprehends what his course of action is likely to have been. He understands that the thief's actions will have been determined not by reason alone, but by something more imaginative, rigorous and compelling – which Dupin suggests is made possible by the Minister being not just a mathematician, but also a poet. Dupin himself, arch analyst, also writes verse, giving him a capacity to transcend the simple logic of those who just follow the rules and to enter into the mind of the other, eventually to trick him and recover the lost object.

Lacan makes use of the story in a variety of ways, appropriating it as an illustration of his argument that 'From the start, and independently of any attachment to some supposedly causal bond, the symbol already plays, and produces by itself, its necessities, its structure, its organisations'.[18] Additionally, and more specifically, the story illustrates the 'inmixing of subjects', the way each subject is penetrated by something else and thus speaks from a position off centre to itself – a reminder of the fragmentary status of the ego which is one of the themes of this book of the seminar. In Lacan's reading, it is the letter itself which penetrates the subject, a causal signifier producing effects: whoever has it in her or his possession is found to be subject to some loss or new relationship. For Lacan, the letter represents the 'pure state' of the symbol, the 'original, radical subject': 'One can say that, when the characters get a hold of this letter, something gets a hold of them and carries them along and this something clearly has dominion over their individual idiosyncrasies.'[19]

Reading the journey of the letter in this literal way, Lacan is able to argue that the impact of the circuit of exchanges documented in the story is to demonstrate how the unconscious disrupts the fixed identity of 'character' or even 'sexual attitude' – how each subject is impossible to place. 'Everything which could serve to define the characters as real – qualities, temperament, heredity, nobility – has nothing to do with the story.'[20] It is the position of the letter that is crucial, who has it and to what use it might be put. Moreover, this position defines not only the status of the subjects, but their sexed identity. So the Minister is feminised in the story when he disguises the letter by putting his own seal on it and addressing it to himself in a feminine hand. Furthermore, when he becomes the duped one from whom the letter is stolen (by Dupin), he takes up the position previously occupied by the Queen:

> The Minister is in what had been the Queen's position, the police are in that of the King, of this degenerate King who believes only in the real, and who sees nothing. The step-wise displacement of the characters is perfect. And simply because he interposed himself in the rest of the discourse, and came into possession of this little nothing of a letter, sufficient to wreak havoc, this most cunning of foxes, this most ambitious of climbers, this intriguer's intriguer, this dilettante's dilettante, doesn't see that his secret will be pinched from under his nose.[21]

The power of the analyst lies in standing outside the game; once one becomes part of it, as the Minister does when he takes the letter, one is caught up in the network of loss and desire through which every subject is structured. Lacan links this with a description of the excessive nature of the anxiety surrounding the letter and of the impossibility of speaking of it; its threat both creates something between Minister and Queen and feminises them both. Why should this thing produce such anxiety, such a sense that if it is lost, one's whole position and identity goes with it? In Lacanian theory, anxiety of this kind is always referred back to the castration complex, understood not just as a configuration of ambivalent emotions but also as a passage from one psychological register to another. Through the castration complex, the subject takes on the weight of culture, thus experiencing the power of an external structure to rupture the fantasy of wholeness and potency around which subjectivity might otherwise be organised. The phallus acts as primary signifier of this state, a source of effectivity which is coveted by all but belongs to no one. At all moments of desire and loss, this shimmering ambiguity is recalled: that that which is most desired is always out of reach. It is, therefore, not surprising to find here too, in the passage of a compromising letter from hand to hand, an evocation of the castration complex as that which sets the symbolic game in motion. The letter creates excessive anxiety because of the effects of its loss, its impact is most potent where it itself is not.

Here Lacan seems to be pursuing the idea of subjectivity –

including (or primarily) sexed subjectivity – as something produced by the position taken up by the subject in the circuit of exchange. However, a different light is thrown on this issue by consideration of what has several times been noted as the most striking feature of Poe's story *omitted* in Lacan's reading, the function of the narrator.[22] Lacan seems to identify Dupin with the position of the psychoanalyst, for example when discussing the issue of payment for services rendered – for advice. Dupin escapes from the game (gives up the letter) when he is paid. Lacan notes that this is also true for the analyst: prices 'have the function of neutralising something infinitely more dangerous than paying in money, namely owing someone something'.[23] Yet, while Dupin has the capacity for imagining another's thought which might be regarded as a necessary underpinning of analytic practice, he is also personally invested in the outcome to a degree which one would not conventionally expect of a psychoanalyst. In fact, every character in the story has a motive impelling them to act in a certain way. The Queen wishes to preserve her position in the eyes of the King; the Minister is a schemer who uses his possession of the letter – and the Queen's knowledge of this possession – to gain political advantage; and the Prefect of Police, who seeks Dupin's advice, is interested in the reward. Dupin, too, is interested in payment, but the end of the tale reveals that he is also motivated by competitive admiration and hatred of the Minister (who once did him an 'evil turn'). He is thus a full player in the game, with an investment in its outcome. This motivated consciousness is also true of the psychoanalyst Jacques Lacan: he had a teaching, he was involved in psychoanalytic politics and he was no pure observer of the scene. Only the narrator of the tale is neutral, the one who, in Lacan's words from elsewhere, 'does not make you speak'. On the other hand, true neutrality lies only with the medium, the system itself. The problem for the Minister is that he believes he is immune to the circuit produced by the letter – that he can hold on to it. This is the source of his defeat. Dupin, on the other hand, knows he cannot hold the letter, so he gives it up on payment. In terms of sexual difference, this suggests that when we strive to be at one with our supposed masculine or feminine being, to find ourselves in a sexed identity, however polymorphous, we risk being duped. We are always in a provisional place, about to be moved.

The seminar on *The Purloined Letter* thus raises numerous questions concerning the structural role of desire, the derivation and motivation of action and the place of the psychoanalyst. It evokes the castration complex as something which does not fix masculinity and femininity in place so much as undermine the possibility of fixedness, opening a space into which both male and female fall and become interchangeable as the letter of desire leaves them grasping after it. In Lacan's reading of this tale, identifications are mobile and multiple, and as each character takes up his or her position they are disrupted by some further movement of the circuit. Moreover, no one is neutral; each of us is infiltrated by what we have to say. The fiction of identity is undermined by the indefatigable pressure of this speaking voice. Taken together with Lacan's other writings on sexual difference and with the general Lacanian stance described earlier, we are left less with the image traditionally credited to him of each subject inhabiting a structure of alienation from which experience is perceived in an unremittingly gendered way, and more with an appreciation of the way all subject positions are nominated by the symbolic system yet are also undercut by the movement of fantasy. In this dynamic there is the possibility of formulating a psychoanalytic theory which does not essentialise subjectivity and ignore society. Moreover, it shows how the very mechanisms at the heart of gender construction – notably, identification – are themselves brokered between the symbolic order of society and the fantasy space of the individual subject. Judith Butler, who is a critic of Lacan on many issues, nevertheless expresses the power of this idea for psychoanalytic gender theory:

> [Lacan] poses the relation between the sexes in terms that reveal the speaking 'I' as a masculinised effect of repression, one which postures as an autonomous and self-grounding subject, but whose very coherence is called into question by the sexual positions that it excludes in the process of identity formation. For Lacan, the subject comes into being – that is, begins to posture as a self-grounding signifier within language – only on the condition of a primary repression of the pre-individuated incestuous pleasures associated with the (now repressed) maternal body.[24]

Identity depends on the occlusion of its conditions of existence, yet the more firmly identity – specifically, here, sexual identity – is clung to, the more precarious is the hold on it. Butler continues: 'The injunction to become sexed in the ways prescribed by the Symbolic always leads to failure and, in some cases, to the exposure of the phantasmatic nature of sexual identity itself.'[25] As the game moves on, as the letter is passed around, our fantasies make us inhabit different positions. Identification makes this possible, but it is not a simple choice; it just happens.

Identification and the provisional

The argument here is that psychoanalysis can be used to undermine claims to fixedness or authenticity, in sex and gender as in every-thing else. Sexed identities, like ascriptions of mastery, are always invitations to dismemberment: as they are declared, so something enters in to disrupt them, to suggest an identification with some-thing else or an origin somewhere else. Psychoanalysis, at least when used in this way, suggests that all our identities are at most 'provi-sional', functioning as scaffolding around which fantasies are built and projections located and held, but ready to dissolve and re-emerge if only we can let them. Benjamin refers to identificatory love as a way forward into recognising the multiplicity of subject positions which are possible, thus undermining the fixed divide of difference. Lacan shows that difference – specifically sexual differ-ence – is contravened by the fragmenting impact of the 'letter of the unconscious', the presence within the human subject of something which is non-sexual yet produces the effects of sexuality. Benjamin focuses on the creative promise of the polymorphism of the psyche; Lacan focuses on its threat. Nevertheless, in their very different ways, both demonstrate that within the desiring space with which psychoanalysis deals can be found a great uncertainty, a rich equiv-ocation concerning what each of us may come to be.

In this work, psychoanalytic though it is, there is a critique of what psychoanalysis becomes when it loses sight of its own discur-sive position. Both Benjamin and Lacan are explicit about this, Benjamin in her castigation of the ideological basis of Oedipal theory:

> Paradoxically, the image of the liberating father undermines the acceptance of difference that the Oedipus complex is meant to embody. For the idea of the father as protection against 'limitless narcissism' at once authorises his idealisation and the mother's denigration. . . . Difference turns out to be governed by the code of domination.[26]

and Lacan in his relentless critique of ego psychology and object relational concepts of 'maturity':

In any case man cannot aim at being whole (the 'total person-ality' being another premise where modern psychotherapy goes off course) once the play of displacement and condensation, to which he is committed in the exercise of his functions, marks his relation as subject to the signifier.[27]

Focused on the issue of gender politics, both these perspectives suggest that psychoanalysis too readily lays itself open to the normalising pressures of familial and patriarchal ideology, not just in the much-commented-upon recourse to explicitly misogynist concepts, but also in the more subtle form of acceptance of the structural assumptions and values of a society built around gender polarisation. Both Benjamin and Lacan, in their radically distinct registers, promote a vision of the dynamism and fluidity of gender construction. Moreover, this work shows that it might (just) be possible to hold on to a radical pursuit of psychoanalysis in which too much 'knowledge' is seen as a symptom of a failure of imagina-tion. Benjamin reveals that Oedipal certainty is ideologically driven and that one has to displace it if one is to articulate a psychoana-lytic account of gendered subjectivity. Lacan, despite his own investment in the Oedipal paradigm and the apparent determinism of the comment which closes the seminar on the purloined letter ('a letter always reaches its destination'),[28] demonstrates the require-ment for an analyst to remain on her or his toes and to continually slip away from any danger of being tied down. When the psychoan-alyst moves from being 'the subject supposed to know' to being 'the subject who knows' (as Lacan does, but not all the time), the critical possibilities of psychoanalysis are lost and it ceases, in the terms borrowed from Marcuse in the last chapter, to be a 'negative' theory. In the context of gender politics, this seems always to involve a forgetting of the historical constructedness of gendered categories and a willingness to pronounce on the correct way to be 'masculine' or 'feminine'.

Enough contributions opposed to this tendency have come from psychoanalysis in recent years to suggest that it continues to be alive to the danger and that it may yet have new things to say about sexual difference, but in order to do so it needs to retain its own disruptive potential in the face of the enormous pressure to bow to the demand to make everything clear and safe. As will be seen in the next section of this chapter, clarity and safety of this kind is no good thing, either for psychoanalysis or for the objects of its gaze.

ON MALE AND FEMALE HOMOSEXUALITY

Psychoanalysis has been engaged with homosexuality from its inception, with Freud struggling manfully against the recognition of lesbianism in his 'Dora' case. His famous footnote added at the end of the case history is an explicit recognition of a blind spot that continued to trouble the vision of psychoanalysts for generations afterwards:

> The longer the interval of time that separates me from the end of this analysis, the more probable it seems to me that the fault in my technique lay in this omission: I failed to discover in time and to inform the patient that her homosexual (gynaecophilic) love for Frau K. was the strongest unconscious current in her mental life. . . . Before I had learnt the importance of the homosexual current in psychoneurotics, I was often brought to a standstill in the treatment of my cases or found myself in complete perplexity.[29]

The complexity of Freud's state of mind when faced with homosexuality in his analysands and others will be outlined below, but this note shows, at least, his capacity for recognition of his analytic failures. It also suggests that, somehow, homosexuality can only be given its proper place retrospectively, not in the heat of the moment of analysis. Only afterwards, reflecting on the end of the work and its failure (Dora walked out on Freud, depriving him of the 'satisfaction' of curing her), could Freud transcend his own transference. Specifically, this meant overcoming his wish or belief that he stood in Dora's fantasy for the significant men in her life, so that he could see that her desire was primarily directed elsewhere. With the advantage of distance, and despite his clear wish to show himself and his methods in a positive light, Freud is able to make a space for homosexuality as a legitimate and significant psychological 'current'. The same cannot be said for many other psychoanalytic writers who, on the subject of homosexuality, have been reluctant to recognise their own investment in failing to understand it or to do anything other than repudiate it. In fact, accusations of homophobia against psychoanalysts as individuals and as a collective abound in the recent literature, making psychoanalysis an object of derision and concern among gay and lesbian activists – even, and especially poignantly, those who turn to psychoanalysis in the hope of finding personal guidance and help. Kenneth Lewes, early in his study of psychoanalytic accounts of male homosexuality, comments: 'The enmity between homosexuals and psychoanalysis is extremely unfortunate, but the blame for its emergence rests squarely on the analytic establishment alone.'[30]

A few statements of the case against psychoanalysis will serve to communicate some of the content of the critique – basically, that homosexuality has been an arena for the display of psychoanalysis' most conformist aspects, revealing the anxieties of psychoanalysts about themselves and their discipline more than it reveals anything worthwhile about homosexuality itself. They also convey something of the pain felt by those who have tried to open psychoanalysts' eyes to the disreputable activity of which they have been guilty or who have felt the perverted gaze of psychoanalysis on their own skin. Here, for example, are the words of Robert Stoller who, despite impressive empirical and psychoanalytic work in the area of sexuality, never managed to transform the American psychoanalytic culture in the way he wished:

> [The] analytic literature is crammed with judgements about 'the homosexual' and 'homosexuality', using a logic that needs to equate homosexual impulses and acts as being, at bottom, made from the same stuff. To obscure things further, a highly abstract, theory-laden, speculation-soaked, scientistic, pseudoexplanatory jargon is offered – and accepted in psychoanalytic circles – as the clinical evidence.[31]

Stoller, in his own words, kept 'hammering' on at the idea that homosexuals are not necessarily more disturbed, neurotically or psychotically, than heterosexuals and hence that the tendency of psychoanalysts to equate homosexuality with pathology was misplaced.[32] Moreover, the generalisation of the category 'homosexual' to include friendships as well as erotic relationships was seen by Stoller as indicative of the flimsy and chaotic state of psychoanalytic knowledge. But his rage seems to have been stimulated most by the incapacity of analysts to learn from their mistakes, to be open to the findings of empirical research or even the straightforward arguments of those who show how wrong most of psychoanalysis' assumptions about homosexuality have been. This suggests some investment on the part of psychoanalysts in maintaining their negative view of homosexuality. Stoller, like many other critics, is fairly sure about where this investment is to be found. In naming it, he also draws attention to another deeply felt

complaint about psychoanalysis: its historic refusal to allow homosexuals to train as psychoanalysts:

> Is it improper to suggest that some analysts' problems in under-
> standing homosexuality have – to put it delicately –
> psychodynamic roots? That would tell me, as the more rational
> explanations do not, why we have by-laws against accepting
> homosexuals as candidates, members of the faculty, or super-
> vising and training analysts. The justification for such regulations
> is our 'knowing' that these people must, by definition, be as
> alleged: fatally flawed psychotic like creatures in states of near-
> annihilation of the self (covered over, of course, by
> normal-appearing behaviour). If we mindlessly judge people that
> way – 'everyone knows it' – then we are very cruel. How many
> grossly, overtly heterosexual candidates have been accepted and
> been graduated who – as their analyses demonstrated and their
> later behaviour confirmed – have severe character defects? We
> have transformed diagnosis into accusation, covering our
> behaviour with jargon. But though it hides hatred, it promotes
> cruelty; jargon is judgement. We should tighten our logic and
> loosen our by-laws.[33]

The intensity of this language is not just the consequence of moral
indignation, but also of a feeling of betrayal: that psychoanalysis,
through its own incapacity to deal with its repressed impulses,
cannot respond to the evidence of psychodynamic and other
studies, to the needs of a specific client group or to the appeals of
those who would wish it to have something useful to say on an issue
of major contemporary interest and concern.

Commenting on the infamous insistence by Charles Socarides
that homosexuality is always pathological and usually signifies
narcissistic disturbance, Richard Friedman connects the scientific
with the personal in a manner usually avoided by psychoanalysts
writing on homosexuality:

> Most behavioural scientists, however, and many psychoanalysts
> reject the hypothesis that predominant or exclusive homosexu-
> ality is associated with pathological narcissism. The basis for this
> rejection is not only that scientific studies do not support the
> association but also that personal experience provides mean-
> ingful evidence to the contrary. ... Many mental health
> professionals do have lasting friendships with gay men, have

shared happiness and sorrow with them, offered support to and received support from them. These professionals dismiss the idea that their friends must be pathologically narcissistic because they are gay.[34]

Interestingly, even in this liberal appeal to personal experience of non-narcissistic relationships with homosexual men, there is a distancing of the gay community from the professional one: the mental health professionals 'have lasting friendships with gay men', but are not themselves gay. The appeal here is for the one community – the professionals – to recognise the mental health of the other. Homosexuality is read as *outside* the mental health community – as indeed, for psychoanalysis at least, is officially the case,

> A homosexual individual who applies to enter a psychoanalytic institute because s/he believes it would offer the best training experience possible could be in for a humiliating shock. The hopeful aspirant may find that s/he is not perceived as an individual with a complex personality and possible talents to offer in the therapeutic field, but as someone with a personality disorder which automatically renders him/her unfit to train as an analyst or psychoanalytic psychotherapist.[35]

Homosexuality has, historically, been an exclusion criterion when it comes to acceptance for training as a psychoanalyst or psychoanalytic psychotherapist, and it probably remains so, implicitly at least, in practice. This may indeed be one of the causes of the continuing pathologising of – and ignorance about – homosexuality among psychoanalysts. It has been pointed out several times that, whereas there were always women analysts who could in principle speak up for women in the institutions of psychoanalysis, the absence of openly gay and lesbian analysts means that pressure from this particular oppressed group could only come from outside.[36] *Why* homosexuals should be denied training rights is a moot point. Freud himself was opposed to any ban. Together with Otto Rank, he wrote as follows to Ernest Jones in 1921 criticising Jones's decision not to allow a homosexual applicant admission to the British Psycho-Analytical Society:

> Your query, dear Ernest, concerning prospective membership of homosexuals has been considered by us and we disagree with you. In effect we cannot exclude such persons without other

sufficient reasons, as we cannot agree with their legal prosecution. We feel that a decision in such cases should depend upon a thorough examination of the other qualities of the candidate.[37]

Yet the ban was made and spread, ostensibly because homosexuals are fixated at an early, pre-Oedipal phase of development and hence would be incapable of dealing with the complex Oedipal transferences characteristic of treatment of heterosexual neurotics. The incoherence of this position is now legendary and one particularly well-worded riposte by 'Rachel Cunningham' (a pseudonym taken by a London psychotherapist presumably out of concern for her own position should she be identified as homosexual) can stand for many:

> Many objections levelled against prospective homosexual trainees could as well be directed at the many analysts who have failed to gain the trust of homosexual patients and have therefore been unable to help them, the result being that analysts pronounce homosexuals un-analysable. That is, they have been too bound by their own sexual mores, having blundered in their countertransferences due to unease about their own possible homosexual tendencies, and have attempted to impose their ideas of 'right' on people who were more in need of understanding, mental and emotional holding and clear-sighted analysis of their conflicts and dilemmas.[38]

This is closely akin to Stoller's point that heterosexuality is no guarantor of mental health and that there are no distinguishable differences in level of pathology between homosexuals, taken as a group, and heterosexuals. Cunningham herself allows that there might be specific difficulties for gay and lesbian therapists in dealing with 'envy of the parental couple', seen particularly by Kleinian analysts as an essential attribute of emotional maturity. The homosexual individual, it is assumed, will be rivalrous for the love of the same-sex parent, thus making it difficult to tolerate the fantasy of a different-sexed pair in loving creative contact.[39] However, Cunningham argues that this is something which can be dealt with during the training analysis, implying that it is to be examined on an individual basis rather than through a blanket debarring of all homosexual training candidates. Moreover, she notes, 'it seems that the ability to hold in central place the notion of creative parental intercourse and the togetherness of the parental couple is a feat of some difficulty for very many people'.[40] Again, the assumption that by the very fact of her or his object choice a homosexual individual will be pathological is at the heart of a central element in psychoanalytic life: not just the treatment of clients, but the selection of analysts themselves.

If one asks what it is that produces this negativity in psychoanalysis, the suggestions which come back from its critics centre on one major idea: it is countertransference, in the traditional sense of the analyst's (and, by the same token, the analytic *movement's*) unworked-through unconscious inhibitions. Several writers argue that homosexuality is split off from the consciousness of psychoanalysis, continuing to trouble individual analysts and the analytic institutions precisely because the homosexual elements of these individual analysts and their institutions are not properly worked through and integrated. That is, rather than the homosexuals being 'insufficiently analysed', it is the analysts who suffer from that trouble. Cunningham comments: '[Homosexuality] seems almost to be, not a repressed entity or complex, but a disavowed one, projected or split off into the external world ("Them") where it can only be seen as threatening, pernicious.'[41]

Noreen O'Connor and Joanna Ryan, similarly, point to the inadequate theorisation of homosexuality and the failure of analysts to articulate a vision of 'an integrated, non-perverse, mature and manifest homosexuality, or of what is required to achieve this' as evidence for the splitting off of homosexuality from the analytic psyche. They go on to comment, from a number of clinical examples, that this defensive pattern can be observed in the detail of therapeutic contacts as well as in the theories and policies of psychoanalytic institutions. In particular, their examples suggest 'how difficult it can be for therapists and analysts working with lesbian or other patients to be able to receive erotic material, either as indirectly reported or more directly in the transference, without unduly defensive reactions being mobilised'.[42] Countertransference issues are rarely discussed in the literature on homosexuality, with the result that all pathology is located firmly in the lesbian or gay client, without proper consideration of the analyst's difficulties. Moreover, many psychoanalysts have in the past taken alteration of a homosexual's object choice as a therapeutic aim – a departure from the traditionally neutral psychoanalytic position that the task of analysis is to enable a patient to become more of an agent, making choices, without prescribing what the content of these choices should be. Why should psychoanalysts be tempted in this way to divert themselves from their usual practice? Because, the argument goes, they are afraid of what homosexuality in their clients brings up for themselves. If this is the case, the active stance of the analyst towards her or his homosexual patient is likely to interfere with the possibility of forming an appropriate treatment alliance or indeed of recognising and responding to the issues troubling the patient as these arise in the transference. This might explain some of the many reports in the literature of homosexual patients finding themselves badly treated by analysts, or of patients who are too 'resistant' for therapeutic progress to be achieved.

Psychoanalysts have to face a considerable amount of disturbance in their patients, as psychoanalysis has always addressed itself to the most distressing and madness-inducing aspects of psychological and social functioning. Why should it be, then, that homosexuality produces such a limited, confused and intellectually impoverished response in a discipline which prides itself on not turning away from the real horrors of human existence? What is it about the love of a person for someone of the same sex that is so unforgivable as to make psychoanalysis (once spoken of by Freud as 'the plague' in terms now resonant with the AIDS vocabulary of homophobia) turn away and join forces with the moralists in repudiating its legitimacy? Cunningham suggests that it is in part because psychoanalysis has bought into an impossible ideal of heterosexual completeness and projected the failure and guilt associated with it into the obvious 'other'. But this can be only part of the story because it does not explain *why* psychoanalysis should act in this way – why homosexuality should be the ground on which it shows itself to be conformist and self deceiving. In this area, the betrayal by psychoanalysis of Freud's most radical positions is at its most obvious, raising the question of whether it is right that the dynamite which is the unconscious should be entrusted to the analytic profession.

Freudian ambivalence

There can be little doubt that Freud's ambivalence over homosexuality was real but it is quite a lesson in the way conformism can creep over a potentially critical discipline to witness the extent to which only one side of this ambivalence – Freud's view of homosexuality as arrested development – has been legitimised in the psychoanalytic literature. This process has been documented in detail in recent years, particularly by Kenneth Lewes. He comments:

> we can see that in the forty or so years from the time of the publication of Freud's *Three Essays* to that of the Kinsey Report, the original revolutionary fervour of Freud's discoveries and the hope that new knowledge could make society more humane had changed into a reactionary attempt to preserve old values and old institutions, even at the expense of honestly acknowledging evidence to the contrary, or of the human sympathy and concern that had motivated the psychoanalytic movement from the very beginning.[43]

This is a general statement, intended to apply to psychoanalysis as a whole and it is partly in line with the argument of other more overtly political studies, such as that of Russell Jacoby.[44] In relation to homosexuality, the drift from Freud is a peculiar mixture of moralising and demonising, linked to a growing adherence to a conservative familial ideology. It is perhaps no surprise that this should be most pronounced in America, where psychoanalysis made a strong and at times successful bid for leadership of the mental health establishment, consequently repressing its own tendency to subversion and political critique. America has also been characterised by a strong gay movement towards which psychoanalysis has taken a defensive and at times abusive posture. Robert Friedman comments about this that American psychoanalysts have acted as if 'any theoretical revisions regarding homosexuality would capitulate to gay ideology and damage the orthodox analytic position',[45] suggesting that psychoanalysis has been more concerned with its purity and its institutional standing than with an honest response to criticism. Indeed, Friedman argues that this stance has led to a growing irrelevance of psychoanalysis in discussions of homosexuality, where its place has been usurped by other disciplines. Whether or not these 'other sciences' have genuinely advanced understanding of homosexuality, it is clearly the case that psychoanalysis, for all its apparent open-minded concern with sexuality in all its forms, has failed to offer any sophisticated response to the new patterns of gay and lesbian consciousness. Moreover, it has to be stated that in adopting a reactionary stance, psychoanalysis was not simply betraying its founder and its own 'truth' in the face of external pressures to conform; it was also living out a particular aspect of itself – the conservative, normalising and pathologising element which can be observed in operation from Freud on. Indeed, the case of homosexuality raises very clearly the spectre that psychoanalysis might be nothing more than an elaborate dressing up of a brutal and repressive ideology.

Freud made some clear statements that homosexuality was not an 'illness' and, as noted above, that it should not prove to be a bar to analytic training. In his famous 'letter to an American mother' who wrote to him expressing concern over her son's homosexuality, Freud stated straightforwardly that homosexuality 'is nothing to be ashamed of, no vice, no degradation, it cannot be classified as an illness'.[46] His own admiration for ancient Greece was one basis for his refusal to see male homosexuality as something abhorrent and his insistence on the existence of 'normal homosexuality' linked to the bisexuality present in every human subject reinforces this. The following comment from Freud's *Three Essays on the Theory of Sexuality* is categorical in this regard:

> Psychoanalytic research is most decidedly opposed to any attempt at separating off homosexuals from the rest of mankind as a group of special character. . . . [It] has found that all human beings are capable of making a homosexual object-choice and in fact have made one in their unconscious. Indeed, libidinal attachments to persons of the same sex play no less a part as factors in normal mental life, and a greater part as a motive force for illness, than do similar attachments to the opposite sex.[47]

In his theoretical system Freud made a clear distinction, lost among later analysts, between 'perversions' marked by disturbances of the sexual aim and homosexuality as 'inversion', in which there is a variation from the norm in choice of object but not otherwise in the structure of sexuality. Indeed, as many authors have pointed out, in the Freudian scheme sexual development is a contingent and erratic series of events, and eventual *heterosexuality* is as much in need of explanation as any homosexual object choice.[48] However, against this liberal–egalitarian tendency in Freud can be set some of the content of his own theorising, in which heterosexuality is set up as the eventual goal of normal development and homosexuality is read pathologically as a fixation or disturbance of the developmental path. For example, the normal period of a boy's love for his mother might be intensified in pre-homosexual boys and, if family relationships and constitutional factors so determine, might be combined with an identification with the mother to produce in the boy a 'narcissistic' object choice. What this means is that the boy takes himself as sexual object instead of taking the 'other' as such; homosexual object choice is thus a choice of 'like' instead of 'different'. The sources of all this are varied but nevertheless traceable in the history of the individual homosexual person:

> Various factors may favour homosexuality in the boy, including the relative strengths of anal fixations, phallic narcissism, castration fears, or even an intense brother rivalry. . . . Freud also implicated typical family patterns as pathogenic. In relation to the mother, excess attachment, seductiveness, or traumatic observations of female genitalia all could conspire toward incest fears and a flight from women. In relation to the father, exaggerated Oedipal fears could result in a wholesale withdrawal from heterosexual competition.[49]

Kenneth Lewes points out that the implications of this theory include the idea that at the root of male homosexuality is an unresolved fixation upon the idealised mother which prevents the 'normal' Oedipal turn away from her as a consequence of the castration complex. Homosexual object choice is thus a way of preserving the loved (pre-Oedipal) mother in fantasy and is based on an unconscious wish to avoid castration; it is thus dominated by anxiety ('horror of the mutilated female genitals') rather than preference.[50] The male homosexual seeks reassurance of the continued existence of his genital through taking as a lover someone who is like him in continuing to posses a penis, so the 'reality' of castration need therefore never be faced. However, such a narcissistic object choice militates against the formation of true object relationships because the other is being used to shore up a fragile sense of integrity rather than being explored as a subject in her or his own right.

In the case of female homosexuality, Freud seems to have emphasised the quality of repudiation, seeing the attraction of a woman for another woman more as a negative thing (neither wants the man) than as a positive. Commenting on Freud's 'Psychogenesis of a case of homosexuality in a woman',[51] O'Connor and Ryan point to Freud's discomfort with the way his young woman patient seemed to have no need of *him*. They link this to the absence of an account of her object choice made in positive terms:

> We are thus presented with some startling forced choices, where

choosing something of one kind (women) means repudiating another (men). The possibility of a woman choosing another woman as a love-object without repudiating men, or femininity, or motherhood, is foreclosed upon, and we are left with female homosexuality as inevitably a negative and reactive choice, based on the exclusion of men.[52]

There has been a strong sense in later analytic writing that lesbian sexuality is barely to be regarded as sexuality at all: not a perversion, not a mode of sexual expression, but something substitute and unreal, produced because of a failure to find heterosexual fulfilment. Discussing a passage in Lacan's paper, 'The meaning of the phallus', in which he states that 'the orientation of feminine homosexuality, as observation shows, follows from a disappointment which reinforces the side of the demand for love',[53] Judith Butler makes the following general comment about the source of such a notion:

> Lacan is perhaps suggesting that what is clear to observation is the desexualised status of the lesbian, the incorporation of a refusal that appears as the absence of desire. But we can understand this conclusion to be the necessary result of a heterosexualised and masculine observational point of view that takes lesbian sexuality to be a refusal of sexuality *per se* only because sexuality is presumed to be heterosexual, and the observer, here constructed as a heterosexual male, is clearly being refused. Indeed, is this account not the consequence of a refusal that disappoints the observer, and whose disappointment, disavowed and projected, is made into, the essential character of the women who effectively refuse him?[54]

We are back, here, with the unresolved countertransference of psychoanalysis, called into play as a repudiation of the homosexual 'other' by the homosexual's refusal to play the game, to bow to the normative vision of psychoanalysis. Mature sexuality is seen as unconditionally heterosexual and any other mode of sexuality is therefore not real sexuality but something substituting for it, a pretence (a notion reinforced by the pejorative connotations of the supposedly technical term 'narcissistic' as it is applied to homosexual object choice). Butler, however, suggests that the desexualising of lesbianism is psychodynamically determined, in that it represents the projection of the feeling of being unwanted and undesired experienced by the male analyst when faced with the lesbian patient. More generally, she is perhaps implying that psychoanalysis itself, rejected by lesbians because its normative assumptions prevent it offering them anything of value, retaliates by declaring that it is lesbians who are not potent, who have nothing to say. To the extent that this is the case, psychoanalysis could be accused of contributing to the disenfranchisement of lesbianism. Out of its own weakness, it writes off the 'other' as illegitimate and even unreal.

A further element in Freud's thought has also been pursued by the post-Freudians responsible for the confusion of psychoanalytic theory in this area. This is a collapse of sexual orientation into sexual division: homosexual object choice becomes bound up with issues of 'masculinity' and 'femininity'. This occurs in large part because object choice is linked with identification and the grounds for identification are given in terms of gender – identifying with the mother means unconsciously taking on her status as sexual female as opposed, for example, to her standing as 'creator' or 'nurturer' or some other aspect of her agency. The homosexual man is less of a man, the lesbian is more masculine than the usual woman; male homosexuality is 'passive', like femininity, and so on. This line, that sexual object choice is an aspect of gender identity, has been swallowed by most post-Freudian analysts despite the obvious category confusions it involves and the everyday evidence that there is no necessary connection between object choice and gender identity – homosexual men and lesbian women may be 'camp' or strongly sex-typed in conventional directions and the varieties of sexual practice which lie within the general rubric of 'heterosexuality' and those which are 'homosexual' encompass all shades of activity and passivity. For example, one contributor to an influential psychoanalytic symposium on male homosexuality in the 1960s *defines* homosexuality as 'the sum total of behavioural attitudes which express a feminine relationship towards the father'.[55] Even a sophisticated recent critic, Richard Friedman, takes as established a link between gender identity disorder in childhood and later homosexuality, stating that 'A strong case can be made for the hypothesis that a feminine or unmasculine self-concept during childhood is not only associated with the emergence of predominant or exclusive homosexuality in men, it is the single most important causal mechanism'.[56] What this neglects is a recognition that the 'samples' from which such data arises are *clinical* samples – patients reflecting back on their childhood experiences or (less commonly) children with gender identity problems followed through into later life. It therefore generalises illegitimately to the wider population of homosexual people, a point that I will return to below.[57] Writers on lesbian sexuality, from Karen Horney to Joyce McDougall, have also emphasised what they see as a 'masculinising' tendency in their patients, built out of a failure to identify with the mother and a fantasy of replacing the father for her. McDougall, whose claims have become more cautious over the years since she was criticised for earlier work generalising from five lesbian patients,[58] still holds to a variant of this view. For example, in her 1995 book, *The Many Faces of Eros*, she comments that some

> lesbian patients convey the conviction that all that is feminine belongs solely to the mother. . . . In some cases, perceiving the impression of being unacceptable in the mother's eyes is interpreted by the little girl as a demand that she should psychically acquire 'masculine' attributes in order to merit her mother's love and attention.[59]

Despite McDougall's careful argument, following Stoller, for maintaining a notion of 'homosexualities' in the plural, so acknowledging the diversity of homosexual experience, comments such as these suggest that she is still working with an understanding of at least some lesbian patients as women who have not been able to enter fully into their feminine heritage.

At least Freud had the grace to express uncertainty about homosexuality and also to admit that nothing could be observed in the childhood histories of homosexuals which could be seen as specific to the formation of that object choice. Later analysts have tended not to be so cautious. The recent critics of psychoanalysis' encounter with homosexuality tell a fairly consistent story of a narrowing of the psychoanalytic vision so that heterosexuality is understood unproblematically as the outcome of normal development, not requiring explanation in the same way that deviant sexualities do. They also tell of the inclusion of homosexuality as a perversion linked with psychopathology, a step which Freud never wholly took. This is in addition to, but presumably linked with, a tendency visible from the 1930s onwards and most comprehensively described by Lewes as 'a shift in tone and rhetoric, a freedom on the part of some analysts to engage in rather sadistic abuse and ridicule at the expense of their homosexual patients'.[60] Over time, the possibility that there might be a variety of outcomes of the Oedipus complex was replaced by a more conservative view that the 'correct' outcome would be heterosexuality and that this was determined both by biological and by social necessity. In addition, the alignment of homosexuality with narcissism – already a pathologising move present in Freud – was supplemented and partly replaced by the idea that homosexuality, as a perversion, might be a facet of borderline or even psychotic personality structures. The rationale for this was, in part, that homosexual object choice is 'pre-Oedipal' and hence 'primitive', and that borderline and psychotic states are similarly primitive in their dynamic structure.

The most influential spokesperson for the pathological nature of male homosexuality was Sandor Rado, whose work in the 1940s laid down the principles of psychoanalytic thinking in this area for decades to come. Robert Friedman provides a brief summary:

> Rado (1949) next spelled out unequivocally that human beings have no innate desire for persons of the same sex. In terse language often repeated by later analysts, he stated that male–female sexuality 'is not only anatomically outlined but, through the marital order, is also culturally engrained and perpetuated in every individual since childhood' (p.205). Exclusive homosexuality, in contrast, is a reparative substitute caused by the fearful avoidance of heterosexuality, arising from excessive parental intimidation of sexual behaviour or masculine assertiveness. 'Only men incapacitated for the love of women by their insurmountable fears and resentments become dependent for gratification upon the escape into the homogeneous pairs' (p.207). Rado also claimed that the original desire for women remained preserved in all homosexual men under their rationalisations.[61]

This position implies that heterosexuality is a naturally given state and that homosexuality always is based on a fear and repudiation of this heterosexual state. This biologistic argument, as well as being evident in the general culture, is also consistent with other psychoanalytic schools – for instance with the Kleinian assumption that the infant is born with innate knowledge of the genitals of the other sex as the complement to her or his own. Heterosexuality is therefore one expectation of the outcome of a successful analysis.[62]

Rado's emphasis on the turning away of the homosexual from heterosexuality through fear became linked to a view that homosexual men come from a specific developmental context in which a dominant mother and a peripheral, weak father combine to 'feminise' the child into a passive, female-identified position. Irving Bieber's famous study of 106 homosexual and 100 heterosexual men in treatment purported to supply empirical foundations for this belief by identifying a triangular constellation in which the boy is made the focus of his mother's sexual attention and the father, excluded, is unable to perform the standard Oedipal rescue act. Lewes summarises Bieber's main findings in this respect:

> First, a significantly greater proportion of homosexuals had what Bieber and his team termed 'close-binding intimate mothers', who were seductive to their sons and also overcontrolling and inhibiting. . . . Second, and perhaps most important, while not all of the mothers of future homosexuals necessarily fit this characterization, a significantly higher proportion of homosexuals reported detached, hostile or rejecting fathers whom they hated or feared during childhood. . . . Third, boys who grew up to be homosexual fit the stereotype of the sissy during latency and adolescence, fearing physical injury and avoiding aggressive activity.[63]

It has been shown many times that these 'findings' are in fact based on complex data subjected to very sweeping generalisations; attempts to replicate them have ended in failure. The most important point, however, is a very simple methodological one which also applies to most psychoanalytic theorising in this area: Bieber's conclusions are based on a sample of homosexual *patients*, preselected for psychopathology. This means that the focus of analysis is the source of *disturbance* in a homosexual population not the source of homosexuality itself. At most, and with many qualifications, one might be able to say that a homosexual group of patients is more likely than a heterosexual group of patients to have the kind of family constellation described by Bieber and that this might contribute to their suffering, but there is no way of moving from this kind of data to a statement about what contributes to their *homosexuality*. Moreover, focusing on patients, as psychoanalysts usually do (of necessity as well as out of choice), makes it much less likely that an account of homosexuality will be produced that emphasises the positive choices and experiences involved. In fact, this approach prejudges the issue: homosexual patients are taken as representative of homosexuals in general, who then are described in pathological terms. Homosexuality ceases to be a 'choice' and instead is viewed as an outcome, a disturbed state of being.

Among numerous critical issues here, one which stands out is the degree to which the idea of homosexuality as signalling a developmental *failure* has dominated the psychoanalytic literature, including and since Freud. The homosexual is a failed man or woman, someone whose identifications have not been sorted out properly. His or her choice of a lover of the same sex is a *narcissistic* choice taken to bolster the self and to avoid reality – a state of mind characteristic of the pre-Oedipal period. In psychoanalytic terms, there are some extraordinary assumptions implied by these views, the adoption of which suggest that some other force is at work driving psychoanalysts towards the most conservative variety of heterosexist ideology available. First, the assumption that object choice defines the quality of object relationship – specifically, that because the homosexual individual chooses a same-sex lover, the relationship between the two must be narcissistic. This is no more obvious, psychodynamically, than it would be to argue that heterosexual relationships are never narcissistic just because they involve an other-sex choice. Clearly, heterosexual relationships can serve both narcissistic and non-narcissistic functions, depending on characteristics of the relationships themselves and on their psychological significance to the participants. In addition, as many analysts and critics have pointed out, there is a homosexual/narcissistic component in many other-sex patterns of relationship, just as there is a strong homoerotic component in the same-sex identifications deemed necessary for the development of heterosexuality. It can only be from a position of having already defined homosexuality as a narcissistic disorder that the generalisation can be made that all same-sex relationships reveal an underlying narcissistic character structure. Stoller's view that homosexuals are no more likely to have disturbed relationships than heterosexuals has already been quoted, but the more general point is that the 'homosexuality equals narcissism/pathology' argument fails to understand that the quality of a relationship might be constituted by its content rather than its form. Homogenising homosexuality loses the richness of the specific relationships which homosexuals form.

The general point here is that sexuality is complex, individual and multiple, and that its meaning for the individual can only be understood through detailed analysis – including, if it is a clinical case, analysis of the transference. Sexuality varies in intensity and breadth of object choice, in mode of eroticism, in its degree of association with aggression and hostility, in its reciprocity and compulsiveness and so on through every possible sexual characteristic. This is true both for homosexuals and for heterosexuals: it is not possible to judge the meaning of any sexual practices without exploring their detailed interpersonal and intrapersonal dynamics. One would have thought this to be an unproblematic notion for psychoanalysts, but what has happened is that heterosexuality has been taken as a biologically given norm. This biological givenness has been established as an essential component of mental health and homosexuality has consequently been defined as a disturbance.

A second, very striking psychoanalytic failure alongside the neglect of meaning and quality of relationship is that this approach leads to the abandonment of fantasy and subjectivity as central facets of psychoanalytic concern. One of the major intellectual contributions of psychoanalysis is to have subverted any simple notions of reality through an appreciation of the way fantasy operates – whether in the clinical situation, in which transference emotions might lead an analysand to experience her or his analyst in ways other than those which might seem obvious from the analyst's behaviour, or in sexual encounters which might actually be dependent upon fantasy for their meaning. However, instead of maintaining this appreciation of the centrality of subjectivity in meaning construction, psychoanalysis has taken what is, ironically, a behavioural turn: the meaning of a sexual relationship is given by its form. Heterosexual relationships are real, homosexual ones are ersatz. This is usually seen as being because homosexuality represents a failure or refusal to deal with the Oedipus complex by identifying with the same-sex parent and accepting the dictates of reality. But what has happened here is that an account of the necessity for a movement beyond the narcissistic dimension of absorption in the other ('mother') has become assimilated to a specific heterosexist familial discourse in which a choice between 'father' and 'mother' is forced and sexual orientation and integrity is seen as following automatically from this choice. As was described earlier in this chapter, critics such as Jessica Benjamin have pointed to the poverty of psychoanalytic thinking when it dichotomises in such a simple way and to the concomitant need to recognise that sexuality and gender identity are both diverse and heterogeneous entities, not right and wrong formulae. Moreover, the unproblematic use of concepts such as 'true', 'healthy' or 'full' sexuality misses the point, made strongly by Nancy Chodorow, that all modes of sexuality are complex and unclear:

> [The] sexual stories and transference processes of heterosexuals are as complex and individualised as those of homosexuals. . . . Clinically, there is no normal heterosexuality: any heterosexuality is a developmental *outcome* reflected in transference, whatever the admixture of biology or culture . . . that may contribute to it.[64]

To state all this at its baldest, *fantasy* is a central attribute of sexual life and can convert any behavioural scenario into something else.

(Homo)sexualising psychoanalysis

Throughout the history of psychoanalysis there have been honourable exceptions to the benighted views and attitudes described above; more so in recent years as the gay rights movement has come into being and (partly as a consequence) following the American Psychiatric Association's decision to exclude homosexuality from their list of psychiatric disorders. Nevertheless, psychoanalysis has been and remains dominated by views on homosexuality which are reactionary and pathologising, and many institutes of psychoanalysis manage to accept homosexuals for training only by fudging the issues. Psychoanalysts such as Charles Socarides, who views all homosexuality as pathology and who has continued to advocate treating homosexuality through psychoanalytic means, speak to considerable constituencies. Various analysts, from Socarides to the much more interesting French analyst, Janine Chasseguet-Smirgel, have ascribed systematic weaknesses in super ego functioning to homosexuals, suggesting a regressive flight from reality. In the case of lesbian sexuality, there is an assumption that it is somehow not 'real' sexuality, just foreplay, based on a narcissistic refusal to accept difference linked with a wish to be masculinised. O'Connor and Ryan also point out that feminist psychoanalysts have shown considerable ambivalence towards lesbianism, as if they fear that somehow their credentials will be called into question – or perhaps, as O'Connor and Ryan put it, 'that feminism will be assimilated to lesbianism, seen in this perspective as the unacceptable face of feminism'.[65] A link between misogyny and homophobia is also very evident in the psychoanalytic literature on homosexuality: it is the 'feminised' homosexual man who is most suspect, suffering from the same narcissistic disorder and weakness of the superego as is supposed to characterise women. Whereas psychoanalysis seems thankfully to have engaged productively with feminism in recent years to develop at least the beginnings of a coherent theory of sexual difference, it has not managed the same shift with regard to homosexuality. Perhaps, indeed, some of its now-repressed violence towards women has been displaced onto homosexuals, making the situation even more fraught than before.

The incoherence of much of the psychoanalytic account of homosexuality is readily apparent. Summarising the points made above, this incoherence arises from the neglect of fantasy and the collapse of sexual orientation into gender identity; the view that homosexuality is linked with narcissism and psychosis and the failure of psychoanalysis to engage with active sexual preference and enjoyment, evident in its insistence that homosexuality is only 'reparative', a way of avoiding heterosexuality. Generalisations have been based on clinical samples rather than populations, thus emphasising the pathology to be found in homosexuals rather than their 'normality'. As Lewes forcefully argues, the willingness of psychoanalysis to ascribe disturbance to homosexuals as a class and to assume the normality of heterosexuality makes one wonder if its wish to assimilate into mainstream American culture may have predominated over its capacity to retain a radical edge. The ferocity of attacks made by psychoanalysis on homosexuality suggest a deep anxiety, present in individuals and institutions alike – perhaps the anxiety of a profession fearing that its interest in sexuality and disturbance will make it an outcast from the society out of which it makes its living. Struggling to be acceptable in a conservative environment, embarrassed perhaps by the subversiveness of their own discoveries and by the secrets to which they are privy and trying to establish their 'professional' credentials, psychoanalysts have – as a breed and with exceptions, of course – too uncritically enacted the homophobia of the dominant culture. By literally excluding homosexuals from the doors of their club, by demeaning homosexuals' capacity for creativity and mature relationships and by insulting them as failed or incomplete human subjects, psychoanalysts have projected into homosexuals some of their own conflicts around acceptance, creativity and sexuality. It is as if the profession has said, unconsciously: 'We may deal with all that is most disturbing and disreputable in the human psyche, but at least we are normal: we hate homosexuals.' To enact this, some basic principles of psychoanalysis as well as of science have been overlooked, but perhaps this has seemed a relatively small price to pay for social acceptance.

Several psychoanalytic writers have, nevertheless, sustained a capacity to think critically about their discipline's approach to homosexuality and in recent years there have been some new hints of ways forward. Some of the most interesting work has come from revaluations of lesbianism, particularly by Luce Irigaray and Judith Butler. Perhaps this is not surprising, as the existence of a set of sophisticated feminist discourses within and around psychoanalysis has provided a language and mode of critical consciousness which can be drawn on when exploring feminine sexuality, including lesbian sexuality. For example, one of Irigaray's major contributions to psychoanalysis has been her opposition to monolithic views of sexuality – to the 'phallocentrism' characteristic of the Lacanianism from which she broke away. This is countered by an emphasis on the multiplicity of sexual and psychic being, expressed by making the diverse modes of bodily experience central to psychoanalytic understanding in place of the monocular 'gaze' of traditional (and Lacanian) theory. In the words of her most famous statement of this sexual plurality:

> This woman does not have a sex. She has at least two of them, but they cannot be identified as ones. Indeed she has many more of them than that. Her sexuality, always at least double, is in fact *plural*.[66]

Whereas looking is a distancing and positioning activity, touching is more diffuse and varied, more 'in touch' and close to the other; it thus subverts the norm, makes it harder to consider desire as closed, truth as achieved.

Irigaray celebrates alternatives to the phallocentric mode of thinking, working to break down the traditional categories of truth and knowledge: the Oedipal categories of psychoanalysis. In so doing, and again through emphasising the multiple desires of the fantasy-infused sexed body, she destroys the positioning of any particular sexual orientation as either right or wrong. That is, heterosexual desire is not in itself superior to homosexual desire, nor is the converse true. Although Irigaray makes women's sexual contact with one another central to her writing, this seems to be a strategy to destabilise all hierarchies of sexual rectitude rather than a statement that lesbianism is in some way purer than, or superior to, heterosexuality:

In her strategy of challenging psychoanalytic theories of sexuality, Irigaray highlights lesbian desires; in so doing she raises questions about sexual differences, gender differences and heterosexuality as well as homosexuality. She is not claiming to legislate for lesbian sexuality as the 'true' female sexuality because, she says, this would be to reinstate the very notions of sameness and univocity which she criticises.[67]

Nevertheless, there is little doubt that the force of Irigaray's critique of psychoanalysis' treatment of lesbian sexuality is to set up a positive rendering of homosexuality through revaluing femininity. Irigaray decentres psychoanalysis, displaying its Oedipal focus on the phallus as a defensive strategy for keeping things under control, for preventing multiplicity and, at the same time, for marginalising femininity – keeping the woman in thrall. Psychoanalysis' neglect and disparagement of homosexuality thus reads as a method for coercing sexuality; the way out of this would be to valorise the diversity of sexual experience. This can be promoted by celebrating the feminine if, as Irigaray claims, the feminine is constituted by those multiple sexualities usually kept from view, that is the despised irrationalities of feminine sexuality are here being reclaimed as the model of a freer way of being. The actuality of bodily experience, riven with fantasy as well as corporeality, exhausts the coercive capacity of disciplines.

While this attitude might at times be read as dangerous, anarchic or destructive (what is the stability of relationships built on these shifting sands?), it is also creatively confrontative, insouciantly displacing social and psychoanalytic certainties over truth, reality and homosexuality. Taken to its logical end, as Judith Butler takes it in her work, it leads to a deconstruction of the binarism of gender (the social and psychoanalytic masculine *versus* feminine) and a reading of lesbian and other 'marginal' sexualities as parodic, constituting a staged strategy for disrupting heterosexual fixations. Homosexuality thus shifts from the position of something repressed and out of sight to the position of display – a carnival which throws into relief the repressing regulatory force of that other sexuality, *heterosexuality*, which is itself not a 'truth', but a performance. In Butler's words:

The construction of coherence conceals the gender discontinuities that run rampant within heterosexual, bisexual, and gay and lesbian contexts in which gender does not necessarily follow from sex, and desire, or sexuality generally, does not seem to follow from gender – indeed where none of these dimensions of significant corporeality express or reflect one another. When the disorganisation and disaggregation of the field of bodies disrupt the regulatory fiction of heterosexual coherence, it seems that the expressive model loses its descriptive force. That regulatory ideal is then exposed as a norm and a fiction that disguises itself as a developmental law regulating the sexual field that it purports to describe.[68]

Gender dimorphic identity is held on to as a way of repressing homosexuality and because homosexuality is repressed, gender dimorphism becomes rigid. Celebrating the carnival aspects of sexual expression – drag, for example, in Butler's work – counteracts the arid casting of sexuality as 'one and only one' and asserts the primacy of the many.

Whether these celebratory renderings of homosexuality are true to the experience of homosexual individuals is not really the point. Rather, they demonstrate the possibility of a psychoanalytically informed re-reading of homosexuality as something which is not in itself pathological but simply expressive of the many potential sexualities available. In so doing, these critiques complement a less radical feminist psychoanalytic strand which again takes issue with the Oedipal fixations of traditional psychoanalysis and attempts to articulate a 'post-Oedipal' psychology open to differences, to plurality and hence to 'alternative' sexualities. Nancy Chodorow, for example, has argued that *all* sexualities – including so-called normative heterosexuality – are compromise formations, so that the differentiation between heterosexual and homosexual personality structures so firmly held by many psychoanalysts – and so poorly supported by empirical data – has no theoretical hold. *Any* sexual outcome or practice, whether heterosexual or homosexual, is 'a compromise formation, a symptom, a defence, a neurosis, a disorder'.[69] This idea explicitly builds upon the work of Kenneth Lewes on male homosexuality. His conclusion, following a logical analysis of the implications of Freud's account of the Oedipus complex, is that 'The mechanisms of the Oedipus complex are really a series of psychic traumas, and all results of it are neurotic compromise formations' – so there is no predeterminedly 'healthy' outcome.[70] This relativises all judgements concerning the relationship between sexual orientation and psychological integrity, returning psychoanalysis to one part of Freud's position: that sexual development is a difficult journey with an uncertain destination.

The idea of a 'post-Oedipal' psychology is most compellingly worked out by Jessica Benjamin, some of whose writing on gender was referred to earlier in this chapter. In the piece described there, 'Sameness and difference: toward an 'over-inclusive' theory of gender development', she elaborates an account of the potential multiple identifications through which children develop. This account acts as a critique of Oedipal theory, with its implicit assumption that there is only one real 'difference', that this is established along gender lines and that it constitutes the direction for sexual object choice as well as personal identity. Benjamin argues that this is too limited a view of difference; indeed, it is not an engagement with difference at all, but a categorical, binary judgement in which there is only that which is 'same' and that which is 'other', with the latter usually (in the form of the mother) being repudiated. Tolerance of difference might better be seen in an appreciation of *likeness in the apparently different* – a point which will be returned to in the discussion of racism below. It is no expression of a sophisticated and integrated acceptance of difference when the marker of like/other is simply an anatomical one: a particular man and woman might be more similar than two men or two women. In more psychoanalytic terms, repudiating an identification with the other-sex parent might best be seen as a failure to come to terms with difference, rather than – as Oedipal theory seems to suggest – an acceptance of reality. Benjamin stresses the importance of recognising likeness: the 'neglected point' in much differentiation theory, she writes, 'is that the difficulty lies in assimilating difference without repudiating likeness, that is, in straddling the space between the opposites'.[71] Without this, heterosexuality is no more 'hetero' than is homosexuality, for what is being pursued is the reassurance of not being the other or perhaps a defence against envy of the other, rather than a full relationship with difference. Summarising, Benjamin marks out the contrast between the Oedipal and post-Oedipal appreciations of difference, the former being a rigid bipolarity, the latter being multivariate, polymorphous and inclusive:

It is possible to distinguish between two forms of complementarity. The earlier Oedipal form is a simple opposition, constituted by splitting, projecting the unwanted elements into the other; in that form, what the other has is 'nothing'. The post-Oedipal form is constituted by sustaining the tension between contrasting elements, so that they remain potentially available rather than forbidden and so that the oscillation between them can then be pleasurable, rather than dangerous.[72]

Put this way, the traditional psychoanalytic disparagement of homosexuality looks like an aspect of masculinist theory, fleeing from the appearance of 'effeminacy' into a rigid, phallic bipolarity. Either yes or no, right or wrong, good or bad, same or other. The Oedipal configuration, seen as the *sine qua non* for healthy adjust-ment, is a waystation at which psychoanalytic theory has got stuck: it bolsters the sense of self by repressing the other, the feminine, either through marginalising male homosexuality as perversion or female homosexuality as barely sexual at all. What Benjamin and the other theorists of the 'post-Oedipal' (perhaps at times 'non-Oedipal') offer is a glimpse of a psychoanalytic approach which does not idealise (thus distorting) heterosexuality, but instead explores the extent to which any manifestation of sexual enjoyment and object choice allows a space for difference and multiplicity, and hence for a relationship to the other which does not reduce to narcissism or disavowal. That psychoanalysis has a long road to travel before it comes to terms with homosexuality can hardly be in doubt, but perhaps the journey begins here.

PSYCHOANALYSING RACISM

If homosexuality has been a topic marked by contention and animosity in psychoanalysis, racism has been straightforwardly neglected. As with homosexuality, this is partly due to the stand-point of psychoanalysis itself. Rooted in a colonising society, it has spoken 'for' others without genuinely allowing itself to *encounter* otherness. Distancing himself from his Jewishness, perhaps as a way of making himself and his new science acceptable, Freud drew on visions of the 'savage' to fill out his speculative prehistories.[73] He also associated the psychology of children with that of 'primitive' peoples, contrasting these two groups with the supposedly more sophisticated and complex psychology of the adult, Western male subject.[74] Other psychoanalysts have specifically adopted the racist discourses of their surrounding culture and have certainly not been immune to the racism found in psychology and other social science disciplines.[75] Although there are probably few psychoanalysts nowadays who would openly or deliberately articulate these values, psychoanalysis as a discipline has found it hard to develop a version of the human subject which is not either racist or at least, in Neil Altman's phrase, 'exclusionary'.[76] In common with the whole mental health industry, psychoanalysis has struggled to develop ways of working which are anti-discriminatory and which actively recognise and validate the experiences of members of ethnically diverse groups. In most respects, this is hardly surprising. Writing and working within a specific cultural tradition, psychoanalysts have found it no easier than anyone else to come to terms with the complexity of 'race', ethnicity and culture and have tended to reduce these to terms with which they are familiar. This systematically discriminates against members of 'other' groups, for example by failing to validate their specific family structures or cultural understanding or by neglecting their experience of racism. Psychoanalysis clearly needs to develop its practice in these areas and works such as Altman's *The Analyst in the Inner City*, in which recognition is given to the constructing power of supposedly 'contextual' factors such as 'race', ethnicity and class, are accordingly to be welcomed.

Of equal urgency with the issue of reforming psychoanalysis' own practice is an answer to the question of whether it can contribute anything substantial to attempts to understand and combat racism itself. In some previous work comparing social psychological and psychoanalytic attempts to understand racism, I drew attention to the paucity of psychoanalytic work on the subject. Through the examples of Adorno *et al.*'s book *The Authoritarian Personality* and Franz Fanon's *Black Skin, White Masks*, I then suggested that psychoanalytic concepts might be used fruitfully to map out a psychic dimension to racism which parallels and interacts with its social dimension. My concluding comments were as follows:

Psychoanalysts, on the relatively rare occasions when they have addressed the issue of racism, have described mechanisms through which racist psychology expresses its emotional charge. They have also developed a portrait of the racist psyche that links it with an intense and violent fear of the structures of the modern environment, and hence positions it socially rather than marginalising it as irrationality. This social positioning is a complex matter, raising complicated questions concerning the modes of action necessary to bring about changes that will reduce the presence of racism amongst individuals and in society. But, however indirectly it has come about, those radical theorists who employ psychoanalytic means to explore racism have opened out the possibility of a full understanding of racist psychology, one which can account both for its subjective intractability and its social force.[77]

Since this was written, there has been a small amount of work in which modern psychoanalytic concepts have been applied to racist psychology. In comparison to the older work of Adorno et al. and Fanon, these have the advantage of a more subtle understanding of projective and other defensive processes, thus moving things on from the relatively simple claim that unwanted 'bad' feelings are projected into a culturally available 'bad object', who then becomes the demonised other of racist discourse. Not that this idea is untrue in any straightforward way, but it is reductive – that is, it does not take full account of the complexity of racist structures of representation nor of the properties of the psychic mechanisms they employ. Perhaps most importantly, the intensity with which the fantasy of the other is invested in by racists is only partially theorised by Adorno, Fanon and their contemporaries. For Adorno et al., the source of this investment lies in a specific family scenario in which an authoritarian father and the absence of affection produces a sadomasochistic personality structure unable to deal with the complexity of the world and insistent on the simplifying products of projection. This creates a world full of hated objects, thus confirming the racist's (or fascist's, in the terms of The Authoritarian Personality) vision of being ensnared in a dangerous situation in which the other has to be wiped out for the self to survive:

> The extremely prejudiced person tends towards 'psychological totalitarianism', something which seems to be almost a microcosmic image of the totalitarian state at which he aims. Nothing can be left untouched, as it were; everything must be made 'equal' to the ego-ideal of a rigidly conceived and hypostatized ingroup. The outgroup, the chosen foe, represents an eternal challenge. As long as anything different survives, the fascist character feels threatened, no matter how weak the other being may be.[78]

For Fanon, the racist passion is spearheaded by sexual repression: whiteness, supported by an ideology of 'purity' and a disavowal of sexuality needs the black 'other' as a repository of its own discontent if it is to survive.

These notions – in which projection of disowned elements of the personality is produced by specific familial and social circumstances – remain useful in understanding the racist psyche, particularly when they are combined with analyses of the *social* symbolic and its constant recycling of racist fantasies and imagery. But the psychoanalytic theories of the 1950s are less adept at managing the remarkable sinuousness of contemporary racism, its capacity to appear as something else, for instance as nationalism or liberationism, and its power to catalyse fantasy and imagination in such a way as to propel nations into civil war. Nation states are explicitly feeding on racist sensitivities to mark out their own boundaries. This is occurring partly in the wake of the collapse of old-style communism but also as a response to migrancy and the multitude of refugee crises produced by what appears to be a 'postmodern' disorder of potentially cataclysmic dimensions. Indeed, the postmodern polyphony of voices and cultures in this arena seems not to be resulting in celebratory enjoyment, but rather to be provoking a counter revolution in which what is sought is safety in mythical but nonetheless concrete boundaries from which otherness can be excluded and denounced.

In this minefield, what psychoanalysis might be called upon to offer is an account of how 'otherness' operates in the subjective geography of the racist psyche. What is produced by this paroxysm of map drawing? What is this other-free, dark-continent-free 'whiteness', this 'purity' which seems so desirable to the racist consciousness? Reversing the usual racist discourse, one might argue that in darkness there is the possibility of subtlety and romance, of the variegated play of one intensity of shade on another, of coolness and refuge, unexpected vocalisation, touch and movement. In darkness there is danger, for sure, but also romance. Turn on the light and in the unblinking stare of whiteness everything looks the same. It seems to be this that is sought after by racism, that nothing unfamiliar and 'other' should survive. Employing the terminology of the previous sections of this chapter, what necessitates this intense affiliation to a dimorphic, 'either-or' mode of relating? What fear prevents movement to a post-Oedipal, 'both-and' perspective in which difference can be available for identification and not just for repudiation?

The terms of this discussion invite a Kleinian analysis and this is offered by Michael Rustin in his book *The Good Society and the Inner World*. Rustin acknowledges fully the social, economic and political sources of racist practices, but insists that 'a crucial means by which such structures are upheld is through irrational mental processes, and that this dimension needs to be recognised and confronted as such'[79] – particularly if antiracists are not to fall victim to exactly the same irrational impulses. Central among these irrational processes are the unconscious mechanisms for warding off anxiety identified by Kleinians as linked with the preservation of the self, that is defences against paranoid or even 'psychotic' disturbances of emotion and the personality. Beliefs about race, writes Rustin,

> when they are suffused with intense feeling, are akin to psychotic states of mind. . . . The mechanisms of psychotic thought find in racial categorizations an ideal container. These mechanisms include the paranoid splitting of objects into the loved and hated, the suffusion of thinking processes by intense, unrecognized emotion, confusion between self and object due to the splitting of the self and massive projective identification, and hatred of reality and truth.[80]

The paranoid nature of racist thinking is apparent in conspiracy theories and fantasies of being flooded by waves of immigration or of being infected by immigrant-borne diseases or poisoned by alien foods and culture. Moreover, this paranoia is given by the *structure* of the thinking process at work here: it is not primarily a cognitive procedure aimed at finding out about the world, but an emotional one, aiming to expel certain feelings and fantasies from the self and evacuating them 'into' the denigrated other. In Kleinian (or, more precisely, Bionian) terms, this is an anti-thought process, a defence against thinking in the constructive sense of making meaningful links between aspects of the world. Racial categories are particularly useful repositories for such anti- or pseudo-thinking, not just because they are socially valorised for political purposes (such as colonialism and economic exploitation), but because they are fundamentally 'empty' categories with very little externally grounded, 'objective' meaning. Rustin comments that virtually no differences are caught by 'black' or 'white'. . . . This is paradoxically the source of racism's power. It is the fact that this category means nothing in itself that makes it able to bear so much meaning – mostly psychologically primitive in character – with so little innate resistance from the conscious mind.[81]

The process of racist ideation is therefore one in which unwanted or feared aspects of the self are experienced as having the power to disturb the personality in so damaging a way that they have to be repudiated and evacuated or projected into the racialised other, chosen for this purpose both because of pre-existing social preju- dices and because, as a fantasy category, racial 'otherness' can be employed to mean virtually anything. Holding onto a subtle and demanding balance of social and intrapsychic levels, Rustin suggests that the projecting impulse might derive from the nature of racist societies but might then be perpetuated and accentuated by the way the personality gets further distorted through its organisa- tion around pseudo-thinking – that is, around a lie:

> The most active process at work in such racisms is the projection of negative, repressed, or inaccessible aspects of the individual and social self. Cultures of racial domination, since they are founded on greed, cruelty and the exploitation of weakness, will have many such hateful states of mind to get rid of somewhere. This process can have a self-reinforcing dynamic, in which the evidence of damage inflicted on projected internal objects gener- ates still more violent persecution, which is again projected onto powerless victims.[82]

Furthermore, the lie becomes something central to the preservation of the individual's personality and identity, deeply invested in and relied upon as a source of support to the self. The more strongly it is held, the more it is needed; the subject comes to be in love with the lie and fearful of anything that challenges it. 'The "lie" in this system of personality organisation becomes positively valued, as carrying for the self an important aspect of its defence against weakness, loss or negative judgement.'[83] Racism, socially originated though it may be, is consequently deeply invested in by the indi- vidual, distorting and disturbing her or his relations with reality and with truth.

Rustin's account of the racist dynamic is fluid, evocative and multilayered, showing an appreciation of the social sources of racist ideology and of the intensity of the emotion with which racist configurations of thought are held. It successfully brings together Kleinian explanatory ideas with suggestions for antiracist practice, for example noting that simple educational procedures are unlikely to do more than provide sources of alarm for racists (contiguity makes things worse or at best leaves intact core racist beliefs by creating exceptions of the 'some of my best friends are . . . ' variety). It is also rooted in a belief in the importance of rationality which is clearly in line with the main psychoanalytic traditions and which forms the backbone of Rustin's own agenda for social progress. Just as psychoanalysts have usually argued that it is possible to employ rational means to investigate the irrationality of the unconscious and that this is a 'therapeutic procedure' to the degree that it makes the subject less in thrall to this irrationality, so Rustin argues the case for a rational, analytically informed account of the irrationality of racism. Racism is 'pseudo-thought', built on the denial of reality and fear of the truth and antagonistic to making real links; antiracist practice needs to incorporate awareness of these irrational forces as a way of dealing with them, rather than risk their replication. Racism is a 'lie' which is experienced as a truth; if racists could tolerate the world as it is, or at least the self as it has become, they would not need to find denigrated objects on whom to dump all their internal mess.

One aspect of Rustin's analysis which seems incomplete is the question of what it is about racism that is *specific*. The mental mechanisms he documents – projective identification, splitting, repudiation – are recognisable in many desperate, 'borderline' conditions, not just in the racist psyche. Additionally, while it makes considerable sense to argue that the social structuring of racism creates an easily available 'other' to be the recipient of negative projections, this argument also applies to other marginalised groups, such as homosexuals, psychiatric patients and the like. Of course, such groups are indeed subject to unwanted projections, but to bunch them all together risks losing the opportunity to document the quality of these projections in each case. What is it, in all this turmoil of dumping and rejecting, that represents the specifically *racist* imagination? Here, a recent paper by Joel Kovel, whose earlier book *White Racism* was an important intervention in the struggle to make psychoanalysis take racism seriously, is of considerable help.[84] Kovel returns to and works with the notion of the 'primitive', using it not as a term of opprobrium but as an evocation of that which is avoided or potentially lost in personal and social history.[85] He first makes a general claim, that the 'primitive' is identified with the 'polycentric' nature of the mind, 'this being associated with an openness of the psyche to the world and, in primitive society at least, an openness of society to otherness'.[86] As modern bourgeois society develops, as modernisation and capitalism come to fruition, so this polycentricity can be observed to be closed down in favour of the rationalist concept of the integrated self, the unified personality. In this view of things, Western modernity is built on the renunciation of alternative possibilities of being; the drive for profit swamps the impulses for pleasure and enjoyment. Noting the need for a specific, socially located explanation of how this renunciation turns into racism as what he calls the 'peculiarly modern form of repressive exclusionism',[87] Kovel asks the following question:

> Could it be that as the western mentality began to regard itself as homogeneous and purified – a *cogito* – it was also led to assign the negativity inherent in human existence to other peoples, thereby enmeshing them in the web of racism?[88]

More precisely and eloquently, he suggests that the focus on reason associated with the advance of modernity has led to a flattening out of experience and a fear of the 'irrational' – the polycentric – which then, presumably through mechanisms of the variety described by Rustin, becomes split off into the being of the derogated racial other. The following passage, redolent of Fanon's ferocious assault on the sensuality-denying, sexually repressed foundations of 'whiteness', powerfully conveys this point of view.

> A persistent shadow had dogged puritanism, the dominant cultural type of the early capitalist order – a spectre of renunciation and rationalisation, of the loss of sensuousness and the deadening of existence. In this context the animality projected onto the black by virtue of his or her role in slavery became suitable to represent the vitality split away from the world in Puritan capitalist asceticism. Sensuousness that had been filtered out of the universe in capitalist exchange was to reappear in those who had been denied human status by the emergent capitalist order. Blacks, who had been treated as animals when enslaved, became animals in their essence, while the darkness of their skin became suitable to represent the dark side of the body, embodying the

excremental vision that has played so central a role in the development of western consciousness. In this way blacks were seen as beneath whites in reasoning power and above whites in sexuality and the capacity for violence.[89]

Kovel is arguing here that a set of economically motivated social circumstances, with slavery and capitalist accumulation at their centre, produced in the West a psychological imperative to disown multiplicity and sensuality and to project it into the black other. The power of this psychosocial organisation is so great that it can 'enter into the evolution of the psyche',[90] closing down the possibility of openness to any new experience which is not in the interests of accumulation. Instead, the repressed sensuousness, preserved unconsciously because otherwise the psyche dries up completely and is 'deadened', is experienced as threatening and subversive, as well as exciting. It is bestial, animal, fit for projection onto those human subjects designated by the complex social drive of capitalist imperialism as non-human – the slaves. Their physical blackness, marking them as distinct, is merged together with already existing psychic defences against what Norman Brown has called the 'excremental vision'[91] to create the ideal object of repudiation. Excrement, mess, animality, anality, polycentric enjoyment, the 'primitive' – all these are denounced by capitalist accumulation and their psychic representation is blackness.

Kovel proposes that the turn of capitalism to Western-style racism is driven by its own power to disrupt the personality, to place selfhood and identity under threat. Again linking with Rustin's analysis and with the wider critique of modernity as exciting and annihilating at one and the same time,[92] Kovel argues that it is at those moments and in those spaces where identity is up against the dissolution of itself by the logic of modernity's brute force, when it most needs the extreme defence against otherness provided by racist ideology. Recognising its own terror, it converts it into loathing, thus feeling it and extruding it in the same gesture. Totally regressive though it is, racism consequently expresses the contradiction of modernity and the desperation of the racist as she or he experiences the threat of loss of self:

> The regime of capital constantly overturns community and existing social relations in its drive to submit everything to the logic of accumulation. This in turn places identity under constant threat, creating a never-ending series of breeding

grounds for racist outbreak – whether of the white variety or otherwise. In this respect, racisms ironically represent a protest against the abstracting logic of capital. Their splitting defines a kind of difference which is then perverted; constructing a degraded race amounts to a kind of clinging to the primitive and the polycentric, though this is recognised only negatively, as delusion and hate.[93]

The racist needs the hated other as a repository of all that she or he has lost and fears losing further: 'Without the spectacle of lost nature to hate and be fascinated by, it is doubtful whether the reduction of the psyche to a homogeneous personality could be sustained.'[94] Just as, in the basic scheme of domination, master needs slave for his mastery to be recognised, so the denuded, alienated and split-off racist consciousness needs its denigrated object for it to feel alive.

The detailed exposition of the racist dilemma proposed by Kovel gains a considerable amount of support from the more general postmodern context in which the claims made by modernism for the superiority of reason are scrutinised and repeatedly deconstructed. Feminism, with its assertion of another voice over and against the rational instrumentality of conventional masculinity, is a prime example of this trend.[95] So is the more general postmodern demonstration of the irrational underpinnings of reason itself, alongside the polyvocality to be detected beneath the apparently smooth surface of rationality. Postmodernism disconcerts any claims to be able to hold on to a single truth of the world, particularly the 'pure' truth claimed by racist politics. With specific reference to racism, Kovel's analysis parallels other accounts that place racism as reason's underside, its repressed dynamic – postulating a primitive other to be colonised and civilised by the superior, more educated and scientific peoples of the West.[96] His additional contribution is that of linking the specific historical trends leading to Western racism, particularly as seen in its American forms, with the psychoanalytic exploration of the workings of the racist psyche. In this regard, he is remarkably positive about the contribution of psychoanalysis, despite acknowledging the racist components of Freud's work and of much post-Freudian psychoanalysis. For Kovel, psychoanalysis returns Western consciousness to a position where it can recognise the polycentricity of the mind (the unconscious, the ego/id/super ego division, the existence of ambivalence, splitting and the like), but armed with new powers of demystification. Moreover, by placing central significance on the unconscious, Freud displaces the claims of the ego; he shows that the ego has a history, an evolution, and is not all that there is to the mind. It seems unlikely that Kovel would follow the Lacanian view that the ego is thereby made specious, a cover-up hiding fragmentation and alienation. Nevertheless, there is a compelling imagery here of the Western claim for rational governance of all the 'primitives' in the world breaking down under the pressure of the sheer *jouissance* of that primitivity, its forceful engagement with what reason represses and also desires.

The argument in this section has been that psychoanalysis, on the rare occasions when it has engaged seriously with racism, has been able to mark out a space for its investigation which is productive and special. Reducible neither to the social forces from which it springs nor to psychological 'givens', racism is a social–psychological complex engendered at the level of social and political relations but also sustained and experienced deep in the individual psyche. Work such as that by Rustin documents the mental mechanisms making racism possible and shows how it is reinforced through cycles of projection and introjection. More historically conscious theorising, represented here by Kovel, identifies the specific dynamic of racist experience as it emerges out of the sociohistorical processes of Western imperialism. Taken to its resting place, this develops into a broad critique of Western rationality – precisely the kind of unsettling insight for which psychoanalysis strives.

Given the potential fertility of psychoanalytic understanding in this area, one is left wondering about the silence over racism which has characterised psychoanalysis through most of its history. Presumably, paralleling the argument tracing psychoanalysis' conformism over homosexuality, this has been because of the domination of the colonising tendency in psychoanalysis over its liberating, expressive tendency. Tempted to play with fire, it has, institutionally, kept the lid on things, buying into the values of its host societies and steering clear of the actual engagements with otherness around which its theories circle. 'Blackness' and otherness of most kinds become invisible in its work. They are treated metaphorically, as if there is no 'real' out there and no material process with which to engage. To some degree, one can see the rationale for this in practice, as psychoanalysis strives to preserve its competence in the one area in which it has legitimacy – the consulting room. However, the caution here is misplaced: it does no service, either to psychoanalysis or to society, to remain silent about the racism sweeping the globe. Perhaps it is only a small beginning, but work such as that presented here suggests that when psychoanalysis releases itself from its self-imposed shackles, it may have something productive and challenging to say about the destructiveness of the racist phenomenon.

ECCENTRIC PSYCHOANALYSIS

The three areas of 'identity politics' surveyed in this chapter – gender, sexual orientation and racism – are three crucial elements in the current social domain. They are also, necessarily, structuring elements in psychoanalytic discourse, for psychoanalysis is produced in the social as an element of interpersonal and political exchange. Kovel puts this clearly in the preface to his article on racism and psychoanalysis:

> The great illusion of psychoanalysis, applying to most contemporary discourse no less than the classical Freudian theory, has been to imagine itself free from society as it goes about its work of producing putatively categorical knowledge about the psyche. Psychoanalytic propositions rarely contain the proviso that the psyche whose innards are being laid out like a patient on an operating table is no physical body but a part of a given social setting at a given time.[97]

The failure of psychoanalysis to theorise its own place in the scheme of things can be seen most clearly in relation to its approach to homosexuality, but more extensive accounts of its gender and race politics would also have revealed the same. Nevertheless, the question we are left with here is not so much whether psychoanalysis partakes of the assumptions, ideological biases and blind spots of the culture out of which it grows, which it obviously does do, but whether it represents or at least contains somewhere inside it a truly critical theory, a way of making sense of the turmoil of contemporary identity. In particular, to borrow Žižek's term again, can it theorise and give voice to 'enjoyment', the fantasy investments through which identity is expressed? Does psychoanalysis still have something important to say at the social level even though it demonstrates strong conformist tendencies, even though its institutions are conservative and inward looking and its practitioners are involved mainly in private practice? In the terms outlined in the previous chapter, does it still address the moments of rupture in experience through which the 'real' is exposed? Is it still capable of provocatively and productively addressing what Anthony Elliott calls 'the interlacing of repressed desire and power-relations, of unconscious passion and cultural reproduction'?[98]

On the evidence of this chapter, the answers to these questions are very mixed. It is a narrow judgement whether the conformist element in psychoanalysis – its tendency to speak from the middle of its social setting, pathologising, judging, supporting social norms dressed up as scientific facts – outweighs its critical possibilities. In the instance of sexual difference, the best-worked-out area discussed here, there is a substantial amount of rigorous and exciting work – mostly feminist in origin and orientation – which has succeeded in destabilising traditional assumptions about gender and opening out a space for more fluid change, more playfulness and more expressive combinations of gender choice. In its theoretical work on homosexuality, however, psychoanalysis is only just, and only tentatively, beginning to find a similar kind of voice. Acting as if its practitioners are afraid of what they might let out of the chest if they open it too wide, psychoanalysis has supported reactionary and normative views of homosexuality in a way which has harmed as well as alienated the gay and lesbian community. Even now, those psychoanalysts and psychoanalytic psychotherapists who have tried to buck this trend have done so mainly by arguing a moral case against conformist psychoanalysis, but they have not developed new concepts in this area to anything but a limited extent. The most exciting exceptions have come more from cultural and literary uses of psychoanalysis, although once again some feminist work disrupting the bipolar gender and sexual categories assumed in traditional psychoanalytic theory, is beginning to beat a new and challenging path.

Finally, in the area of racism there is now some very compelling work which not only uses psychoanalytic ideas to make sense of the psychology of racist individuals, but which also theorises social processes in an increasingly explicit and exact way. Here attention has been paid in a particularly fertile manner to the energy with which racist ideology is held on to, with the consequent elaboration of links between individual psychic defences and the challenge posed to identity by the dislocating power of contemporary society. To some degree, and despite the fact that there is so far only a limited amount of work on the psychoanalysis of racism, this has meant that this area has shown what might be achieved as psycho-analytic concepts are applied to the political arena. Where psychoanalysis breaks free of its tendency to seek acceptance in a normative society, it still possesses a capacity to reach out to 'other-ness', to the disruptive moments in which desire comes loose from its moorings and the erotic, unwilled unconscious can be heard. It can then face up to the excess and to the elements of human social functioning which are not easily reduced to economic or political or even moral terms but which require a comprehension of the degree to which people's lives are governed by fears, wishes and fantasies. Acting in that register, it can offer a language and set of concepts through which alternative identities can be imagined and the foun-dations installed upon which new relationships between individuals and the social order might be built. Whether this remains a pious hope or is translated into some kind of effective reality will soon, no doubt, become clear.

Conclusion

Chapter 9

For or against?

As with other parts of this for-and-against study of psychoanalysis, presenting a conclusion is a precarious process, if I am not to offer too many hostages to fortune. Thinking about it with a friend, he suggested that I had three choices: I could say either 'psychoanalysis is good', or 'psychoanalysis is bad', or something in between. My response is to want to say *both* of the first two – not to take up a moderate, 'in between' position but to argue for a passionate encounter with psychoanalysis. At this point, having surveyed so many areas (and acknowledging the absence of others which could have been included, such as developmental theory or psychoanalytic literary criticism), it seems obvious to me that the arguments 'against' and 'for' psychoanalysis are in a tight balance with one another. The 'againsts' include psychoanalysis' authoritarian training and institutional structures, its confusions over evidence, its poor documentation of clinical material, weak research base, limited outcome and process literature, ethnocentricity and tendency towards normative moralising. The 'fors' are, among other things, its engagement with subjectivity and emotion, concern with agency and intentionality, widening of the scope of rationality, critical awareness of the limits of consciousness, fluid and complex interpersonal focus, appreciation of fantasy and therapeutic integrity. But there is no simple balance sheet here. Rather, what I want to advocate is an intense and, if possible, ambivalent engagement with the psychoanalytic project of mapping the unconscious, of articulating a new rationality which is based on *reason* (and so is not mystical) but which is also respectful of emotion and irrationality – 'unreason' – and which does not close its eyes in the dark. Psychoanalysis keeps open a route to the underside of experience and this is why, when it betrays its subject, the betrayal feels so appalling. Having great hopes can lead to great disappointments. On the other hand, if one is not bothered about what psychoanalysis might offer, about the questions it raises and the emotions it probes, then an opportunity to explore some core elements of human subjectivity is missed.

FANTASY AND SCIENCE

In the Introduction to this book, I described some of the tensions in psychoanalysis, focusing especially on that between its institutional authoritarianism and its critical vision. What has become clearer through the working out of the argument in the rest of the book is how much of this tension stems from the centrality of unconscious fantasy in psychoanalytic work. Instead of turning to the regulating practices of the external world for its explanations of human conduct, psychoanalysis portrays the individual as imbued with fantasy structures which have causal significance – that is, they are the most appropriate focus of psychological explanation and the true source of human agency. To understand a person, one must be able to give an account of that person's unconscious life, of her or his wishes, dreams, anxieties and conflicts. It is in interaction with these that the great forces of society operate – that is why we are not all the same, even when the social world strives to make us so. Conversely, society is inhabited by fantasies born out of the inescapability of subjectivity: the interpersonal and the physical environment take their meaning from the conscious and unconscious interpretations placed upon them by people. Myths, narratives of historical origin, anxieties about security or images of power and revenge are the stuff not only of contemporary psychotherapy, but also of politics and human geography. All political and personal relations are infused with phenomena of this kind. When we love or hate someone, when we draw together in communities or hide in isolation from others, when we seek or refuse help, we are enacting fantasies, unconscious structures of meaning.

Steeped in this messy, uncontrollable, uncontainable material, it is perhaps not surprising that psychoanalysis should turn out also to be messy, uncontrolled and uncontained. In many situations, it operates as if its wild and radical vision of the constitution of human subjectivity is just too hot to handle. Then, psychoanalysis takes on a constricting role, as if its moral task is that of defending against its own fire or at least of channelling it safely away from the surrounding gunpowder. The authoritarianism of psychoanalytic training, the self-satisfied knowingness of some of its clinical practice, its social conservatism and reactionary elements (for instance its homophobia) are all examples of this tendency. Thus, in Chapter 1, I argued in part that the institutional structures of psychoanalysis have been put to use in perpetuating a self-sustaining, inward-looking and relatively dissident-free enclave for its practitioners in which trivial disagreements ('how many sessions per week are necessary for genuine psychoanalysis?') are endlessly worked over and form the source of controversy and competition, while big questions ('does psychoanalysis offer a public service?' 'is the unconscious a lie?') are defended against. The lack of imagination of many psychoanalysts is not necessarily a major criticism of the discipline, as the same is true of most professionals in most areas of work (try economists or lawyers, for example), and it could be legitimately argued that there are at least as many examples of creative individuals in the psychoanalytic community as in any other. Nevertheless, the intensity of its closure of ranks and its impermeability to public scrutiny or criticism is certainly an indicator of anxiety and insecurity. Is this because psychoanalysts do not really believe in what they do, or is it because they are sometimes scared to fully know what they usually only partly glimpse? That, faced with the power and fluidity of unconscious fantasies, their own regulatory practices are puny and their claims to mastery incoherent? What I am suggesting here is that psychoanalysis is often caught in a flight from its own subject: the restlessness and subversiveness of unconscious life.

As described in Chapter 2, the assertion that there is such a thing as a dynamic unconscious explodes all claims to absolute knowledge. If there is always unconscious activity, then one can never stand outside the system in order to observe its operations in a perfectly 'objective' way. Rather, as each claim is made, as each moment of discovery is realised (whether by Freud or a lesser mortal), the unconscious tricks its way in: an ambition appears, a wish, a blind spot or a self-serving interpretation. There is, *in principle*, no way to escape this, because human understanding is always intricately entwined with the workings of the unconscious. It is this intrinsic subjectivity that so challenges the traditional modes of scientific thought. As both Gellner and Grünbaum show, in their different ways, the circularity of psychoanalytic theory is such that it can never be established on a 'scientific' basis, if what is meant by that is a discipline in which immaculate and uncontaminated evidence is available for rational and judicious critical scrutiny. Psychoanalysis suggests that under the best conditions this would be a pious hope as, given the contradictions and confusions of the human psychological states with which psychoanalysis deals, it is never going to be possible to find an objective place to stand. Reflexivity, reactivity, subjectivity – whichever of these terms is preferred, the 'fact' is that psychoanalysis accentuates rather than obliterates the investment of the researcher or therapist in the material with which she or he deals.

The reflexivity of psychoanalysis is a double-edged sword. On the one hand, it leaves psychoanalysis open to the various critics of its scientific status. Because one can never separate the claim from the claimant, one can never attest to the objective validity of the theory in question. In simple terms, psychoanalysts can wriggle out of anything by appealing to the trickery of the unconscious. On the other hand, psychoanalysis can also be seen to be exemplary for the emerging 'new paradigm' approaches in the social sciences, which take as a major topic of interest and concern the investment of the researcher in the material she or he is exploring. A strong version of this position is to be found in the argument that 'scientific' understanding, at least of human phenomena, has to be built around an act of imagination in which human meanings are observed and articulated by investigators with the capacity to imagine themselves into the position of the observed 'subject'. This is a relatively old argument, present in the hermeneutic distinction between *Naturwissenschaften* (natural sciences) and *Geistesswissenschaften* (moral or human sciences), the idea being that the human sciences require an interpretive stance and that the methods of the natural sciences (to which, historically, psychology and some branches of psychoanalysis have aspired) are inappropriate in that arena. As social scientists and psychologists return to this idea, so the psychoanalytic 'take' on interpretation comes back into the limelight, in all its sophistication.

What is at issue here is the conceptualisation of science itself. Is it something defined by a specific method, for example the formal hypothetico–deductive procedures of positivist empiricism, or by a set of concerns – the unveiling of information and the generation and testing of theory through the most appropriate means given the material of interest? If the former, then psychoanalysis and new paradigm psychological research both fail the test of scientificity, although in doing so they also accuse science of neglecting central aspects of human experience. If, however, the latter approach to science is accepted, then psychoanalysis suggests numerous concepts and procedures – transference, countertransference and interpretation, for example – which may prove to be crucial in the development of a human psychological 'science' which pays due attention to the interior workings of people, to their subjective, fantasy-filled inner lives.

Psychoanalysis has an enormous amount to contribute to the study of contemporary human consciousness, built out of its own special appreciation of the postmodern orthodoxy that regards the rationalist division between subject and object as only partially sustainable. In particular, it offers powerful concepts for use in theorising intersubjectivity and for appreciating the 'inmixing of subjects' which occurs at a psychological level whenever one person is engaged with others, whether as therapist or researcher. None of this can take place in a vacuum, however. It is one thing to argue that the working definition of 'science' could be expanded to include interpretive ventures based on a scrupulous practice of imagination and subjective understanding, but quite another to claim that the chaotic and often patently speculative outpourings of dogma to be found in the psychoanalytic literature constitutes such a scrupulous practice. If psychoanalysis is to offer a model for a 'human science' in which the significance of unconscious fantasy is appreciated and in which meanings are treated as causes – a science of 'intentionality' in the current jargon – then its own theories and practices have to be open to scrutiny, rooted in observation and argument and painstakingly documented. As described in Part I of this book, the very important British tradition of infant and child observation offers an important positive model of such carefully grounded practice. The literature also contains sophisticated recent debates about scientific method and about the complex formulations of 'clinical facts'. However, to fully tap the potential of psychoanalysis as a 'new paradigm science' requires more rigour in both description and interpretation than is often evident in the published literature. In particular, if it is the case that the subjectivity of the 'researcher' has to be deployed to make sense of the phenomena researched, then this has to be documented and analysed in an open and detailed way.

THERAPEUTIC INVENTIVENESS

Psychoanalysis offers itself to the world not just as a method of discovery of psychological truths, but as a therapy. Part II dwelt on this at considerable length, balancing the remarkable fertility of psychoanalytic ideas about therapy against the relative banality of everyday practice and – more ominously – the absence of convincing evidence that psychoanalysis, as a therapy, *works*. The debate here is possibly the most heated in all the areas of controversy surrounding psychoanalysis. Psychoanalysis is criticised for its procedures, which in the most extreme characterisation are seen as domineering, constricting, expensive, elitist, speculative, intrusive, patriarchal and socially oppressive. It is also criticised in terms of its therapeutic value because, despite all the conviction of analysts and the personal attestations of at least some analysands, the effectiveness of psychoanalysis has never been persuasively demonstrated. Those who come out cured of their ailments would probably have done so given any other reasonably coherent form of treatment – and perhaps more quickly. Moreover, psychoanalysts have shown themselves incapable of predicting in advance which patients will improve or of explaining the mechanisms of improvement in those who do get better during therapy. Given this situation, the argument goes, the length, expense and downright weirdness of the psychoanalytic endeavour is inexcusable, at least in the public mental health arena. 'Supportive' psychotherapy is likely to be at least as effective as psychoanalysis, without all the attendant humbug, and some other forms of therapy might be more powerful, at least for some kinds of difficulty.

There is much to be said in support of these dismissive arguments for it is in fact the case that the evidential base for psychoanalytic psychotherapy is extremely weak, especially when one considers that this is not a new therapy but, in something resembling its present form, has a hundred-year history. By now, one has the right to expect something tangible to show for all those talking hours, all those transference interpretations, training analyses, supervision sessions and fees. One might also, as described above, wish to see less dogmatic assertions of what goes on in psychoanalysis and more careful documentation and open-minded exploration of the therapeutic encounter – for example, of what evidence there is for the effects of interpretations of various kinds or of the specificity of countertransference emotions or the relative impact of 'containing' versus 'interpretive' stances. Of course, there has been work on all these issues but it is generally equivocal in its findings and often too divorced from the standard psychoanalytic situation to impact or reflect upon practice with any great power. What we are left with is an elaborate set of esoteric practices, lacking any convincing evidence to demonstrate their utility, but institutionalised in a variety of closely related forms and rationed through 'closed shop' arrangements so that their purveyors can charge fees high enough to sustain a middle-class professional lifestyle. Talking to themselves in a sophisticated jargon, these analysts convince one another that they are working on something substantial and meaningful. In addition, they make themselves available to pronounce on some of the centrally troubling issues of contemporary life – violence, child abuse, sexual distress – acting as if they know what they are talking about. But, the argument might run, they do not know anything except their own opinions. It is all a self-deceiving fraud.

Offsetting this critique, one might draw attention to the vivacity of the therapeutic procedures themselves, especially when contrasted with the reductive and mechanistic activities which pass for therapy in some other approaches. Attending scrupulously to the moment-by-moment fluctuations of the therapeutic relationship, analysts have developed a subtle vocabulary to express the complex variations in attitudes, beliefs and emotions as they materialise in the consulting room. Taking seriously the sophistication of each individual's mental apparatus, they have immersed themselves in intense personal encounters with their patients and have not backed away into the defensive distancing devices of drugs or didacticism. For sure, there are many examples of bombastic and rigid practice – what else would one expect when the work relentlessly demands openness to all varieties of lie, abuse, hatred and desire? Even for an analyst, this can get too much. But in the main, psychoanalysis is marked by care and patience, by the capacity of analysts to wait and observe, to see what comes and accept it for what it is and to recognise that behind every apparently trivial or mad moment there might be something crucial painfully raving.

Psychoanalysis also places the intersubjective realm at the centre of its concerns. This means that it grants pride of place to the social aspect of human functioning, treating the therapeutic situation as a special instance of this. What happens between one person and another? The answer to this is given in terms such as containment or interpretation – making safe and moving on – with analytic procedures (transference, countertransference and the like) being exemplars of the infiltration of relationships by deep and potent fantasies. Psychoanalytic psychotherapy is therefore not something done *by* one person *to* another; rather, it is something offered, an opportunity, a route towards hope. Written up like this, it is not surprising that simple methods of measuring change are insufficient to pick up the impact of psychoanalytic therapy nor that appropriate tools for measuring psychoanalytic 'process' should be so difficult to develop. Each therapeutic encounter is different, each moment brings about a change, one thing does not necessarily lead straightforwardly to another and what happens might be incomprehensible to an observer. Try to pin this thing down as it moves and you are the boy who kills the dove.

What is obvious from the foregoing is the double face of psychoanalysis. It is turned towards pragmatism and poetics at the same time, caught in their material contradictions and disputes. Attending to the nuances of human psychological experience means abandoning any aspiration to know what the outcome of a psychotherapy might be, for one can never be sure where a relationship will lead. Unfortunately, however, a public mental health service needs to know exactly that; it must have a reasonable amount of confidence that the funds invested in a particular method of therapy will produce desirable results. Psychoanalysis has never been able to promise that and probably never will. Whether other therapies can manage better is still not clear, but they can hardly manage much worse. Yet, psychoanalysis continues to live because it recognises and answers the need for distress to gain a response, for the voice of confusion and despair to be heard. Perhaps this is a real 'for and against' of psychoanalysis as therapy: it offers nothing, but at least it does not run away.

IDENTITY POLITICS

Finally, Part III considered psychoanalysis on a wider stage, in its applications to some social and political concerns. While the central investment of psychoanalysis has always been in clinical activity, the tradition of broader application began with Freud and has continued unabated, producing some of the most fertile and provocative work in the social sciences. Gradually, it has become clearer that the strength of psychoanalysis in this respect does not lie in the reductionist interpretation of social phenomena as outcrops of the psychodynamics of individuals, nor even, in any simple way, in the application of concepts derived from individual work to social events. Instead, psychoanalysis claims its place as a social theory through the recognition that social processes are imbued with the unconscious structures of subjectivity in a dialectical way. Features of the social world – particularly what is generally referred to as 'ideology' – are 'absorbed' by individuals as fantasies. They are also invested in by individuals through the projection of fantasised emotions and aspects of the self. This is why psychoanalysis might have something important to contribute to the new 'identity politics', with its focus on the construction of selfhood through processes of social location.

As discussed in Chapter 7, the particular set of issues with which psychoanalysis might be concerned is that related to questions of 'excess', to the fragmenting, unstable and provocative intermixing of public and private fantasies as part of the grain of social and political life. Psychoanalysis does not replace social and economic analysis here, but it addresses the margins left untouched by these other methods, margins which are nevertheless causal and crucial – as can be witnessed in all the otherwise inexplicable prolongations of passionate and often internecine conflict within and between communities around the world. Rationality does not sufficiently explain what goes on as people struggle for generations to make real some kind of dream (or nightmare, depending on one's position in all this); something else is usually at work, irreducible to economic or political cause. Here, perhaps, is the arena for an applied and progressive psychoanalysis, taking its place as the discipline devoted to exploring the fissures and contortions of subjectivity and their workings in the social world.

As was described in Chapter 8, the response of psychoanalysis to the challenge of articulating a 'psychology of excess' has been decidedly patchy. Its dialogues and debates with feminism have been enormously creative, at least in their impact on the development of theory; their effect on the practice of psychoanalysis in clinical settings is less clear. Leaving this last point aside, psychoanalytic ideas have been irreversibly influenced by the growth in awareness of the constructed nature of sexual difference and by the increased consciousness of the structures of patriarchy and their impact on women and on men. 'Masculinity' and 'femininity', never completely taken for granted by Freud, are widely understood as mobile and contingent constructs, and examination of the factors contributing to their development has become an issue of considerable psychoanalytic interest. Conversely, psychoanalysis has contributed a vocabulary and set of concerns to feminist theory as it advances a view of gender in which subjectivity is central. This interchange of ideas is by no means cosy. In neither camp are the disputes now resolved and there are many feminists who repudiate psychoanalysis just as there continue to be psychoanalysts who employ deterministic and normative views of gender as guidelines for mental health. But at least psychoanalysis continues to be alive in this area, discussed and developed, used to enhance understanding and to a considerable degree open to influence itself.

In the other two areas considered in the last chapter, the outlook is less sanguine, for different reasons and to differing degrees. The history of psychoanalysis' involvement with homosexuality bears witness to the power of the normalising tendencies in the psychoanalytic movement, to its conformism and to the ease with which the radical elements of Freud's teachings could be lost. Basically, faced with homosexuality, psychoanalysis gave up its critical vision and instead appointed itself a guardian of traditional morals; even more cynically, one might argue that it attempted to ride to social respectability on the back of its repudiation of 'deviant' or 'perverse' sexuality. The impact of this on the lives of homosexuals has been significant, as has been the consequent and understandable antagonism of much of the gay and lesbian community towards psychoanalysis. Among other things, psychoanalysis lost sight of the centrality of fantasy when it came to consider homosexuality. It acted behaviourally, as if there are no complex inner meanings, no ways, for instance, in which the taking of an 'objectively' heterosexual partner might have homosexual meaning to a particular person or vice versa. More generally, the case of psychoanalytic homophobia demonstrates that if it is to retain its critical capacity, psychoanalysis has to constantly reassess its own values and to become suspicious when they look too much like those of society as a whole.

The tension between the critical and conformist aspects of psychoanalysis is also present in its approach towards 'race' and racism. Until recently, there was very limited work in this area and the classical texts of psychoanalysis showed rather too much freedom in their use of colonialist notions of the 'primitive', the 'savage' and the like. There are now some positive developments towards recognising the culturally specific and 'racialised' elements of psychoanalysis and towards exploring their effects. Nevertheless, the ethnocentrism of psychoanalysis remains an issue of great clinical and theoretical concern. In the last section of Chapter 8, the focus was on a more promising area: some new psychoanalytic work devoted to understanding racism itself. This work demonstrates the viability of an approach in which racism is theorised as a social phenomenon yet which also highlights the ways in which the racist 'state of mind', invested in by individuals, fuels and sustains racist ideology and activity. Racism does not operate simply by deceiving citizens into a false perception of the inferiority of people from outside their own group; rather, it builds on deep fantasies – anxieties about otherness, about envy and destructiveness, about contamination and disintegration. Psychoanalysis, used imaginatively by some creative social critics, has done much recently to trace the way this process occurs and in the course of this, psychoanalysis' own capacity to theorise the recurring issue of the relationship between 'internal' and 'external' worlds has been extended.

FOR AND AGAINST

This really brings me back to the beginning. It is never obvious where one should start with psychoanalysis. As I have pointed out several times, its concepts are slippery, its foci various and its attitudes and procedures multiple and often contradictory. In my encounters with psychoanalysis, I have always been thrilled by its versatility, by the acuteness of its intelligence and the challenge it presents to conventional ideas. I have been entertained by its speculations, amused by its wildness and moved by many of its insights. I cannot imagine how to understand late modernity without recourse to its major concepts – the unconscious, fantasy, repression, projection and the like. I have also been irritated by its conventional morality, by its authoritarianism and by its arrogance – for instance, by the conviction with which people who sometimes seem to have incomplete insight into themselves pronounce on the ethical and mental health of others. In the public health arena, I remain convinced that psychoanalytic psychotherapy has important things to offer, but concerned by the extent to which this has to be based on conceptual and anecdotal evidence rather than on systematic documentation and research.

As it passes into its second century, psychoanalysis is very much alive but perhaps it needs to aim some more kicks at itself to make sure that it remains so. A good place to start would be with the reminder that when Freud introduced the notion of a dynamic unconscious, he brought a demon into the modern world which will not let anything alone, but which continually disrupts the things we take for granted and subverts the things we assume to be true. Psychoanalysis, one hopes, will never exclude itself from the sphere of this demon's activities.

Notes

CHAPTER 1: THE PSYCHOANALYTIC HERITAGE

1 Masson, J. (1992) 'The tyranny of psychotherapy', in W. Dryden and C. Feltham (eds) *Psychotherapy and its Discontents*, Milton Keynes: Open University Press, 21.

2 Rose, J. (1996) *States of Fantasy*, Oxford: Clarendon Press, 34.

3 I take this as being Breuer, J. and Freud, S. (1895) *Studies on Hysteria*, Harmondsworth: Penguin (1974).

4 Rieff, P. (1959) *Freud: The Mind of the Moralist*, Chicago, IL: University of Chicago Press (1979).

5 Freud, S. (1930) *Civilisation and its Discontents* Harmondsworth: Penguin (1985), 339.

6 Steiner, R. (1995) 'Hermeneutics or Hermes-mess?' *International Journal of Psycho-Analysis*, 76: 435–46, (p. 439).

7 Rustin, M. (1991) *The Good Society and the Inner World*, London: Verso, 139.

8 Freud, S. (1905) 'Fragment of an analysis of a case of hysteria', in S. Freud (1977) *Case Histories*, Harmondsworth: Penguin, 157–8.

9 Sandler, J., Dare, C. and Holder, A. (1973) *The Patient and the Analyst*, London: Maresfield, 47.

10 Gellner, E. (1985) *The Psychoanalytic Movement*, London: Paladin, 53.

11 *ibid.*, 55.

12 Lacan, J. (1972–3) 'God and the *jouissance* of the woman', in J. Mitchell and J. Rose (eds) (1982) *Feminine Sexuality*, London: Macmillan, 139.

13 Obholzer, A. (1994) 'Authority, power and leadership: contributions from group relations training', in A. Obholzer and V. Roberts (eds) *The Unconscious at Work*, London: Routledge, 41.

14 See Roudinesco, E. (1986) *Jacques Lacan and Co.*, London: Free Association Books (1990).

15 Lacan, J. (1958) 'The meaning of the phallus', in Mitchell and Rose, *Feminine Sexuality*, 82.

16 Bion, W. (1970) *Attention and Interpretation*, London: Tavistock, 42.

17 *ibid.*, 51.

18 Bion, W. (1962) *Learning from Experience*, London: Maresfield, 36.

19 For a discussion of these claims and a comparison with the equivalent truth claims of academic psychology, see Frosh, S. (1989) *Psychoanalysis and Psychology*, London: Macmillan.

20 Gellner, E. (1992) 'Psychoanalysis, social role and testability', in Dryden and Feltham *Psychotherapy and its Discontents*, 41.

21 Freud, S. (1923) *The Ego and the Id*, Harmondsworth: Penguin (1984), 368.

22 See Symington, N. (1985) *The Analytic Experience* London: Free Association Books, 293.

23 For an extended discussion of these issues, see Sandler, J. and Dreher, A. (1996) *What Do Psychoanalysts Want?*, London: Routledge.

24 Gellner, *The Psychoanalytic Movement*, 73.

25 e.g. Frosh, S. (1987) *The Politics of Psychoanalysis*, London: Macmillan; Frosh, S. (1991) *Identity Crisis*, London: Macmillan.

26 Guntrip, H. (1968) *Schizoid Phenomena, Object Relations and the Self*, London: Hogarth Press, 422.

27 See, for example, Hobson, P. (1995) 'The intersubjective domain: approaches from developmental psychopathology'; and Fonagy, P. (1995) 'Psychoanalytic and empirical approaches to developmental psychopathology', both in T. Shapiro and R. Emde (eds) *Research in Psychoanalysis*, Madison, CT: International Universities Press. Both these researchers draw on attachment research to develop psychoanalytically driven models of infant mental states. Fonagy is trained in the Freudian tradition, Hobson in the Kleinian. Sandler and Dreyer, in *What Do Psychoanalysts Want?*, also discuss the convergence of different psychoanalytic schools on intersubjectivity.

28 Rustin, M. (1995) 'Lacan, Klein and politics: the positive and negative in psychoanalytic thought', in A. Elliott and S. Frosh (eds) *Psychoanalysis in Contexts*, London: Routledge, 226.

29 *ibid.*, 241.

30 Rieff, P. (1966) *The Triumph of the Therapeutic*, Harmondsworth: Penguin.

31 For a more radical reading of similar tendencies to those documented by Rieff, see Jacoby, R. (1975) *Social Amnesia*, Sussex: Harvester.

32 Gellner, *The Psychoanalytic Movement*.

33 Lacan, J. (1953) 'The function and field of speech and language in psychoanalysis', in J. Lacan (1977) *Écrits: A Selection*, London: Tavistock, 65.

34 Gallop, J. (1985) *Reading Lacan*, Ithaca, NY: Cornell University Press, 20.

CHAPTER 2: SCIENCE, MYSTICISM AND SUBJECTIVITY

1 Freud, S. (1933) *New Introductory Lectures on Psychoanalysis*, Harmondsworth: Penguin (1973), 219.

2 *ibid.*, 193.
3 *ibid.*, 194.
4 *ibid.*
5 *ibid.*, 195.
6 Eysenck, H. (1985) *Decline and Fall of the Freudian Empire*, Harmondsworth: Viking, 208.
7 Gellner, E. (1992) 'Psychoanalysis, social role and testability', in W. Dryden and C. Feltham (eds) *Psychotherapy and its Discontents*, Milton Keynes: Open University Press 43.
8 The argument here is well worked over by Parker, R. (1995) *Torn in Two: Mothering and Ambivalence*, London: Virago. See also Frosh, S. (1989) *Psychoanalysis and Psychology*, London: Macmillan.
9 Wiggins, J. (1973) *Personality and Prediction: Principles of Personality Assessment*, Reading, MA: Addison-Wesley.
10 Stern, D. (1985) *The Interpersonal World of the Infant*, New York: Basic Books.
11 Parker, *Torn in Two*, 192.
12 *ibid.*, 195.
13 Waddell, M. (1988) 'Infantile development: Kleinian and post-Kleinian theory, infant observational practice', *British Journal of Psychotherapy*, 4: 313–28, (pp. 313–14).
14 For a full account of these issues, see Guba, E. and Lincoln, Y. (1994) 'Competing paradigms in qualitative research', in N. Denzin and Y. Lincoln (eds) *Handbook of Qualitative Research*, London: Sage.
15 Henwood, K. and Pidgeon, N. (1992) 'Qualitative research and psychological theorizing', *British Journal of Psychology*, 83: 97–113, (p. 99).
16 For an overview of qualitative research methods, see Denzin and Lincoln *Handbook of Qualitative Research*.
17 Strenger, C. (1991) *Between Hermeneutics and Science: An Essay on the Epistemology of Psychoanalysis*, Madison, CT: International Universities Press, 149–50.
18 Henwood, K. and Pidgeon, N. (1995) 'Remaking the link: qualitative research and feminist standpoint theory', *Feminism and Psychology*, 5: 7–30, (p. 9).
19 Riessman, C. (1993) *Narrative Analysis*, London: Sage.
20 Wetherell, M. and Potter, J. (1992) *Mapping the Language of Racism*, London: Harvester Wheatsheaf.
21 Hollway, W. (1989) *Subjectivity and Method in Psychology*, London: Sage, 78.
22 Popper, K. (1959) *The Logic of Scientific Discovery*, London: Hutchinson.
23 Spence, D. (1987) *The Freudian Metaphor*, New York: Norton, 73–4.
24 Rustin, M. (1991) *The Good Society and the Inner World*, London: Verso, 115–16.
25 Will, D. (1980) 'Psychoanalysis as a human science', *British Journal of Medical Psychology*, 53: 201–11, (p. 205).

26 See Chapter 1 in Frosh, *Psychoanalysis and Psychology* for a description of this debate.
27 Spence, *The Freudian Metaphor*, 74.
28 *ibid.*, 80.
29 Rustin, *The Good Society and the Inner World*, 139.
30 Gellner, E. (1985) *The Psychoanalytic Movement*, London: Paladin, 53.
31 *ibid.*, 83.
32 *ibid.*, 152.
33 *ibid.*, 164.

CHAPTER 3: KNOWLEDGE AND INTERPRETATION

1 Grünbaum, A. (1984) *The Foundations of Psychoanalysis: A Philosophical Critique*, Berkeley, CA: University of California Press.
2 A good example here comes again from Rustin, M. (1991) *The Good Society and the Inner World*, London: Verso, 122: 'Psychoanalysts believed themselves to be discovering objective conditions of human development, comparable to those imposed by biological or material limits; it was the discovery of these new "unconscious" limits to human freedom that explained psychoanalysis' revolutionary impact on Western culture. On the other hand, hermeneutic approaches – including those related to psychoanalysis – deny the relevance of causal models in the human sphere. They are inherently voluntaristic: conceiving, in place of causal factors of one kind or another, that distorted understanding and communication are the chief obstacles to the fulfilment of human purposes and desires.' Compare this with Grünbaum, *The Foundations of Psychoanalysis*, 58: 'the generic disavowal of causal attributions advocated by the radical hermeneuticians is a nihilistic, if not frivolous, trivialisation of Freud's entire theory.'
3 Freud, S. (1920) *Beyond the Pleasure Principle*, Harmondsworth: Penguin (1984), 295: 'What follows is speculation, often far-fetched speculation, which the reader will consider or dismiss according to his individual predilection.'
4 Grünbaum, *The Foundations of Psychoanalysis*, 6.
5 *ibid.*, 109.
6 *ibid.*, 113.
7 *ibid.*, 139–40.
8 *ibid.*, 140.
9 Strenger, C. (1991) *Between Hermeneutics and Science: An Essay on the Epistemology of Psychoanalysis*, Madison, CT: International Universities Press, 17.
10 Freud, S. (1917) *Introductory Lectures on Psychoanalysis*, Harmondsworth: Penguin (1974), 452.
11 Freud, S. (1925) 'Negation', in S. Freud (1984) *On Metapsychology*, Harmondsworth: Penguin.
12 Grünbaum, *Foundations of Psychoanalysis*, 277.

13 Kernberg, O. (1994) 'Validation in the clinical process', *International Journal of Psycho-Analysis*, 75: 1193–200, (pp. 1195–6).
14 *International Journal of Psycho-Analysis*, vol. 75 (1994).
15 Tuckett, D. (1994) 'The conceptualisation and communication of clinical facts in psychoanalysis: foreword', *International Journal of Psycho-Analysis*, 75: 865–970, (p. 865).
16 Tuckett, D. (1994) 'Developing a grounded hypothesis to understand a clinical process: the role of conceptualisation in validation', *International Journal of Psycho-Analysis*, 75: 1159–80, (p. 1161).
17 Spence, D. (1994) 'The special nature of psychoanalytic facts', *International Journal of Psycho-Analysis*, 75: 915–26, (p. 920).
18 O'Shaughnessy, E (1994) 'What is a clinical fact?' *International Journal of Psycho-Analysis*, 75: 939–48, (p. 945).
19 Ornstein, P. and Ornstein, A. (1994) 'On the conceptualisation of clinical facts in psychoanalysis', *International Journal of Psycho-Analysis*, 75: 977–94, (p. 978).
20 *ibid.*, 977–8.
21 Sandler, J. and Sandler, A.-M. (1994) 'Comments on the conceptualisation of clinical facts in psychoanalysis', *International Journal of Psycho-Analysis*, 75: 995–1010, (p. 1008).
22 O'Shaughnessy, 'What is a clinical fact?', 944.
23 *ibid.*, 941.
24 Spence, D. (1987) *The Freudian Metaphor*, New York: Norton, 78.
25 *ibid.*, 91.
26 *ibid.*, 111.
27 *ibid.*, 112.
28 *ibid.*
29 Freud, S. (1905) 'Fragment of an analysis of a case of hysteria', in S. Freud (1977) *Case Histories*, Harmondsworth: Penguin. For evidence of the range of alternative 'narrative truths' which can be developed from the Dora case, see C. Bernheimer and C. Kahane (eds) (1985) *In Dora's Case*, London: Virago.
30 Ricoeur, P. (1974) *The Conflict of Interpretations*, Evanston: North Western University Press.
31 Strenger, *Between Hermeneutics and Science*, 188.
32 *ibid.*, 42.
33 Habermas, J. (1975) *Knowledge and Human Interests*, London: Heinemann, 261.
34 Grünbaum, *Foundations of Psychoanalysis*, 27.
35 Steiner, R. (1995) 'Hermeneutics or Hermes-mess?', *International Journal of Psycho-Analysis*, 76: 435–46, (p. 441). On the topic of the internecine squabbles among psychoanalysts, Steiner also comments: 'In our own psychoanalytic institutions situations have existed, and still exist, where attempts to explore new avenues have led and still lead colleagues to feel their professional identity is put at risk from all sorts of pressure from within the psychoanalytical establishment, local societies and groups. Patient referrals have and can still be used to try

to silence creative but dissenting voices' (*ibid.*, 439). Clearly, agreement on how to 'read' psychoanalytically is still some way off.

36 Brook, A. (1995) 'Explanation in the hermeneutic science', *International Journal of Psycho-Analysis*, 76: 519–32, (p. 525).

37 Freud, S. (1900) *The Interpretation of Dreams*, Harmondsworth: Penguin (1976), 672, 186.

38 Flax, J. (1981) 'Psychoanalysis and the philosophy of science', *Journal of Philosophy*, 78: 561–9, (p. 566).

39 Moore, B. and Fine, B. (eds) (1990)*Psychoanalytic Terms and Concepts*, New Haven, CT: Yale University Press, 99.

40 Freud, S. (1933) *New Introductory Lectures on Psychoanalysis*, Harmondsworth: Penguin (1973), 112.

41 Flax, J. (1990) *Thinking Fragments*, Berkeley, CA: University of California Press, 66.

42 For example, Klein describes the way the 'epistemophilic impulse' is derived from the desire to explore the inside of the mother's body and is derived from anal–sadistic wishes to appropriate the contents of the womb. See Klein, M. (1928) 'Early stages of the Oedipus Complex', in J. Mitchell (ed) (1986) *The Selected Melanie Klein*, Harmondsworth: Penguin, 72.

43 Hamilton, V. (1984) *Narcissus and Oedipus: The Children of Psychoanalysis*, London: Karnac (1993), 238

44 Flax, *Thinking Fragments*, 53.

45 *ibid.*, 75.

CHAPTER 4: PSYCHOANALYTIC PSYCHOTHERAPY

1 Masson, J. (1992) *Against Therapy*, London: Fontana, 24.

2 Winnicott, D. W. quoted in Sandler, J. and Dreher, A. (1996) *What Do Psychoanalysts Want?*, London: Routledge, 76.

3 Quoted in Jacoby, R. (1975) *Social Amnesia*, Sussex: Harvester, 124.

4 *ibid.*, 122. See my detailed account of this debate in Frosh, S. (1987) *The Politics of Psychoanalysis*, London: Macmillan.

5 Masson, *Against Therapy*, 42.

6 For example, Eysenck, H. (1985) *Decline and Fall of the Freudian Empire*, Harmondsworth: Viking.

7 Masson, J. (1984) *Freud: The Assault on Truth*, London: Faber and Faber.

8 Masson, *Against Therapy*, 25.

9 Masson, J. (1992) 'The tyranny of psychotherapy', in W. Dryden and C. Feltham (eds) *Psychotherapy and its Discontents*, Milton Keynes: Open University Press, 16

10 Freud, S. (1905) 'Fragment of an analysis of a case of hysteria', in S. Freud (1977) *Case Histories*, Harmondsworth: Penguin.

11 For example, Trowell, J. and Bower, M. (eds) (1995) *The Emotional Needs of Young Children and their Families*, London: Routledge.

12 Garland, C. (1991) 'Emotional disasters and the internal world: an

approach to the psychotherapeutic understanding of survivors', in J. Holmes (ed.) *Handbook of Psychotherapy for Psychiatrists*, London: Churchill Livingstone.

13 Marcuse, H. (1955) *Eros and Civilization*, Boston, MA: Beacon Press (1966), 245.

14 Wax, M. (1995) 'How secure are Grünbaum's *Foundations*?', *International Journal of Psycho-Analysis*, 76: 547–56, (p. 550).

15 Steiner, R. (1995) 'Hermeneutics or Hermes-mess?', *International Journal of Psycho-Analysis*, 76: 435–46, (p. 444).

16 *ibid.*, 442.

17 Freud, S. (1933) *New Introductory Lectures on Psychoanalysis*, Harmondsworth: Penguin (1973), 109–10.

18 Freud, S. (1937) *Analysis Terminable and Interminable*, London: Hogarth Press, 354.

19 See Shepherd, M. (1985) *Sherlock Holmes and the Case of Dr Freud*, London: Tavistock. For an account of a joint case taken on by these two fictitious Victorian characters, see Oatley, K. (1993) *The Case of Emily V.*, London: Minerva.

20 Freud, 'Fragment of an analysis', 114.

21 Sandler, J., Dare, C. and Holder, A. (1973) *The Patient and the Analyst*, London: Maresfield Reprints (1979), 115.

22 Freud, *New Introductory Lectures* , 112.

23 Moi, T. (1989) 'Patriarchal thought and the drive for knowledge', in T. Brennan (ed.) *Between Feminism and Psychoanalysis*, London: Routledge, 196–7.

24 Of particular relevance here is Klein's late essay: Klein, M. (1957) 'Envy and gratitude', in M. Klein (1975) *Envy and Gratitude and Other Works*, New York: Delta.

25 Klein, M. (1955) 'The psychoanalytic play technique', in Klein, *Envy and Gratitude and Other Papers*, 133.

26 Klein, 'Envy and gratitude', 231.

27 Elliott, A. (1996) *Subject to Ourselves*, Oxford: Polity, 77.

28 *ibid.*

29 See Sandler and Dreher, *What Do Psychoanalysts Want?*

30 Rieff, P. (1966) *The Triumph of the Therapeutic*, Harmondsworth: Penguin

31 For examples, see Hoffman, L. (1993), *Exchanging Voices: A Collaborative Approach to Family Therapy*, London: Karnac; and Parry, A. (1991), 'A universe of stories', *Family Process*, 30: 37–54. For a critique of the use of postmodernist theory in family therapy, see Frosh, S. (1995) 'Postmodernism versus psychotherapy', *Journal of Family Therapy*, 17: 175–90.

32 See, for example, Leary, K. (1994) 'Psychoanalytic "problems" and postmodern "solutions"', *Psychoanalytic Quarterly*, 63: 433–65.

33 For example, Elliott, A. and Spezzano, C. (1996) 'Psychoanalysis at its limits: navigating the postmodern turn', *Psychoanalytic Quarterly*, 65: 52–83.

34 Bouchard, M. (1995) 'The specificity of hermeneutics in psychoanalysis',

International Journal of Psycho-Analysis, 76: 533–46, (p. 543). Bouchard goes on to state that 'rhetoric in the psychoanalytic setting is concerned with discourse as revealing occurrences of "procedures of subjectivity", through displacement and condensation, symbolism and transference. While these phenomena do not, strictly speaking, qualify as linguistic, they are nevertheless expressed symbolically (or are sometimes acted out) in the form of intersubjective narratives.'

CHAPTER 5: THE RULES OF THE GAME

1 Winnicott, D. (1955) 'Clinical varieties of transference,' in D. Winnicott (1958) *Through Paediatrics to Psychoanalysis*, London: Hogarth Press, 279.
2 Laplanche, J. and Pontalis, J.-B. (1983) *The Language of Psycho-Analysis*, London: Hogarth Press, 2.
3 Steiner, J. (1993) *Psychic Retreats*, London: Routledge, 132.
4 *ibid.*, 133.
5 Bion, W. (1962) *Learning from Experience*, London: Maresfield, 36.
6 Steiner, *Psychic Retreats*, 133.
7 *ibid.*, 141.
8 *ibid.*, 145.
9 Winnicott, D. (1955) 'Clinical varieties of transference', in Winnicott, *Through Paediatrics to Psychoanalysis*, 281–2.
10 Little, M. (1985) 'Winnicott working in areas where psychotic anxieties predominate: a personal record', *Free Associations*, 3: 9–42, (p. 21 and p. 27).
11 Segal, H. (1981) *The Work of Hanna Segal*, New York: Jason Aronson, 80.
12 Guntrip, H. (1968) *Schizoid Phenomena, Object Relations and the Self*, London: Hogarth Press, 350.
13 For example, Guntrip, *Schizoid Phenomena*, 360: ' "Analysing" is a male function, an intellectual activity of interpretation. . . . Ultimately "being there for the patient" in a stable and not a neurotic state is the female, maternal and properly therapeutic function.'
14 Benjamin, J. (1995) 'Sameness and difference: toward an "over-inclusive" theory of gender development', in A. Elliott and S. Frosh (eds) *Psychoanalysis in Contexts*, London: Routledge, 118.
15 *ibid.*, 119.
16 Laplanche and Pontalis, *The Language of Psycho-Analysis*, 227.
17 *ibid.*
18 Sandler, J., Dare, C. and Holder, A. (1973) *The Patient and the Analyst*, London: Maresfield (1979), 110.
19 Castoriadis, C. (1995) 'Logic, imagination, reflection', in Elliott and Frosh, *Psychoanalysis in Contexts*, 28.
20 See the discussion of this in Chapter 2 of Frosh, S. (1994) *Sexual Difference: Masculinity and Psychoanalysis*, London: Routledge.
21 Bouchard, M. (1995) 'The specificity of hermeneutics in psychoanalysis', *International Journal of Psycho-Analysis*, 76: 533–46, (p. 543).

22   Lacan, J. (1952) 'Intervention on transference', in J. Mitchell and J. Rose (eds) (1982) *Feminine Sexuality*, London: Macmillan, 62–3.
23   See Laplanche and Pontalis, *The Language of Psycho-Analysis*, 456.
24   For a detailed description and discussion of the Lacanian view of psychosis as produced by the 'foreclosure' of the symbolic order, see Chapter 6 of Frosh, S. (1991) *Identity Crisis*, London: Macmillan.
25   For example as described in Bion, W. (1970) *Attention and Interpretation*, London: Maresfield.
26   Sandler *et al.*, *The Patient and the Analyst*, 47.
27   Lacan, J. (1972–3) 'God and the *jouissance* of the woman', in Mitchell and Rose, *Feminine Sexuality*, 139.
28   Hinshelwood, R. (1991) *A Dictionary of Kleinian Thought*, London: Free Association Books, 465.
29   Klein, M. (1952) 'The origins of transference', in M. Klein, *Envy and Gratitude and Other Works*, New York: Delta, 53.
30   Segal, H. (1981) *Introduction to the Work of Melanie Klein*, London: Hogarth Press, 120–1.
31   Laplanche and Pontalis, *The Language of Psycho-Analysis*, 93.
32   Quoted in Sandler *et al.*, *The Patient and the Analyst*, 64.
33   Heimann, P. (1960) 'Counter-transference', *British Journal of Medical Psychology*, 33: 9–15, (p. 10).
34   Hinshelwood, *A Dictionary of Kleinian Thought*, 255–6.
35   Laplanche and Pontalis, *The Language of Psycho-Analysis*, 93.

CHAPTER 6: THE OUTCOME OF PSYCHOANALYTIC PSYCHOTHERAPY

1   Felman, S. (1987) *Jacques Lacan and the Adventure of Insight*, Cambridge, MA: Harvard University Press, 119.
2   Kantrowitz, J. (1995) 'Outcome research in psychoanalysis: review and reconsiderations', in T. Shapiro and R. Emde (eds) *Research in Psychoanalysis: Process, Development, Outcome*, Madison, CT: International Universities Press, 315.
3   Bachrach, H., Galatzer-Levy, R., Skolnikoff, A. and Waldron, S. (1991) 'On the efficacy of psychoanalysis', *Journal of the American Psychoanalytical Association*, 39: 871–916, (pp. 906–7).
4   Cooper, A. (1995) 'Discussion: on empirical research', in T. Shapiro and R. Emde (eds) *Research in Psychoanalysis: Process, Development, Outcome*. Madison, CT: International Universities Press, 385.
5   This has been reported in many places, particularly by Robert Wallerstein. The fullest account is in Wallerstein, R. (1986) *Forty-Two Lives in Treatment*, New York: Guilford.
6   *ibid.*, 304–5.
7   *ibid.*, 305.
8   For example, Blatt, S. (1992) 'The differential effect of psychotherapy and psychoanalysis with anaclitic and introjective patients: the Menninger Psychotherapy Research Project revisited', *Journal of the*

American Psychoanalytic Association, 40: 691–724. Blatt claims that 'anaclitic patients, whose pathology focuses on disruptions of interpersonal relatedness and who use primarily avoidant defenses' have significantly greater positive change in non-psychoanalytic psychotherapy. 'Introjective patients, whose pathology focuses on issues of self-definition, autonomy, and self-worth and who use mainly counteractive defenses' have significantly greater positive change in psychoanalytic psychotherapy.

9 For example, Bachrach *et al.*, 'On the efficacy of psychoanalysis'; Denman, C. (1995) 'Questions to be answered in the evaluation of long-term therapy', in M. Aveline and D. Shapiro (eds) *Research Foundations for Psychotherapy Practice*, Chichester: Wiley.

10 For example, Bachrach *et al.*, 'On the efficacy of psychoanalysis', 904: 'If anything, studies ... suggest that analysts are likely to be more critical about their results than patients or outside observers.'

11 Kantrowitz, 'Outcome research in psychoanalysis', 319–20.

12 *ibid.*, 317.

13 *ibid.*, 318–19.

14 *ibid.*, 324.

15 Bachrach, H. (1995) 'The Columbia Records Project and the evolution of psychoanalytic outcome research', in Shapiro and Emde, *Research in Psychoanalysis*, 288.

16 A relationship between treatment length and outcome is also revealed in the studies reported by Peter Fonagy and Mary Target of children treated for both emotional and disruptive disturbances at the Anna Freud Centre in London. Emotionally disturbed children did better than those with more conduct-based disturbances. See Fonagy, P. and Target, M. (1994) 'The efficacy of psychoanalysis for children with disruptive disorders', *Journal of the American Academy of Child and Adolescent Psychiatry*, 33: 45–55; Target, M. and Fonagy, P. (1994) 'The efficacy of psychoanalysis for children with emotional disorders', *Journal of the American Academy of Child and Adolescent Psychiatry*, 33: 361–71; Target, M. and Fonagy, P. (1994) 'The efficacy of psychoanalysis for children: prediction of outcome in a developmental context', *Journal of the American Academy of Child and Adolescent Psychiatry*, 33: 1134–44.

17 Bachrach *et al.*, 'On the efficacy of psychoanalysis', 871.

18 Denman, 'Questions to be answered'.

19 In England, the NHS Executive 1996 document, *NHS Psychotherapy Services in England: Review of Strategic Policy* is very polite in this way, but it also firmly reveals the writing on the wall for unevaluated treatments.

20 For a traditional, empirically minded review of the field, see Roth, A. and Fonagy, (1996) *What Works for Whom? A Critical Review of Psychotherapy Research*, New York: Guilford Press.

21 Kantrowitz, 'Outcome research in psychoanalysis', 325.

22 See Kantrowitz, J., Katz, A. and Paolitto, F. (1990) 'Follow-up of psychoanalysis five to ten years after termination: III. The relation

between the resolution of the transference and the patient–analyst match', *Journal of the American Psychoanalytic Association*, 38: 655–78; Kantrowitz, J., Katz, A. and Greenman, D. (1989) 'The patient–analyst match and the outcome of psychoanalysis: A pilot study', *Journal of the American Psychoanalytic Association*, 37: 893–919.

23 For example, evidence that patients benefit when they see their therapists 'as trustworthy, as respectful of their patients, and as likeable and encouraging'. See Conte, H., Buckley, P., Picard, S. and Karasu, T. (1994) 'Relations between satisfaction with therapists and psychotherapy outcome', *Journal of Psychotherapy Practice and Research*, 3: 215–21.

24 Orlinsky, D. and Howard, K. (1986) 'Process and outcome in psychotherapy', in S. Garfield and A. Bergin (eds) *Handbook of Psychotherapy and Behavior Change* , 3rd edn, Chichester: Wiley, 371.

25 Orlinsky, D., Grawe, K. and Parks, B. (1994) 'Process and outcome in psychotherapy – noch einmal', in A. Bergin and S. Garfield (eds) *Handbook of Psychotherapy and Behavior Change*, 4th edn, Chichester: Wiley, 352.

26 *ibid.*, 359–60.

27 Shapiro, D., Harper, H., Startup, M., Reynolds, S., Bird, D. and Suokas, A. (1994) 'The high-water mark of the drug metaphor: a meta-analytic critique of process-outcome research', in R. Russell (ed.) *Reassessing Psychotherapy Research*, New York: Guilford, 2.

28 An accessible source for these and other approaches is Shapiro, T. and Emde, R. (eds) (1995) *Research in Psychoanalysis*, Madison, CT: International Universities Press.

29 Henry, W., Strupp, H., Schacht, T. and Gaston, L. (1994) 'Psychodynamic approaches', in Bergin and Garfield (eds) *Handbook of Psychotherapy* , 4th edn, Chichester: Wiley, 475–6.

30 Howard, K., Orlinsky, D. and Lueger, J. (1995) 'The design of clinically relevant outcome research', in M. Aveline and D. Shapiro (eds) *Research Foundations for Psychotherapy Practice*, Chichester: Wiley, 4.

31 Elliott, R. and Anderson, C. (1994) 'Simplicity and complexity in psychotherapy research', in Russell, *Reassessing Psychotherapy Research*, 65.

32 Stiles, W. and Shapiro, D. (1989) 'Abuse of the drug metaphor in psychotherapy process-outcome research', *Clinical Psychology Review*, 9: 521–43; Stiles, W. and Shapiro, D. (1994) 'Disabuse of the drug metaphor', *Journal of Consulting and Clinical Psychology*, 62: 942–8.

33 Stiles and Shapiro, 'Abuse of the drug metaphor', 525.

34 Stiles, W., Shapiro, D. and Harper, H. (1994) 'Finding the way from process to outcome', in Russell, *Reassessing Psychotherapy Research*, 40.

35 See, for example, Greenberg, L. (1994) 'The investigation of change', in Russell, *Reassessing Psychotherapy Research*, 118: 'In fact, intensive and rigorous observation of how change takes place has probably been the most sorely neglected. We need to observe the process of

change in order to observe patterns that will lead to the kind of explanation that involves new understanding of what actually occurs,
instead of automatic theoretical explanations from our favourite
(often too strongly held) theory.'

36 Howard, Orlinsky and Lueger, 'The design of clinically relevant
outcome research', 7.

37 Russell, R. (1994) 'Critically reading psychotherapy process research',
in Russell, *Reassessing Psychotherapy Research*, 171.

CHAPTER 7: PSYCHOANALYSIS AND THE POLITICS OF IDENTITY

1 For example, *Totem and Taboo, The Future of an Illusion, Civilisation
and its Discontents*. See the three volumes collected in the Penguin
Freud Library and published in 1985 as *Civilization, Society and
Religion, The Origins of Religion* and *Art and Literature*.

2 Some outstanding recent British books on some of these topics (with
apologies to the many omitted) include Rustin, M. (1991) *The Good
Society and the Inner World*, London: Verso; Giddens, A. (1991)
Modernity and Self-Identity, Cambridge: Polity; and Rose, J. (1996)
States of Fantasy, Oxford: Clarendon Press. There are papers on
imagination, authority, feminism, nuclear war, racism and politics in
Elliott, A. and Frosh, S. (1995) *Psychoanalysis in Contexts*, London:
Routledge.

3 Rustin, *The Good Society and the Inner World*, 71.

4 *ibid.*, 60.

5 See, particularly, Frosh, S. (1989) *Psychoanalysis and Psychology*,
London: Macmillan.

6 Segal, H. (1973) *Introduction to the Work of Melanie Klein*, London:
Hogarth Press, 14.

7 Žižek, S. (1990) 'East European republics of Gilead', *New Left
Review*, 183: 51–2. This quotation is taken from Rustin, M. (1995)
'Lacan, Klein and politics', in Elliott and Frosh, *Psychoanalysis in
Contexts*, 234–5.

8 *ibid.*

9 Žižek, S. (1994) *The Metastases of Enjoyment*, London: Verso, 78.

10 Rose, J. (1996) *States of Fantasy*, Oxford: Clarendon Press, 5.

11 See my detailed discussion of this debate in Frosh, S. (1987) *The
Politics of Psychoanalysis*, London: Macmillan.

12 Jacoby, R. (1975) *Social Amnesia*, Sussex: Harvester Press.

13 Marcuse, H. (1955) *Eros and Civilisation*, Boston, MA: Beacon Press
(1966), 6.

14 Jacoby, *Social Amnesia*, 31.

15 Lacan, J. (1958) 'The meaning of the phallus', In J. Mitchell and J.
Rose (eds) (1982) *Feminine Sexuality*, London: Macmillan, 81–2: 'In
any case man cannot aim at being whole (the 'total personality' being
another premise where modern psychotherapy goes off course) once

the play of displacement and condensation, to which he is committed in the exercise of his functions, marks his relation as subject to the signifier.'

16 Žižek, *The Metastases of Enjoyment*, 82.

17 For example, Adorno, T., Frenkel-Brunswik, E., Levinson, D. and Sandford, R. (1950) *The Authoritarian Personality*, New York: Norton (1982); Fanon, F. (1952) *Black Skin, White Masks*, London: Pluto Press (1986). Other, particularly influential radical texts include Fromm, E. (1942) *The Fear of Freedom*, London: Routledge and Kegan Paul; Reich, W. (1946) *The Mass Psychology of Fascism*, Harmondsworth: Penguin; Marcuse, H. (1955) *Eros and Civilisation*, Boston, MA: Beacon Press (1966); and Brown, N. (1959) *Life Against Death*, London, Routledge and Kegan Paul. There is a review of some of this material in Jacoby, *Social Amnesia* and also in Jacoby, R. (1983) *The Repression of Psychoanalysis* New York: Basic Books. See also Frosh, *Psychoanalysis and Psychology* for a discussion of the books by Adorno *et al.* and Fanon.

18 For example, Foucault, M. (1977) *Discipline and Punish*, London: Allen Lane; (1979) *The History of Sexuality*, vol. 1, Harmondsworth: Penguin.

19 For a review of the relationship between psychoanalysis and postmodernism, see Frosh, S. (1991) *Identity Crisis: Modernity, Psychoanalysis and the Self,* London: Macmillan.

20 Elliott, A. *Psychoanalytic Theory: An Introduction*, Oxford: Blackwell, 7–8.

21 *ibid.*, 168.

22 The remainder of this chapter draws on material first published as 'Postmodernism and the adoption of identity', in A. Elliott and C. Spezzano (eds) *Psychoanalysis at its Limits: Navigating the Postmodern Turn*, Northvale, NJ: Jason Aronson, 1997.

23 Erikson, E. (1965) *Childhood and Society*, Harmondsworth: Penguin.

24 Lacan, J. (1954–5) *The Seminars of Jacques Lacan, Book II: The Ego in Freud's Theory and in the Technique of Psychoanalysis*, Cambridge: Cambridge University Press, 155. The 'Irma' dream is to be found in Freud, S. (1900) *The Interpretation of Dreams*, Harmondsworth: Penguin (1976).

25 Freud, S. (1923) *The Ego and the Id*, Harmondsworth: Penguin (1984), 368.

26 Castoriadis, C. (1995) 'Logic, imagination, reflection', in Elliott and Frosh, *Psychoanalysis in Contexts*, 29.

27 Winnicott, D. (1967) 'The mirror-role of mother and family in child development', in D. Winnicott (1980) *Playing and Reality*, Harmondsworth: Penguin.

28 Lacan, J. (1949) 'The mirror stage as formative of the function on the I as revealed in the psychoanalytic experience,' in J. Lacan, *Écrits: A Selection*, London: Tavistock (1977), 2. Many writers have pointed out that a major element in Lacan's influence on contemporary thought has been his capacity to express something of the contingency and

confusion of the experience of being a subject under the conditions of late capitalism. This aspect of Lacan's writing may indeed be more important than its actual content, which sometimes has raised obscurity to an art form. Here is Elliott's appraisal in Elliott, A. (1994) *Psychoanalytic Theory: An Introduction*, Oxford: Blackwell, 30: 'What has been especially influential in Lacan's writings is the point that the imaginary and symbolic dimensions of psychical life are themselves the ideological carriers of culture and history. . . . Lacanian theory offers a powerful account of the organisation of personal life by the social institutions of modern culture. The Lacanian emphasis on the decentring of the subject grasps the inherent difficulties of forging a core of personal selfhood in the late modern age. Caught between the narcissistic traps of the imaginary and the structural positioning of the socio-symbolic order, the portrait of the human subject in Lacanianism is in certain respects an apt characterisation of how personal life is globally outstripped by social, political, and economic mechanisms.'

29 Klein, M. (1946) 'Notes on some schizoid mechanisms', in M. Klein (1975) *Envy and Gratitude and Other Works*, New York: Delta.

30 Lacan, 'The mirror stage', 4.

31 Lacan, 'The Seminars of Jacques Lacan', 205.

32 Žižek, S. (1991) *Looking Awry: An Introduction to Jacques Lacan Through Popular Culture*, Cambridge, MA: MIT Press, 29.

33 *ibid.*, 32.

34 Kristeva, J. (1983) 'Freud and love', in T. Moi (ed.) *The Kristeva Reader*, Oxford: Blackwell. After birth, claims Kristeva, the infant experiences the maternal object as encompassing and potentially annihilating. The 'abject' is the term she applies to this elementary, presubjective object. In Kristeva's thought, the infant subject is preserved when the mother has an object of her own to turn towards, allowing a space for growth. But treating the whole thing metaphorically, one might say that the world of symbols preserves the infant from disappearing into this black hole. Faced with the abyss, the subject builds a bridge over it – usually but not necessarily a linguistic one. Human symbolic activity covers over the horror of falling into space, a space which will not give us any bearings, but instead faces us with the impossibility of self location and identity.

35 Kristeva, J. (1988) *Strangers to Ourselves*, London: Harvester Wheatsheaf (1991), 192.

36 *ibid.*, 76.

37 Foucault, M. (1973) *The Birth of the Clinic*, London: Tavistock.

38 For psychoanalytic readings of this material, see, for example: Frosh, *Identity Crisis*; Žižek, *Looking Awry*; Brennan, T. (1993) *History after Lacan*, London: Routledge; Frosh, S. (1994) *Sexual Difference: Masculinity and Psychoanalysis*, London: Routledge; and Elliott, A. (1996) *Subject to Ourselves*, Cambridge: Polity.

39 Rustin, *The Good Society and the Inner World*, 60.

CHAPTER 8: PSYCHOANALYTIC AGENDAS

1 I have written about this in three previous books: *The Politics of Psychoanalysis*, London: Macmillan (1987); *Psychoanalysis and Psychology*, London: Macmillan (1989); and *Sexual Difference*, London: Routledge (1994).

2 Freud, S. (1914) 'Totem and taboo', in S. Freud, *The Origins of Religion*, Harmondsworth: Penguin (1985).

3 For an account of this debate, see Hirst, P. and Woolley, P. (1982) *Social Relations and Human Attributes*, London: Tavistock.

4 This section is based on material first published as 'Psychoanalytic challenges: a contribution to the new sexual agenda', in L. Segal (ed.) (1997) *New Sexual Agendas*, London: Macmillan; and in *Human Relations*, 50: 3 (1997).

5 Mitchell, J. (1974) *Psychoanalysis and Feminism*, Harmondsworth: Penguin.

6 See, for example, Benjamin, J. (1988) *The Bonds of Love*, London: Virago (1990); Chodorow, N. (1994) *Femininities, Masculinities, Sexualities*, Kentucky: University Press of Kentucky; Mitchell, J. (1984) *Women: The Longest Revolution*, London: Virago.

7 Freud made few bones about this, as is clear from the conclusion to his last significant paper on femininity. See Freud, S. (1933) *New Introductory Lectures on Psychoanalysis*, Harmondsworth: Penguin (1973), 169: 'That is all I had to say to you about femininity. It is certainly incomplete and fragmentary and does not always sound friendly. But do not forget that I have only been describing women in so far as their nature is determined by their sexual function. It is true that that influence extends very far: but we do not overlook the fact that an individual woman may be a human being in other respects as well. If you want to know more about femininity, inquire from your own experiences of life, or turn to the poets, or wait until science can give you deeper and more coherent information.'

8 The single most important volume in this regard in the English-speaking world was probably Juliet Mitchell and Jacqueline Rose's collection *Feminine Sexuality* (London: Macmillan, 1982). Jane Gallop's book of the same year, *Feminism and Psychoanalysis* (London: Macmillan) created quite a stir, as did her later *Reading Lacan* (Ithaca, NY: Cornell University Press, 1985). Elizabeth Grosz, in her *Jacques Lacan: A Feminist Introduction* (London: Routledge, 1990) offers a balanced description and evaluation of this area. The impact of post-Lacanian French feminism, some sympathetic to Lacan and some opposed but always engaged with him, has been enormous in intellectual circles (see, for example, the contributions to Brennan, T. (ed.) (1989) *Between Feminism and Psychoanalysis*, London: Routledge), and is perhaps even creeping into an influence on psychoanalytic practice. However, in Britain, at least, Klein remains dominant in the feminist clinical sphere – see, for example, Maguire, M. (1995) *Men, Women, Passion and Power*, London: Routledge.

9 Most famously in Irigaray, L. (1977) *This Sex Which is Not One*, Ithaca, NY: Cornell University Press (1985).
10 Žižek, S. (1991) *Looking Awry: An Introduction to Jacques Lacan Through Popular Culture* Cambridge, MA: MIT Press.
11 For example, Segal, L. (1990) *Slow Motion: Changing Masculinities, Changing Men*, London: Virago.
12 Lacan, J. (1958) 'The meaning of the phallus,' in Mitchell and Rose, *Feminine Sexuality*. See the discussions of this paper in Frosh, *Sexual Difference*; and Gallop, *Reading Lacan*.
13 Benjamin, J. (1995) 'Sameness and difference: toward an 'over-inclusive' theory of gender development, in A. Elliott and S. Frosh (eds) *Psychoanalysis in Contexts*, London: Routledge, 120.
14 Particularly Fast, I. (1984) *Gender Identity*, Hillsdale, NJ: Analytic Press.
15 Benjamin, 'Sameness and difference', 106.
16 *ibid.*, 114.
17 Lacan, J. (1954–5) *The Seminars of Jacques Lacan, Book II: The Ego in Freud's Theory and in the Technique of Psychoanalysis*, Cambridge: Cambridge University Press.
18 *ibid.*, 193.
19 *ibid.*, 196.
20 *ibid.*, 205.
21 *ibid.*, 203.
22 For example, Gallop, *Reading Lacan*.
23 Lacan, *The Seminars of Jacques Lacan*, 204.
24 Butler, J. (1990) *Gender Trouble*, London: Routledge, 44–5.
25 *ibid.*, 56.
26 Benjamin, *The Bonds of Love*, 135.
27 Lacan, J. (1958) 'The meaning of the phallus', in Mitchell and Rose, *Feminine Sexuality*, 81–2.   ·
28 Lacan, *The Seminars of Jacques Lacan*, 205.
29 Freud, S. (1905) 'Fragment of an analysis of a case of hysteria', in S. Freud, *Case Histories I*, Harmondsworth: Penguin (1977), 162.
30 Lewes, K. (1989) *The Psychoanalytic Theory of Male Homosexuality*, London: Quartet Books, 21.
31 Stoller, R. (1985) *Observing the Erotic Imagination*, New Haven, CT: Yale University Press, 95.
32 Stoller's work on perversions led him to a strongly negative view of the prospects for any 'healthy' sexuality: 'I do not find heterosexuals in the mass to be more normal than homosexuals. When it comes to the expression of sexual excitement, *most* people, whatever their preference, often appear to be quite hostile, inept, fragmented, gratified only at a considerable price, and deceptive with themselves and their partners'. (*ibid.*, 97)
33 *ibid.*, 182–3.
34 Friedman, R.C. (1988) *Male Homosexuality: A Contemporary Psychoanalytic Perspective*, New Haven, CT: Yale University Press, 183.

35   Cunningham, R. (1991) 'When is a pervert not a pervert?', *British Journal of Psychotherapy*, 8: 48–70, (p. 49).
36   Lewes, *The Psychoanalytic Theory of Male Homosexuality*, 238: 'There has not been in the history I have sketched a single analytic writer who could identify himself as a homosexual. . . . The psychoanalytic discourse on homosexuality has been and still is formulated by nonhomosexuals about homosexuals, and the direction of observation, judgement and control extends in one direction only.'
37   Quoted in Lewes, *The Psychoanalytic Theory of Male Homosexuality*, 33.
38   Cunningham, 'When is a pervert not a pervert?', 63.
39   Cunningham describes the scenario thus in *ibid.*, 53–4: 'It seems that a pivotal factor militating against analytic training of homosexuals is the assumption of the presence of anti-parents, anti-baby fantasies at the centre of unconscious homosexual life. It is one of the tenets of psychoanalysis, particularly in the Kleinian school, that the hallmark of mental health and emotional maturity is the tolerance of the notion of the parental couple in reproductive sexual intercourse. . . . The worry seems to be that the homosexual, in wanting to be like the parent of the opposite sex, is actually enviously usurping the identity and position of that parent and falsely claiming it as his/her own, at the same time claiming the remaining parent as love object.'
40   *ibid.*, 54.
41   *ibid.*, 50.
42   O'Connor, N. and Ryan, J. (1993) *Wild Desires and Mistaken Identities: Lesbianism and Psychoanalysis*, London: Virago, 9, 184.
43   Lewes, *The Psychoanalytic Theory of Male Homosexuality*, 139.
44   Jacoby, R. (1975) *Social Amnesia*, Sussex: Harvester.
45   Friedman, R.M. (1986) 'The psychoanalytic model of male homosexuality: a historical and theoretical critique', *Psychoanalytic Review*, 73: 483–519, (p. 485).
46   Freud, S. (1951) A letter to 'A grateful mother' dated 9 April 1935, *International Journal of Psycho-Analysis*, 32: 331.
47   Freud, S. (1905) 'Three essays on the theory of sexuality', in S. Freud (1977) *On Sexuality* Harmondsworth: Penguin, 56 (footnote added in 1915).
48   The quotation from 'Three essays on the theory of sexuality' continues: 'Thus from the point of view of psychoanalysis the exclusive sexual interest felt by men for women is also a problem that needs elucidating and is not a self-evident fact based upon an attraction that is ultimately of a chemical nature.' (*ibid.*, 57)
49   Friedman, 'The psychoanalytic model of male homosexuality', 487–8.
50   Lewes, *The Psychoanalytic Theory of Male Homosexuality*, 43.
51   Freud, S. (1920) 'Psychogenesis of a case of homosexuality in a woman', in S. Freud, *Case Histories II*, Harmondsworth: Penguin (1979).
52   O'Connor and Ryan, *Wild Desires and Mistaken Identities*, 42.

53 Lacan, J. (1958) 'The meaning of the phallus,' in Mitchell and Rose, *Feminine Sexuality*, 85.

54 Butler, *Gender Trouble*, 49.

55 Pasche, F. (1964) Contribution to symposium on homosexuality, *International Journal of Psycho-Analysis*, 45: 203–19, (p. 210).

56 Friedman, *Male Homosexuality*, 74.

57 To be fair to Friedman, later on in his important book he makes this point in a very forceful way: 'There are many subgroups of homosexuality, phenotypically similar but with different origins, mental functions, courses, and responses to psychotherapy and psychoanalysis. One subgroup, under-studied by psychoanalysts to date, is made up of men who have always been predominantly or exclusively homosexual in fantasy and/or activity and whose character structure is integrated at a high level . . . these men appear to have character neuroses comparable to those of heterosexual men. Other homosexual men, integrated at an even higher level, find their way to a positive sense of gay identity. These men experience stable representational worlds, empathic object relationships and highly functional ego mechanisms.' (*ibid.*, 180–1)

58 See Ryan, J. (1992) 'Lesbianism: clinical perspectives', in Wright, E. (ed.) (1992) *Feminism and Psychoanalysis: A Critical Dictionary*, Oxford: Blackwell.

59 McDougall, J. (1995) *The Many Faces of Eros*, London: Free Association Books, 36–7.

60 Lewes, *The Psychoanalytic Theory of Male Homosexuality*, 97.

61 Friedman, 'The psychoanalytic model of male homosexuality', 490.

62 See Klein, M. (1950) 'On the criteria for termination of a psychoanalysis', in M. Klein, *Envy and Gratitude and Other Works*, New York: Delta, 1975.

63 Lewes, *The Psychoanalytic Theory of Male Homosexuality*, 208.

64 Chodorow, N. (1992) 'Heterosexuality as a compromise formation: reflections on the psychoanalytic theory of sexual development', *Psychoanalysis and Contemporary Thought*, 15: 267–304, (p. 295).

65 O'Connor and Ryan, *Wild Desires and Mistaken Identities*, 215.

66 Irigaray, L. (1977) 'Ce sexe qui n'en pas un', in E. Marks and I. de Courtivon (eds) *New French Feminisms*, Sussex: Harvester (1981), 102.

67 O'Connor and Ryan, *Wild Desires and Mistaken Identities*, 151.

68 Butler, *Gender Trouble*, 135–6.

69 Chodorow, 'Heterosexuality as a compromise formation', 269.

70 Lewes, *The Psychoanalytic Theory of Male Homosexuality*, 82.

71 Benjamin, 'Sameness and difference', 106.

72 *ibid.*, 117.

73 The roots of psychoanalysis in Jewish culture has been compellingly described in many publications, including Roith, E. (1987) *The Riddle of Freud*, London: Tavistock; and Bakan, D. (1958) *Sigmund Freud and the Jewish Mystical Tradition*, London: Free Association Books (1990). Linking this tradition with opposition to racism, Pajaczkowska and Young comment: 'It has been suggested that

psychoanalysis was forged from the cumulative wit of hundreds of generations of Jewish survival, and that the systematic understanding of the psyche was initially the need to understand the oppressor, to anticipate the next blow, in order to deflect it and continue with self realization.' (Pajaczkowska, C. and Young, L. (1992) 'Racism, representation, psychoanalysis', in J. Donald and A. Rattansi (eds) *'Race', Culture and Difference*, London: Sage, 198)

74 See, for example, Freud, 'Totem and taboo', 141–2: 'If children and primitive men find play and imitative representation enough for them, that is not a sign of their being unassuming in our sense or of their resignedly accepting their actual impotence. It is the easily understandable result of the paramount virtue they ascribe to their wishes, of the will that is associated with those wishes and of the methods by which those wishes operate.'

75 See Billig, M. (1978) *Fascists*, London: Harcourt Brace Jovanovich.

76 Altman, N. (1995) *The Analyst in the Inner City*, Hillsdale, NJ: The Analytic Press.

77 Frosh, S. (1989) *Psychoanalysis and Psychology*, London: Macmillan, 249. The references to Adorno *et al.* and Fanon are: Adorno, T., Frenkel-Brunswik, E., Levinson, D. and Sandford, R. (1950) *The Authoritarian Personality*, New York: Norton, (1982); Fanon, F. (1952) *Black Skin, White Masks*, London: Pluto Press, (1986).

78 Adorno *et al.*, *The Authoritarian Personality*, 324–5.

79 Rustin, M. (1991) *The Good Society and the Inner World*, London: Verso, 71.

80 *ibid.*, 62.

81 *ibid.*, 63.

82 *ibid.*, 66.

83 *ibid.*, 69.

84 Kovel, J. (1984) *White Racism*, London: Free Association Books (1988). The more recent paper is Kovel, J. (1995) 'On racism and psychoanalysis', in Elliott and Frosh, *Psychoanalysis in Contexts*.

85 Kovel, 'On racism and psychoanalysis', 221: 'The term "primitive" is not much used these days, owing to the pejorative connotation of being backward and childish. This, of course, is a direct product of western ethnocentricity. We might as well think of primitive as "primary" and original. In any case, we append the sense of "state-free" to assert the distinguishing feature of primitive life, the absence of social class and the superordinate social regulation of the state which inevitably attend social class.'

86 *ibid.*, 211.

87 *ibid.*, 212.

88 *ibid.*

89 *ibid.*, 217.

90 *ibid.*, 212.

91 Brown, N. (1959) *Life against Death*, Middletown, CT: Wesleyan University Press.

92 See Berman, M. (1983) *All That is Solid Melts into Air*, London: Verso.
93 Kovel, *On racism and psychoanalysis*, 219.
94 *ibid.*, 218.
95 For a detailed examination of the problematic dovetailing of rationality and masculinity, see Seidler, V. (1993) *Unreasonable Men*, London: Routledge.
96 See Cohen, P. (1989) 'Reason, racism and the popular monster', in B. Richards (ed.) *Crises of the Self*, London: Free Association Books, particularly p.246: 'In fact, it is not the sleep of reason which has produced 'monstrous races', rather, it is the creatures of the racist imagination which have periodically aroused the European intelligentsia from its slumbers, if only in order to rationalise them as the basis of new technologies of surveillance and control over subject populations. The dominant forms of scientific rationality in western society are not only consistent or complicit with racist ideas, they have played an active role in producing and relaying them.'
97 Kovel, *On racism and psychoanalysis*, 205.
98 Elliott, A. (1994) *Psychoanalytic Theory: An Introduction*, Oxford: Blackwell, 166.

Name index

Subject index